D1524455

The Experience of Culture

Theory, Culture & Society

Theory, Culture & Society caters for the resurgence of interest in culture within contemporary social science and the humanities. Building on the heritage of classical social theory, the book series examines ways in which this tradition has been reshaped by a new generation of theorists. It also publishes theoretically informed analyses of everyday life, popular culture, and new intellectual movements.

EDITOR: Mike Featherstone, *Nottingham Trent University*

THE TCS CENTRE
The Theory, Culture & Society book series, the journals *Theory, Culture & Society* and *Body & Society*, and related conference, seminar and postgraduate programmes operate from the TCS Centre at Nottingham Trent University. For further details of the TCS Centre's activities please contact:

Centre Administrator
The TCS Centre, Room 175
Faculty of Humanities
Nottingham Trent University
Clifton Lane, Nottingham, NG11 8NS, UK
e-mail: tcs@ntu.ac.uk
web: http://tcs.ntu.ac.uk

Recent volumes include:

Occidentalism
Modernity and Subjectivity
Couze Venn

Simulation and Social Theory
Sean Cubitt

The Contradictions of Culture
Cities, Culture, Women
Elizabeth Wilson

The Tarantinian Ethics
Fred Botting and Scott Wilson

Society and Culture
Principles of Scarcity and Solidity
Bryan S. Turner and Chris Rojek

Modernity and Exclusion
Joel S. Kahn

The Experience of Culture

Michael Richardson

SAGE Publications
London • Thousand Oaks • New Delhi

SAGE Publications Ltd
6 Bonhill Street
London EC2A 4PU

SAGE Publications Inc
2455 Teller Road
Thousand Oaks, California 91320

SAGE Publications India Pvt Ltd
32, M-Block Market
Greater Kailash - I
New Delhi 110 048

British Library Cataloguing in Publication data

A catalogue record for this book is
available from the British Library

ISBN 0 7619 6650 1

Library of Congress control number available

Typeset by M Rules
Printed in Great Britain by The Cromwell Press Ltd,
Trowbridge, Wiltshire

Contents

PREFACE

According to Aztec myth, culture came into being after the immortal spirits had been sacrificed and were no longer present to mortals. To alleviate the people's mourning, Tezcatlipoca appeared to one of them and informed him to go to the sun's house and bring back singers and instruments. The man travelled to the land of the sun and came across singers and musicians playing. Seeing him approach, the sun told his singers to ignore the man, since he was a thief. However, the man began to sing and so beautifully that the sun's musicians, entranced, could not resist following him, playing their drums and pipes as they accompanied him on his return to earth. From that time on, people have performed music to honour the spirits, who periodically come down from the skies to join in their dances.

This myth locates culture as a mediating process that serves communication and acts as an intermediary between different realities. This provides us with the basis of what culture is, and it may legitimately be said that human beings alone have culture because only we are imbued with a lack of self-sufficiency that entails a necessity to communicate with other beings in order to subsist in the world. This is both our condition and our restriction. In writing this book I have tried to be faithful to this communicative function in looking at the way culture unfolds in multifarious ways in modern life.

Culture as a topic has generated a vast critical literature over the past century and especially during the last two decades. Most of the debate is concerned, in one way or another, with theories of what culture is, and this often reveals wide divergences. Culture has different meanings in different contexts, and it is often difficult to find common ground among competing notions of it. This book makes no attempt to answer questions of what a theory of culture might be, but takes culture for granted as human activity in its generality and material forms. It examines the issues raised by the way the culture becomes manifest in and through individual and collective experience and how this affects the dynamic of culture itself. It looks at these issues through themes that exemplify some of the cultural exigencies that are raised in relation to the history of ideas.

In this respect, it does not try to 'explain' culture or to provide a comprehensive view of it, something that may be impossible since we experience culture at virtually every moment of our lives. At least, the experience of culture is too vast to be explored fully in a single book, and no doubt important omissions will be pointed to – especially, perhaps, in the light of current debates, any real discussion of gender divisions. Such omissions have been dictated by the shape the book took and do not imply any denial of their importance. The aim has been to engage culture phenomenologically, treating it *as* experience. It seeks to show that culture does not emerge from out of human activity, but rather is co-extensive with it; that human experience is, essentially, culture. As it draws upon debates and combines approaches from a range of disciplines, it tries to place human experience at the heart of concepts of culture in a general way, and it is to be hoped that such a wide scope does not lead to a superficial viewpoint. In engaging with philosophical issues, in particular, it makes no claim to do so with philosophical exactitude, and strives to be a study of ideas in their social context rather than of ideas in themselves.

It is particularly concerned with the interrelation between cultures, seeking to locate the places where they meet or diverge, inquiring into what they have in common or otherwise. Taking culture as a lived process means to chart out a terrain whereby it becomes possible to grasp what it may be in its generality against the tendency towards fragmentation that has tended to be the feature of much recent cultural analysis. In particular, the book tries to engage with how culture has been made cosmopolitan in today's world and especially how Western culture has been opened up to the people of other cultures. In such a situation, what do cultural identity and integrity mean?

In this respect, the issues raised emerge especially from my own experience of teaching a wide range of students of different social and cultural backgrounds over the past few years. Without the participation of my students, it would have been impossible for me to have been able to have conceptualised the issues raised with whatever precision has been achieved. It seems invidious to single out particular students among so many, but I feel I need to mention Yoko Nagao and Naoko Yoshida, whose critical perspectives were instrumental in initially allowing me to conceive this material as a book and recognise that it had relevance to a wider audience.

THE MANIFESTATION OF CULTURE
IN HUMAN LIFE

Human beings, in being born, are – uniquely among living creatures – cast into a world of culture. Other animals are born into a physical universe in which survival is the primary concern. They need to learn no more than how to subsist in an unknown – and at times hostile – environment. The legacy of previous generations does not weigh upon them: each new generation is born anew, free of any burden of the past, and adapts iself to whatever circumstances it finds confronting it. For the human child it is very different. Survival in a physical world is likely to be the least of its worries, which will mostly be taken care of by its parents. What the child will need above all are social skills: the human child must know how to exist in a world humans themselves have created. It is this world of human creation that we call culture. Almost from the moment the child emerges from the mother's womb, it is being acculturated into human society. This is a complicated task that will place a tremendous burden on the child's parents. Most animals are ready to face life on their own very soon after their birth. Humans, in contrast, require sixteen or more years. And these years will be spent learning a whole series of complicated cultural forms that will be necessary for survival in a complex and sometimes violent human world. Moreover, this task of enculturation will never be completed: all of us are still learning about culture at the moment we die.

Geneticists tell us that the aim of life is to reproduce itself. This may be true, but if it is, a study of culture soon reveals that it is so in an extremely complex way because the webs of culture that human beings have created – which necessarily serve the aims of life – often conflict with or place obstacles in the way of this elemental aim. The existence of culture shows us that human beings are not exclusively or even primarily concerned with reproducing themselves. They also want to preserve themselves, to impose themselves on their environment, and to shape their own destinies. If their sole concern were to reproduce themselves, culture would be an unnecessary extravagance, as it is for other animals. Indeed, if the only aim of life was to reproduce itself, then living beings would have no reason to exist once they had reproduced. That this is not the case, that most of life – and human beings most especially – is also concerned with asserting a self-identity in actions that are irrelevant – or even detrimental – to genetic reproduction, is a fact that is fundamental to any understanding of the nature – indeed of the enigma – of culture. A preliminary consideration of what culture involves leads to an inescapable conclusion that human needs go much further than the reproduction of the species. If the aim of life is to reproduce itself, the complexity of human culture reveals that human existence is not coterminous with the needs of life. Indeed, there is a tension between the fact of life itself and the particular form of life that is existing at a specific time and place. Human existence is founded on a particular consciousness: that we enter and depart the world alone and yet we shall always be striving to transcend that awareness in numerous ways.

Despite the enormous advances in understanding of the evolution of life on earth, it has never been possible to identify what exactly makes humans different from other animals. Why and how have language and culture arisen to separate us from all other species on earth? It may be argued that we are not so different, that language and culture are not unique to humans. Other species may certainly be said to have a potential for language (we even speak of the 'language of birds') or culture (a wide variety of species from bees to beavers construct items for their use from the natural world). Yet even if we accept that this may constitute an elementary form of culture, human culture can still be distinguished from that of any other creature in numerous ways. Possibly, most importantly, human culture is productive. We not only make tools to serve us; we also preserve and reproduce them for future use. As we do so, this means that we are not living exclusively in the present, as other animals are. Our being is also imbued with past experience and future possibilities. A conception of the future, indeed, seems to be the essential prerequisite for the development of cultural forms. Without it, culture would remain in a rudimentary form, serving only immediate needs.

On this basis we may say that culture is simply what human beings produce and the means by which we preserve what we have produced. The result, however, is far from simple. *Homo sapiens* is *the* productive animal, and this productive capacity defines us in complicated ways. No other creature produces in the way humans do. From birds to tigers by way of fishes, the only substantial productive activity of other animals is devoted to the sustenance and reproduction of the species and the only real trace they leave behind them is in the form of their descendants. On the other hand it seems that, even in their very earliest days, humans sought to inscribe themselves and their existence on to the structure of the world. From the cave paintings left by Palaeolithic people to the complex forms of our present-day society, human culture has been involved with a will to confront and place some distance between us and our mortality. This seems to represent another crucial feature making us different from other animals: we have an awareness that we shall die, and we strive to deny, delay or come to terms with the fact of our own annihilation.

The very definition of a human depends on a concept of culture. We are, literally, inconceivable as a species without it. Culture is the totality of all that characterises us. It includes the tools and objects we create, the structures and institutions we fashion, the concepts and ideas we develop, and the way these take shape as customs and beliefs, all of which must be taken into account for any comprehensive sense of what culture is and how it lies at the very root of human society. In addition, these elements are not static, held separate from other cultural elements, but are in constant communication with one another, so that a continuous interrelation exists between all of the elements that may be said to constitute culture.

To define it, then, we may say that culture is the material form assumed by humanity's social activity. If it is what we produce, this production has specific aims. In particular, culture is shaped by the form of whatever we create in the course of our social lives to serve or respond to the purposes of social communication: the way we build our houses, the way we eat our food, the way we establish work patterns, practise religion or create art are all elements of culture. Almost all human activity serves culture in one way or another and results in the production of cultural evidence. This, not the fact of culture itself, is what really distinguishes us as a species. But it is not the activity itself; it is the way we carry it out that imprints social forms with characteristic cultural patterns that may be said to constitute the essential element that defines the human being and provides the evidence – as provisional as it may be – that we exist as a species apart.

The extent of culture is quite extraordinary, permeating every aspect of our lives.

Everything we construct is a cultural artefact, marked with significance. The building in which I am currently writing this book is not simply a place in which to live; it also tells the story of the society that built it a century ago. It has a history of its own that is tied in with the lives of the people who have lived here, it stands as a mark of the culture of society at the time it was built, and has gained resonances through the time that has elapsed since it was built. Any cultural construction is also part of the autobiography of those within it: our lives participate in the universal unfolding that constitutes culture. Human beings produce nothing that is not inscribed in one way or another with the identity of the person who created it, and, furthermore, this primary inscription is reinscribed by each person who comes into contact with whatever it is that has been created. This is even the case with today's mass-produced products, which reflect the needs of modern society. Though they may appear to be bland in terms of content, concerned only with attracting attention by the image they project, they still need to be clearly distinguished from the products of their competitors. In deciding to buy any product at all, our decision will be conditioned as much by how it is presented as by what it actually is: when purchasing even something like a tin of apricots, we pay attention to the cultural form within which the tin is placed. We are unlikely to buy a simple tin devoid of any inscription but the words 'apricots' to tell us what it is. Unless we are striving and desperate for any food, we are not content with sustenance itself; we also demand that it is presented to us with a certain image or attractiveness. That is, we expect it to be given form and meaning within a human system of signs through the way it is presented, and this affects the choice we make, even if we know that all tinned apricots are more or less the same.

This reveals another essential characteristic: all culture, even in its earliest human forms, is constituted as part of an all-embracing symbolic system. And the essential feature of a symbol is to provide a vehicle for the transmission of different meanings within which the complexity of culture takes shape.

Symbolic meaning is not directly generated by the elements of culture themselves, but by the associations they embody through the links they make with other cultural forms. In themselves the buildings I see from my window *mean* nothing: they are merely constructions of bricks and mortar. They assume *meaning* only when compared with other buildings and human constructions. I can draw a whole tableau of cultural significance by probing into associations evoked by the different buildings I can see along the street. Simply by comparing them, I can tell something about their purpose and the life of the people who inhabit them. Delving deeper, I can study the activity carried on inside the buildings and how their different inhabitants interact, which will tell me a considerable amount about the greater society (the porter on the door has a very different relationship to the building than do the people who live in it, or the postman who visits it each day, or the burglar who would like to break in). I can make such a study only because of the trace that human beings always leave behind them in the way they respond to, and create, culture. Objectively formed by human activity, culture is experienced subjectively by each individual, and this interaction provides the dynamic that founds the complexity and richness of culture. Other animals may build: birds form nests, bees hives, beavers complex irrigation systems. But they do so in a species-defined way: their creations leave behind no trace and have no *symbolic* meaning; any resonance they have is always manifest, always practically defined to serve the needs of the species and apparently – at least as far as we can see – with no subjective element to distinguish the particular individual creature that creates them. Birds' nests tell us little more than the obvious fact that they are built to facilitate the process of reproduction, providing a safe haven for the gestation of the egg. Differences between different nests tell us no more than that for practical purposes different birds have a different way of making nests. The way in which other animals construct appears to leave no possibility for the introduction of any subjective individual element.

As far as we can tell, animal behaviour is determined and uniform and anything that may be considered to be cultural activity is overwhelmingly the result of genetic factors. What is learned and transmitted from one generation to another independently of genetic factors is, on the other hand, a crucial aspect of human behaviour. Cultural rules, not genetic instinct, determine much of human conduct, even with something as elemental as eating: we eat not only when we are hungry but in accordance with rules that have been internalized and learned through practice. Our elemental needs, indeed, are modified by the demands of culture: our feeling of hunger is mediated by the fact of when we expect to eat. Whether we can understand anything about what we are from study of our genetic and biological make-up, this means little if it is sundered from the impact of culture, even if it can be shown that culture as such has little direct effect upon our genetic and biological make-up. Functionally this may be true. In the way in which our genetic and biological constitution is *directed* in the course of our lives, however, it makes an enormous difference.

In distinction to animals, then, humans irrevocably imprint themselves upon the world. Unlike other animals, too, we are uniquely *social* creatures, and our everyday interaction is fundamentally organised into social forms. Sociability may be important to other animals, but not to the extent of determining their existence as a species. In human society, if someone does not accept the basic established social rules, they will be unable to participate or even survive. Without socialisation it is arguable whether we could become human beings at all. We start to become socialised the moment we are born. Other animals do not teach their young social behaviour: their instruction is limited to showing them how to survive in the world, how to fend off predators, find food, and so on. But as humans it is also essential that we learn to survive in society, and we have to be taught what is considered to be the proper behaviour towards our fellows which, though it may vary considerably in its details in different societies, always entails a complex orientation programme involving social responsibilities and expectations. Such learning also has an ethical component: certain behaviour is morally unacceptable and children have to be taught what this is.

Culture is also the way this learning process becomes manifest as fundamental to the life of societies. In this respect, it involves many contingencies, but can perhaps most satisfactorily be defined as providing a set of shared ideals, values and standards of behaviour. However, though they are shared, these ideals and values are neither uniform nor generally explicitly defined but subject to considerable variation, both within a particular culture and between different cultures.

Culture is always learned; it is defined by the fact that it is not biologically given but is constituted by social action. Transmitted through individuals and collectives, it is based on symbols and signs, notably language. This symbolic form is what is to be distinguished from what is supposedly naturally given. Culture takes shape from the social nature of human development. Our existence in the world relies on the existence of other beings to a far greater extent than other animals, which are largely self-sufficient. To perceive the world, it is necessary for us to engage with it. This entails also engaging with other people, who may have different desires and needs to us. To cope with the resultant conflict of interests, we need to negotiate our relations with others. Culture also becomes what emerges from such negotiation, mediating our social reality and being an essential feature by which we establish our own sense of identity. It reflects a constant need for renegotiation of the dialectical relationship between individual and society and between different classes and interests within a given society. In addition, culture can be said to provide the conduit through which we construct reality. Reality is not a pre-formed thing into which we are born, nor is it something that is given to us at birth. It is rather what is formed through the relationship we construct with the world, which is shaped through our learning of culture. It is therefore by means of our interaction with culture that we construct our sense of reality.

Culture is also connected with the development of civilisation. Etymologically it is derived from cultivation of the land, and a division is often made between culture and nature; in this view, culture also represents an aspiration to dominate nature. The distinction between nature and culture may, with some reservations, be considered universal, although it is often conceptualised in different terms in distinct contexts: it may be seen in terms of a separation between hearthside and the wild, the internal and the exter-nal, the raw and the cooked, public and private, nakedness and clothing. Others, those whom we do not consider to be human, are characterised as indulging in non-cultural behaviour: they eat raw meat, go around naked or lack a sense of private space.

The separation between nature and culture is a central theme in myths across the globe. One of the most striking is perhaps the Celtic legend of Melusine. The daughter of Elinas, the King of Scotland, and the nymph Pressine, Melusine, having avenged a wrong done to her mother by her father, is cursed to become a snake up to the waist every Saturday. Meeting Raimond de Lusignan beside a fountain, she agrees to marry him on condition that he does not inquire into what she does on Saturdays. Ultimately, unable to con-tain his curiosity, he follows her to the cave into which she retires and discovers her bathing in a green tub, her lower body like a snake. Distraught that Raimond has betrayed her, Melusine weeps and stretches out her arms, which are transformed into wings as she disappears into the air, uttering ter-rible cries of distress.

Melusine – who represents irreducible otherness, but also our link with nature, the protective fairy whose true nature must remain hidden from human profanity – reveals the double aspect of human becoming through interplays of otherness, a process that is denied by the way in which we have assumed culture. In a remarkable analysis of the Melusine myth, Jean Markale shows how it reveals a primal repression of the possibility of being both male and female at the same time, asserting the separation of the sexes as the essential human quality, with maleness being erected as the preferred condition: 'The male does not admit the feminisation of the male, but does admit the – superficial – masculinisation of the female' (1983: 197). This reflects an underlying impatience with the possibilities of existence, inserting a human will (situated as male) as the motivating aspect of progress at the expense of a harmonious expansion of potentiality. It requires that culture yield to a repression of essential integrality and in the process founds an atti-tude of separation and dissemblance that is at the root of the dualisms of exclusion found most explicitly in the Christian tradition of the angry all-seeing and all-knowing God who refuses any ceding to an otherness of experience.

This leads us to forming our self-definition as humans within a framework in which we set ourselves against what we perceive as the 'wildness' of nature. Socialisation expressly comes to be about 'civilising' our children, as tempering their natural wildness, and making them social and cultural beings. In identifying the wildness not only of children but of any 'other' that does not fit our social framework as being uncivilised, we also equate them with nature. Yet with culture also comes the most uncivilised of behaviour: the crimes committed by humanity, which by implication are also committed in the name of culture, dwarf anything we are aware of in the natural kingdom. In comparison, animals who are lacking in culture have little to fear from their own kind, and few creatures will of their own volition hurt one of their own species. Human beings, in contrast, are dangerous.

In the final analysis, however, culture cannot be opposed to nature. Both remain discrete phenomena that participate in the unfolding of existence and are mutually dependent. In interacting with the world, the human produces culture and transforms nature, but even so whatever is produced is of natural origin. It may be that producing culture is our natural state. In so doing we transform ourselves, sharing our personal and collective identities, and it is this that makes it possible for us to engage with the world. Culture is the repository of all that is experienced by human life in its encounter with the world. And all cultures are characterised by universal features: all cook food and have inscribed ritual behaviour.

If other animals have culture, it may be said that it is only in a rudimentary form, as a potentiality that has not been realised. However, to say this is to assert no more than a *human* truth: culture is what we perceive to distinguish us. Other animals may simply have chosen not to develop such a capacity, for while, on the one hand, culture can be said to open up vistas and provide us with what we perceive as the means to master the world, it also reveals a breach between us and the world that is at the source of most human problems: the acquisition of culture implies an endless striving that is undoubtedly as much a curse as it is a blessing. It means that, unlike other animals, we are unable to relate directly to the world: food has to be cooked or otherwise prepared in order to be fit to eat. We lack the means to make an unmediated judgement as to whether we can safely eat something. This lack is something that the process by which we assume culture is intended to remedy, and emerges from processes of socialisation that rely on the fact that human beings can only exist in fellowship with other humans and need, as a determinant of their existence, to form societies and provide the means by which all individuals are enabled to enter and contribute to and participate in those societies.

2

ENTERING CULTURE

As individuals, we are born into culture. We emerge from an undifferentiated state in which we identify with our surroundings, comfortable in the safety of our mother's womb, into a world that is strange and alien. We strive at first to re-establish the primal comfort we have known, identifying with our new surroundings and not making a clear distinction between what constitutes our self and what does not, but we are forced little by little to come to terms with the separation birth involves: the fact that, ultimately, we are alone in the world. This is not easy to accept. The experience of birth – perhaps for all beings – is traumatic. As Otto Rank (1993) has shown, in being born we are in a sense violently forced into exile. The process is itself threatening: we struggle for breath at a moment of shock as we are rudely disturbed and taken out of our relaxed state. Coming into the world, we desire a return to the bliss we have lost, and this institutes a primal anxiety that, as Rank demonstrates, remains with us throughout childhood at least. We therefore come into the world disturbed and discountenanced, and our psychic development during childhood involves a process of repressing the memory of the pre-natal state, playing out representations of it in order to cope with the anxiety it leaves as a residue within us so as to prevent regression to foetal nature. In addition, we must deal with this new and intimidating world into which we are reluctantly cast.

We are born into a world that is alien to us and that would like to impose itself on us in numerous ways. The most immediate imposition comes from our parents: what they wish us to be will never be commensurate with what we are. People rarely, if ever, have children for the sake of the child that is to be born. It would be fanciful to think they could. A child, prior to conception, is for the parents a pure abstraction and remains such until probably quite some time after birth. Often it is not until the child has developed into an adult that the parent feels able to accept it as an independent being, and in all probability most people, at least within the context of the Western family structure,[1] never reach the stage of being entirely comfortable with the fact that their children have an existence that is separate from their own; there is a parallel process at work by which both child and parents must come to terms with their separate existences in the world. In most cases, having children is not a free choice. Frequently, it even takes place against the will of the parents: they may not have wanted a child at all, or they may have wanted one of the opposite sex. Even when it is freely chosen, it still occurs under pressure of one sort or another. This may be biological (to reproduce the species), cultural (to reproduce the culture) or individual (to reproduce oneself). In most cases it is a combination of all three. This means that the child is born with a set of expectations and needs imposed on it. It has not chosen these and they may be antithetical to its own natural destiny, if such a thing exists. Of course, even if the child does have a natural destiny, it is something impossible: in the absence of its parents – or at least someone who will assume that role – it will die. It relies on others for its growth, its membership of society, and its becoming as a human. But this may not be accepted easily by the child: from the beginning there may be an elemental struggle between the wants of the child as an active agent and how the individual parents, society and species would like to mould it. The extent to which this tension is present is subject to enormous cultural variation, but it is always present; in fact it is a conflict that is necessary for life to develop and assume a shape as culture. Freud's discussion of the Oedipus complex in this sense undoubtedly contains a fundamental truth, feeding into the way that essential oppositions are imposed upon us as a condition of our very existence. From this – cultural – point of view, whether the Oedipus complex is universal or not is irrelevant: the myth it embodies – which may take multiple forms depending on the form of society – is simply one manifestation of this elemental tension between the continuity of existence and the demands of the different human individuals comprised in it.

Our identity takes shape in relation to how we accept or react against the conditioning imposed upon us. The nature of that conditioning, combined with the child's experiences in its early years, will mark the child in ways that will be difficult if not impossible later to erase or modify. Whether or not there is something within us constituting a personality of our own that is independent of socialisation is impossible to say, because the shape our personality will take as we enter society emerges from the confrontation between our internal being and the impact the external world makes upon us, a confrontation that is violent in ways that, from our later perspective as adults, we will find difficult to conceive, even though we have ourselves passed through this experience.

One of the many difficulties of reconstituting childhood experience is that the child's formation as a human also involves the way in which the parents respond to it and what their expectations are. From the moment of birth our becoming is not in our own hands, and even our experience of the world is not ours alone. A child is conceptualised by its parents as an extension of themselves, not as an individual in its own right. Only with birth does it become possible for the parents even to perceive the child as having any reality of its own, as being an individual that is different from them. If the child's separation from the mother (and from the surrounding world) is traumatic, the acceptance of the separation of the child from themselves is no less so for the parents. For the parents there is a tension: often a desire that the child should be an extension of themselves and achieve what they themselves have been unable to is combined with a recognition that the child is different from them and that they have no right to make such an imposition on it. This sets up an inevitable tension, one that may be further accentuated by the fact that each of the parents may have different hopes for the child. It is a tension that is never entirely resolved and further feeds the child's neurosis; it must fight for recognition.

If the parents can only relate to the newborn child as an abstraction, then so too for the child the parents are equally abstract. A child does not choose its parents, any more than it chooses the fact of its birth; the separation it fights against is that which severs it from a wholeness it experienced in the womb – the mother is the last remaining link between the child and eternity.

For the child, the world into which it is born is strange and alien, but it strives, at first, to deny this. It must reconstitute itself as something integral to itself. It perceives a continuum between itself and its perception of the world: the child *identifies* with what surrounds it, most immediately with what nourishes it, that is, the mother's breast, which has replaced the sanctuary of the womb. But the comfort of the breast, unlike the womb, is not constant: the mother allows us to take solace from it only intermittently, and as time passes she has to wean us away from it altogether. In so doing, she confronts us, in a brutal way, with our own isolation. The process of our self-constitution has begun, which is founded in an alienation from the continuity of the world. As we are faced with this gradual realisation, there are still further pressures that act upon us by means of others, not simply those of our parents, but of all those coming from the surrounding society, although generally the parents are the primary conduit of such pressures.

Above all, we become marked with the imprint of the past, which is nothing other than the cultural heritage of the society into which we have been born. Our initial exposure to culture is the experience of *another's* culture; our parents and those around us bring to us the experience of what they have themselves experienced. We never construct our own culture; the most we can do is to mould a culture that has already been created into a shape that to some extent responds to *our* needs. Faced with the burden of the past, with the fact that we have been born into a world that has been formed in our absence, how do we establish our own individual identity and ability to act in the world? We are not simply thrown into this world as undifferentiated beings able to make of it what we will and dependent only upon what we ourselves are (whatever this may mean), but must respond to multiple social and cultural demands. We also take from our parents a genetic structure – which places limits on us as it also governs many of our qualities – that will not be easily exceeded. As much as we may not accept that our genetic make-up determines what we are and hold that the possibility of going beyond what is given to us remains open, we still have to act within the limits set by a framework that our genetic structure, together with our social and cultural situation, imposes on us. The limits these set may make it impossible for us to achieve our hopes. They may even make it impossible for us to fulfil the hopes our parents have of us, which can result in further elementary tensions being introduced into all of our relationships.

Consequently, the process of self-definition is an exceedingly complex one of differentiation and growing awareness of our separateness from – and, correspondingly, our reliance upon – what surrounds us. All experience of the self is an experience of the other: self-creation takes shape only in relation to what lies outside our grasp. This process begins at the moment we are born, if not earlier. It establishes a veritable vortex of conflicting sensations that undermine and yet at the same time underline the need we have for security.

The unborn child lives in an enclosed universe that is coterminous with itself. At first the self extends limitlessly in all directions: we do not recognise a separation between what we are and what the world is. This egocentric and timeless realm is ruptured upon first contact with the world, but only gradually is the child able to recognise and come to terms with the separation this involves. Many creation myths reveal elements of this primary sense of disorientation. The myth of expulsion from the Garden of Eden, for instance, is clearly in part a psychological rationalisation of this process: encountering the otherness of the tree of knowledge revealed through the auspices of the serpent, Adam and Eve experience the shock of recognition that they exist in a world that is alien to them. This alien quality of the world is the first shock; there follows that of the recognition of an otherness that exists as a category of things emerging from our sensibility as the child learns to perceive the surrounding world. The world, that is, is given to us not whole, but as a series of fragments that we must learn to put into some form of order if we are to establish it with a solid foundation that accords with our perceptions as well as (through a process of negotiation) with those of other people and the way in which what surrounds us responds to our presence in the world.

The other – manifested in many different ways as a primal presence – is the means by which we realise our sense of cultural identity; it also, at the same time, presents a threat to it. Established in distinction to the self, the other is both its extension and its limit; both its actuality and its negation. Self and other are created in dynamic relation and can exist only within the terms of that relation. As such, the other is the apprehension of difference and exists only in relation to what is self. Self-identity cannot be established if the individual is sundered from this relation, for in this case the self and the other are cast into a formless and featureless limbo. And the identity of the self and the other reciprocally transpire only as long as the relation continues: once the bond is broken, that particular avenue of identity formation is cut. We may thus be said to establish different selves in relation to each of the different others we encounter, and it is through this process that we can form the means by which to recognise our self and place ourselves in the world with something resembling equilibrium. Otherness therefore represents the negative essence of the self, what the self both desires and is repelled by, and what impels us to accept the challenges that life offers rather than collapsing back into the certainty of the pre-natal state.

The importance of the process of self-definition by differentiating what we are from what is other, of creating ourselves in recognition of what we are not – and the dangers this process entails – can be seen in the extensive myths relating to forms of twinning: mirrors, shadows and doubles. The mythologies surrounding these phenomena share intriguing characteristics that throw considerable light on the process by which we establish an identity. Mirrors not only reflect our appearance but may also be gateways to another world. They may provide protection against the evil eye but may also be used to conjure up magic forces. They copy images but also absorb and contain them. To break a mirror is an inauspicious sign and may bring seven years bad luck. Similarly, to lose one's shadow, or to meet with one's double, is widely believed to be a portent of death. What lies behind all such superstitions is the relation between self and other, and it is something that touches on and gives us an understanding of how we create and maintain our sense of self-identity.

At the root of myths connected with mirrors, shadows and doubles lies the biological phenomenon of twins. The belief that there is something troubling about twins is extensive, and most cultures have myths concerning them. Mirrors and twins in particular have in common the fact that both offer a perfect, yet elusive, likeness. A face resembles our own but it is not our own; both fool us by offering identical features that are not us at all. What we see in a mirror – a reversed image of ourselves – parallels what each twin sees in its sibling. Twins confound expectations and disconcert in ways that are linked to the disturbance our view of ourselves in the mirror establishes in regard to our sense of what we are. They appear to be the same but aren't, and their relation involves a complex inter-relation of similarity and difference. They are not superimposable but nor are they opposites or complementary to one another; they have separate personalities but respond to one another in ways that are out of the ordinary. In addition, twins are troubling in their demeanour: they may – intentionally or unintentionally – confuse us about their respective identities; each can assume that of the other and use such uncertainty to their own advantage.

There is a widespread belief that twins are immortal. Most traditions see their birth as either a good or a bad sign. Only rarely is it considered to be a normal event. Twins are often associated with the full moon and may be seen as having a special relationship either with the supernatural or with the natural world. They may be considered to have divine powers or the ability to transform themselves (into animal forms: to become werewolves, for instance). These powers may be benevolent: they may have rain-making capabilities, or have control over thunderbolts, fertilisation and the protection of travellers. But they can also be malevolent: they may use their powers of magic and sorcery for evil ends. It is also perhaps significant that many of the twins in mythology are characterised by the fact of being born of an immortal father and a mortal mother: they represent the clash of the possible and the impossible, a realisation of the scandal of reality.

There is a suggestion that the process of establishing a sense of otherness may begin in the womb. In this respect one of the most interesting myths of twinning is that of the Marassa. This is found in several African and American cultures. One element of this myth especially pertinent to discussion of the constitution of identity is that at conception everyone has a twin, but that most of us kill our twin in the womb. It is this event that makes us a human being and takes away our supernatural qualities. Babies born as twins have failed to carry out this act of separation and thus remain supernatural beings. They are thus not properly human. That is, they have not established themselves as differentiated beings. Recent scientific work has raised the possibility that there may be some truth in this (at least x-rays taken very early in the birth cycle apparently frequently appear to reveal the presence of two foetuses, one of which later mysteriously vanishes), but in any event the symbolism represented by twin mythology undoubtedly has very real psychological consequences and tells us much about the process by which we form ourselves not simply as what we are but also by what we are not. Indeed, there is a sense in which the memory of our lost twin – whether imaginary or not – continues to haunt us through our lives. In this respect we only have to think of the way we often construct ideas by means of imaginary conversations with ourselves, or may feel we have a guardian angel who watches over us. This can take more sinister forms in people who hear voices, especially when those voices tell them to act in particular ways, or even to commit terrible crimes. The mythology surrounding twins and also that associated with mirrors, shadows and doubles represents a significant attempt to account for the fact of our dual nature (vampires, we may recall, having no twins, neither cast shadows nor produce reflections in a mirror).

The mirror reflection embodies a latent displacement between the image, which we perceive as nothing but an empty property that provides the evidence of our material existence in a passively reflexive way (by providing proof of what we look like, it reveals our self as an autonomously established being existing in a stable universe), and an unstable likeness that may assume the form of an entity, coming to life in the double, which in the process rudely reminds us of our mortality and may thereby be seen as announcing our death. This is why the double represents both what is desired and what is feared. Not only does it give proof that we exist, it also stands in for the state of non-differentiation that we wish to return to and yet also dread. This drama is played out in one way or another in all of our relationships, with the other person standing in for the reflection. In choosing our friends, we are careful to ensure that they are similar to us but not too similar; that they are different from us but not too different. The security of our existence relies upon a primal linkage, but also the retention of a basic distinction, between myself and you. It is for this reason that unity with the double is fatal but so too is total separation from it. And this is given particular force in love, where we desire overwhelmingly and impossibly to fuse completely with the beloved whilst remaining distinct from him or her.

Whatever the objective truth that myths surrounding doubles and twins contain, therefore, they certainly provide resonant ideas about the unfolding of identity construction throughout the life process. The Oedipus complex itself, seen as being founded in a primal crime (not unlike the killing of the twin in the womb) in which we unknowingly kill our father and are sexually drawn to our mother, represents but one, culturally specific, element of it. In Lacanian psychology the infant's confrontation with the mirror is elemental, and Lacan's idea can be explored as providing further pointers to the way in which identity is shaped through the encounter with the image.

Lacan indeed considered the way we respond to mirrors as the key to understanding the foundation of culture and as representing a stage of development through which all humans pass. The human child at first does not recognise a distinction between itself and the world; it exists in an imaginary universe in which it is merely one element among others, without a notion of its own individual reality or that of others. It is through identification with the mirror image that we become really human. This was seen by Lacan as a crucial distinguishing feature that separates our sensibility from that of animals. A baby monkey and a human baby are equally fascinated at first by their mirror images, but once the monkey realises the image is empty it loses interest in it, while the human child continues to identify with it and seeks to penetrate its meaning.

The mirror stage is a primordial moment that effects the separation between the world of formless undifferentiation and that of a manifest, though symbolic, realm of shape and form that is objectified by means of the dialectic of identification with and isolation from the other. It serves to conceptualise this problematic distinction: as we recognise the reality of the other as what is distinct from us, so we seek to close the gap this sets up by means of language, which establishes a means of communication with the other, and also, in so doing, restores a sense of provisional continuity, by this very process further separating us from the world. This gives rise to a need to resolve the discordance with our own reality, which is correlatively formed as a loss, projected into infinity. Lacan explains the result of this problematic as follows:

> . . . [T]he formation of the *I* is symbolized in dreams by a fortress, or a stadium – its inner arena and enclosure, surrounded by marshes and rubbish-tips, dividing it into two opposed fields of contest where the subject flounders in quest of the lofty, remote inner castle whose form (sometimes juxtaposed in the same scenario) symbolizes the id in a quite startling way. Similarly, on the mental plane, we find realized the structures of fortified works, the metaphor of which arises spontaneously, as if issuing from the symptoms themselves, to designate the mechanisms of obsessional neurosis – inversion, isolation, reduplication, cancellation and displacement. (1977: 5)

We will look at this more closely in the next chapter. For now, let us simply note how the individual comes to take shape as an enclosure, an entity that is separate from others.

Lacan's conception of the mirror stage is suggestive and contains essential elements that help to explain how we shape our identity in our early years by means of this encounter with social and cultural forms. The way we respond to mirror reflections (which are in effect the manifestation of the Other, not simply, or necessarily, an actual mirror) undoubtedly has an essential bearing on the way our relation with other people develops and correlatively serves to found our own identity. The legend of Echo and Narcissus gives us an example of what may occur should we misrecognise, or draw faulty conclusions about, the nature of otherness contained by the mirror. Failing to distinguish between his own reflection and the reality of the Other, Narcissus in effect collapses back into a state of undifferentiation, rejecting otherness in the form of Echo and becoming one with his double, thereby mistaking the status and nature of the world. The story of Echo, who loves Narcissus but is separated from him due to his self-absorption and by her own inability to establish a sense of her own personality, gives shape to a corresponding failure of recognition: for her everything is other, including her own self, to the extent that she exists only as a reflection, as a mirror image with no substance and no possibility of achieving recognition of her self-identity, which consequently remains in a latent state. From this we can see the double imperative that faces the child, who needs not only to fathom the other's desire, but also to recognise its own. Essential to this process, too, is that we need recognition from the other of our own existence. The to-and-fro of this relation is incredibly complex.

The legend of Echo and Narcissus presents several important aspects of relations between self and other in terms of the apprehension of mirrors, but does not exhaust the implications. The mirror not only reflects an image of ourselves but also acts upon us directly, having, in a sense, its own energy source. We have seen that an evil spirit may reside in it, or, on the other hand, that it may have the power to deflect the evil eye. There is also a superstition that a mother should not allow a young child to see its mirror reflection because it does not have sufficient strength to resist the temporary separation of the soul that such an encounter entails, for mirrors have power and may also be doors to the other world. For this reason, also, they should be covered after death so as not to allow one of the living to be snatched away by a spirit of the other world. In East Asian philosophy, too, the mirror is regarded as having its own light source that it projects into objects, for the mirror effectively exists in the mind as a common human principle. To look into a mirror is therefore not necessarily a narcissistic exercise; it may be a meditative process based on the common principle that unites self and other in their integrality. The mirror image is not only reflective, but also illuminating. In this conception, the mirror stage is not simply a process of self-consciousness but the realisation of how dependent we are on the other: the self is not constituted in this process, but remains forever suspended in the relation between its own identity and that of the other.[2]

We do not need to see our own image in order to learn to recognise the ways in which we differ from the Other and, perhaps even more crucially, from the image of the Other. The fact that we groom ourselves to make ourselves as presentable as possible confirms this. For us as humans there is an inextricable link between what we are and the image we present to others, but there is also a realisation that there is a disjunction between our self and our image: we are also Other to ourselves. This is nicely expressed by Kenneth Patchen in a novel about the constitution of culture: 'I have forgotten my mask, and my face was in it' (1941: 11). Our identity is never one, but remains plural and flexible; we choose different masks and guises that are appropriate for different circumstances. We have a plurality of identities, and manifest ourselves differently in different situations.

What we call personality is a mask we assume that is protean and variable. It is created as a shell that both conceals and reveals what we are and is shaped in different ways by the different relationships we have with others and what we want from them. The self emerges in relation to experience and has no reality other than through the ways it is shaped by the experience of existing in society. In order to establish a sense of identity, the child must learn not only what it is but also how to fathom the Other's desire, for all human relations are predicated on the different forms of relation we establish, not simply with other people, but also with the world as a whole.

These relations with what is Other are always at the same time provisional, and we need to remain aware that the aspect the Other reveals to us corresponds only partially to the integral reality of that person: we each construct ourselves anew in every social and cultural encounter. But the being that presents itself to us is also never identical with itself. Rather, it acts as an enticement to reaffirm our own identity in the form of a new relationship. In this respect, identity is not determined but remains constantly open and mutable. Each time we enter into relations with another person we create a different form of exchange that affects our personality in relation to our immediate environment.

The process of life can thus be seen as an image of movement: we pass from one point to another until, ultimately, we die. In earlier societies the staging posts in this journey – a journey that calls for constant realignments of our relation with the external world – were clearly marked by initiatory rituals. Such initiatory stages were perceived as a primary confrontation with Otherness within one's being: one became a different person for having undergone the specified ritual. In today's society such initiation is discreet, if it exists at all. Rituals do exist in the form of anniversary celebrations, weddings, and so on, but in a degraded, empty form. Such rituals are largely devoid of significance and are not characterised as preparing the person involved for a new stage of life (this is due to the fact that one of the myths of modern society is that we exist as determinate and fixed beings with a self that inalienably belongs to us). In today's society, rather than ourselves being adapted to new circumstances by ritual processes given to us by society, we are expected naturally to adapt ourselves to them, it being assumed that we can easily do so without our personality being affected, since it should remain stable and constant. We are never given any support in coming to terms with how to confront Otherness. Rather, everything is done to ease the transition by pretending it does not exist, in order to maintain familiarity in the world at all costs. This tacit adaptability adds a secondary neurosis of great tenacity that becomes an inherent aspect of the modern condition.

As open as we are to new possibilities, these remain within the framework of a secure personal identity that keeps Otherness on a leash. We may seek an encounter with what is 'different', but this tends towards a vicarious experience of something outside ourselves that is separable from us, involving no real risk of psychic contamination. This reflects a will to deny that the birth trauma is constantly being repeated in the life cycle. For, in contemporary society little help is available to come to terms with it other than by shoring up individual identity and offering a sense of personal aspiration that helps to allay the primary neurosis we never entirely leave behind. For the modern individual, the urge to leave home is an essential element of the assertion of personal identity, the sign that one is no longer part of the enclosure the parents provide. This process provides the equivalent of what was once ritually established by initiation: the preparation and acknowledgement of a change of life circumstances.

In the life journey, a perpetual encounter with what is alien is mediated by ideas of the familiar that set up a tension by which our personality is shaped and transformed. The sense of home has to be broken up and made open to new possibilities in order for movement to take place and to prevent stagnation from occurring. Familiar and strange, safety and danger have to be balanced, and we exist in the gap that is always being opened up between them. It is how we situate ourselves within that gap, giving contour and purpose to our situation, that ultimately provides the basis for our (provisional) sense of identity based upon a conviction that it provides us with a stable 'self'. We form friendships, choose careers and interests, get married and even make decisions about which football clubs to support in accordance with how we want to situate our sense of identity, and it is through such attachments that we gain a sense of security in what we are. Indeed, it is these relationships, not what we ourselves are, that ultimately determine our sense of ourselves.

As secure as we may seek to make it, the identity we establish nevertheless remains contingent and shaky. We will always be pulled by contrary flows that respectively wish to hold us in our secure environment and at the same time to pull us away from our mooring towards new vistas. We do not cross a bridge or visit an unfamiliar place without experiencing a certain displacement, no matter how much of a seasoned traveller we may be. We experience it, too, each night, when we sleep, and most especially when we dream, an event that is itself an experience of Otherness that again brings into question the fundamental stability of the human personality. In sicknesses, too, especially in psychological disorders such as schizophrenia, the dynamic between familiar and alien breaks down, the self collapses into a state in which it can recognise neither, but constructs its own egocentric world of resemblance which is essentially a world of pure undifferentiation. To witness such a state is to see the extent to which the human personality is a fragile construction that may collapse at very little prompting.

Lacan's image of the self as an enclosure surrounded by treacherous reaches that divide the subject from itself is therefore a resonant way of thinking about the problematic inscribed at the heart of identity formation. Whether we remain tight within our self-enclosed world or whether we strike out boldly towards new horizons, we are still faced with a problematic bearing upon our own process of self-discovery and self-affirmation. This turns on our relation with Otherness, especially upon how we deal with the ineluctable alienness of the Other and make it meaningful in terms of the framework of our own lives. Are we able to accept Otherness, broadening our frame of reference in order to accommodate the different perspectives of the other people we encounter, or do we seek to fix others into our own frame of reference, forcing them to accommodate themselves to us as the price of our recognition? This raises fundamental issues about our relation with the world: how do we accept what other people have to offer us while allowing them to retain their identity as Other, and without seeking to turn them into pale imitations of ourselves? To what extent should we expect other people to accept our reality, and to what extent should we accept theirs without compromising either our own or their own integral being?

In this there is a need to recognise difference and its irreducibility. There is also, concomitantly, a need for communication across such differences. True communication arises from the existence of these differences and the distance that inevitably separates my cultural experience from yours. The faculty to apprehend the existence of different realities existing in the tangible world we encounter is by no means as easy as it may appear; it requires conscious engagement if we are to forge meaningful relationships with others and make our world one that contains the richness life has to offer. The failure of such recognition is what leads to elemental conflict. All movement, all of the changes that occur in the course of a lifetime, involves some engagement with the Other, an engagement that frequently places our own sensibility at stake, and this Other exists as much within us as outside in the world. Otherness is not an abstraction existing separately from the processes of life. Rather, it is inscribed within those processes.

Each movement placing us in a fresh environment represents something of a secondary birth: finding ourselves in an unfamiliar situation, we respond as the newborn child does to its new situation, striving to come to terms with it while simultaneously wanting to flee it. The response of the Other is similarly ambivalent, seeking to place our intervention into their familiar situation. There is a natural inclination to fail to recognise how alien this encounter is and to try to elude it. Each would like, impossibly, to allow things to continue as they were before, reducing the Other to an object having no bearing on him- or herself.

This facile initial turning away from encounter needs to be overcome to establish genuine communication with the Other, to recognise the Other as a subject with as rich and complex a sensibility as one's own. There is a need to negate the initial moment of alienating consciousness and to welcome the strangeness that all encounters with the Other initially introduce. Human life is fundamentally dialogical, and we need to encounter other people in order to form our own sense of identity. We become human agents through the acquisition of languages by which to communicate with others. This provides us with a bridgehead by which we are able to understand ourselves and define what we are. Language itself is learned through exchanges with others. We acquire these languages not through self-reflection but through interaction. The human mind takes shape by means of dialogical activity.

This shaping does not simply serve our own purposes, even if we are expected to develop our own ideas, attitudes and viewpoints independently of others'. When we define our identity, we do so in dialogue or in struggle against others. We either succumb to or struggle against what others see in us. And this dialogue continues, in some cases, with people who are especially important to us, like our parents or our lovers, until the day we die. Those who care for us early in life will inevitably shape our personalities, in either a positive or a negative sense. Even as we strive against this influence, we must admit its importance. Any original identity needs the recognition of others and suffers if this is withheld. This leads us to understanding of the extent to which identities are formed by means of interaction and the images that are created by means of it. We can demean others by forming inaccurate images of them, or simply forming images of them that do not accord with their own self-image. This may even be internalised, to the extent that the debased image can be accepted as true by the subject. All of our relationships are implicated in processes of self-discovery and self-affirmation.

In the modern world, we are acutely aware of the latter difficulty, and this consciousness has given rise to a politics of difference, in which each unique identity is expected to be recognised. The difficulty with this is that it breaks down communicative processes, instituting a suspicion of Otherness that leads away from communication to a polarisation of difference accepted in its self-similitude, rather than as an aspect of each person's self-identity.

Whether we like it or not, our personality is formed against and in harmony with multiple elements of Otherness. We are not inscribed with difference: we become different by contrasting and judging ourselves against others. Even our own experiences become Other to us as we develop. The childhood sensibility is open to a vast range of experience that we shall never know as our development closes down possibilities as it makes us into the adult we shall become. In a moment of profound insight, Freud recognised how socialisation retards rather than civilises:

> It is hardly to be believed what goes on in a child of four or five years old. Children are very active-minded at that age; their early sexual period is also a period of intellectual flowering. I have an impression that with the onset of the latency period they become mentally retarded as well, stupider. (1959: 215)

The person we were as a child is not different from our present self but is an element of ourselves that has become distant from and alien to what we now are: it is an aspect of Otherness, being what we have passed through in the process of our becoming, and what we once were can never be recovered. We are never identical with ourselves, no matter how much we believe we are.

The experience of life is strange and disorientating, and as much as we might believe that we can establish a sense of equilibrium, life will always be apt, often at the most unexpected times, to undermine it. It is the play with multiple senses of Otherness that enables the provisional equilibrium to be established. Society is formed at the point at which we accept a common vision or, in the absence of such common vision, when one succumbs to the viewpoint of the other. This conflict is elucidated by Hegel's master and slave dialectic, which reveals how, as part of the socio-psychological process, human conflicts result in certain ideas and people emerging triumphant. The masters may emerge victorious because they have dared to prefer death to servitude while the slaves have preferred servitude to death, but the relationship between them is symbiotic: they depend on one another and also need recognition from one another. This involves a power relation that is at the heart of human oppression and injustice. The master's recognition is conquer or die; the slave's is submit and remain alive. But this relation distorts social relations, leading to a denial of our true reality. We live in a state of limbo, subject to delusions. Both master and slave are, in a sense, slaves: they are each trapped within their respective states. It is only through a daily struggle to correct this relation that we can hope to attain genuine freedom, and this elemental struggle reveals the dilemma of otherness.

In the final analysis, we know nothing of the Other: what defines otherness is that its experience is hermetically sealed from us and will always remain alien and unknown to us. This involves a disjunction at our very heart, to the extent that we are detached from ourselves: there is an Otherness within us. The only experience of the Other we have is what has been translated into terms that make sense within our own frame of experience. This is the most we can do. We can extend our own experience to try to encompass that of the Other; we can empathise with what it is they have undergone. But the actual experience remains uniquely Other. Ultimately all of us are alone in the universe and condemned to remain so, even being, in the final analysis, disconnected from our own self. When we ask 'Who am I?' we are faced, ultimately, with a blank. 'I', as Rimbaud asserted, 'is another.'

Notes

1. This may of course be quite different in societies in which the nuclear family is not dominant, or in which socialisation is the primary responsibility of the greater society, not of the enclosed family. In such cases the sense of identification between parent and child may be very differently configured.
2. I am indebted to Han-Rog Kang for this insight.

3

THE DIFFERENTIATION OF CULTURES

As humans, we are born not only into culture, but also into a particular culture: we are given a set of culturally specific defining features into which we are expected to fit or to which we are expected to adapt ourselves. More accurately, we are born into several cultures, each of which acts upon us in different ways, expecting different things from us and making different demands to which we are forced to respond. Moreover, such demands, and the extent to which we are constrained – or, on the other hand, inclined – to accept them, vary enormously in their intensity and insistence, to the extent that we must constantly weigh up the ones to which we will give priority. In many we have little or no choice: sex, race, nationality, are given to us at birth and we ignore at our peril the imperatives they place upon us.

Cultural difference remains a mystery, something that once more seems to separate us from other animals. How do we explain it? Other species appear homogeneous: they do not separate into different groups who may establish a hostile relationship to one another. If it is true that dogs, for instance, are, if anything, more variegated as a species than humans (in physical appearance and also in demeanour an Alsatian is far more distinct from a Pekinese than a Londoner is from a New Guinea highlander), they remain relatively unvarying in their species behaviour. Humans are a restless species, endlessly seeking to extend their domain and constructing different cultural patterns wherever they go. And each community they form establishes different norms of judgement that may be incompatible with those of other, neighbouring, communities. Why should the diffusion of humans lead to the establishment of so many different cultures differentiated in such stark ways? Why should human beings need to belong to societies at all or identify with abstract entities like tribes and nationalities? Consideration of culture here once again leads to doubt about how important genetic factors are in the constitution of what we are. For, if we are genetically determined, all cultures should follow the same path. Yet this is patently not the case. Cultural factors clearly act in such a way as to affect the aspirations and assumptions of different cultural groups in different ways. A will towards differentiation is central to human culture: we define ourselves not only by what we are, but also by what we are not. And a double movement is necessary to effect this: we must establish ourselves as social beings while at the same time maintaining a sense of ourselves as individual entities separable from – although dependent upon – society.

As much as we must fit in with the needs of society, we also need to establish a sense of our being as individuals, both in our own right, but also in relation to the different cultural formations of which we are part or strive to be part. Individuation is crucial and is based on the fact that we want to be like others while simultaneously wanting to be different from them, to fit in with our group and at the same time to be sufficiently distinct from it to feel that we exist also as individuals in our own right. This dual pull is central to our identity, which has to be seen as being both individual and collective, and there is both a dialectical tension and unity in the way in which individual and collective demands have an effect upon the way we constitute ourselves. How important this is may vary across cultures, but its tension is always present to some extent.

Recognition of this tension does not always come easily. If the whole of our life is centred on our relation with others (what do we want from them? what are we prepared to give?), there is a concurrent process that causes us to want to withdraw into ourselves, or even back into species undifferentiation. As we have seen, this may be equated with the death instinct of Freudian psychology, and it affects not only individuals but also collectives. As much is recognised by many societies, and not only such practices as sacrifice but also the prohibitions that pertain in human society – especially the apparently universal institution of the incest taboo supported by complex rules of endogamy and exogamy – are required to maintain a balance of social interaction by which the society is renewed without losing its coherence, as well as to prevent it from collapsing into itself. The complexity of modern society has its own means of instilling discipline in its citizens to ensure that the society is able to reproduce itself in an effective way.

We each have a need to assert our identity as an individual that is separate unto itself, differentiated from all others, and yet at the same time we desire to belong, to be accepted and respected by others. This double imperative at the basis of our assertion of identity requires that we move in and out of different cultural formations at certain moments and in certain places, establishing complex and different relationships that serve our sense of self and of belonging.

To explore this, we need to return to consider further the relation between self and other, a relation that is primordial to our becoming as humans, but that also feeds back into the way in which society itself develops. Our entry into culture requires us to exteriorise our subjectivity, something that, according to Lacan's idea of the mirror stage, as we have seen, occurs by means of a dialectic of identification with the Other. If the ego can achieve a unified state only by means of misrecognition of the image in the mirror, which allows it to gain a self-coherence that is founded in a neurotic sense of identification with the Other's desire, so assuming the Other's unity as its own through a procedure of displacement by which the anticipation or projection of integration is assumed, then the child's identity that emerges is founded as a social entity held together only provisionally, tormented by lack and surrounded on all sides by the symbolic system of language.

Desire, as a craving for recognition and love, can be satisfied only by an abstraction that has been established in the interaction with the Other, a desire animated both by the wish to be desired by the Other and by the self's projection of its own desire upon the Other. This primary identification is therefore formed consequent upon the relationship with the Other, whose identity *vis-à-vis* the subject is itself shaped within a web of signifiers that comes to be articulated in language.

As we have seen, a discordance is thereby instituted that the subject must try to resolve within the self if it is to establish its own stable identity, which thus cannot be seen as being purely an emanation from within the subject. As the self is formed as a fortress with an inner arena and enclosure, surrounded by a treacherous marshland, which the subject must strive to negotiate in quest of the inner area represented by the unconscious, so the Other is constituted as the object of the subject's desire and this establishes a mutual need through which we strive to maintain an appearance of coherence and completeness as we identify with the culture around us. But, as often as not, and no matter how strong our will, this is a process that controls us rather than one that we control: the environment captures us and forces us to do its will. We see this all around us in the demands society makes upon us as it requires us to work and make a contribution to society, forcing us into configurations of relationships we have not chosen.

As the process of identity formation requires the self to form as an enclosure separate from other beings with certain characteristic properties that, whether innate or acquired, are intrinsic, so it is equally acted upon by racial and sexual as well as national or class factors. The notion of the individual is inseparable from the associations it either establishes or else fails or is unable to establish, such associations revealing paths that open us up to certain cultural worlds while closing off others. This process is also associated with an essential element of our entrance into History, Time and Society, and provides for us a template by which we can comprehend our social identity and fix our individual identity within it.

This rather schematic account of self-becoming developed from Lacan's understanding hopefully sets up an account that is sufficiently precise to provide a valuable and resonant description of how the self and other relation is played out in the general framework of the life process. We may doubt some of the specifics of Lacan's analysis – especially the importance of the play of signifiers as the self's only tangible reality, something that has been effectively questioned by Castoriadis, who saw the imaginary not as a reflected image of something but as fundamentally in its very nature being undetermined and creating images from out of this undetermined nature; the self is thereby generated by the other as much as it is a reflection of it. We shall also later raise doubts about the primacy and irrevocability of the symbolic world in analysing Saussurian assumption of the arbitrariness of the sign. Nevertheless, Lacan's theory of development contains a clear enough analysis of self-formation to provide an effective means for understanding how culture enters the individual consciousness, directing the individual into structures that are allowable as the foundation for identity formation within the particular social and cultural situation of that individual.

What is significant here is the way in which, from the moment we are born, as we engage with what is external to us, we are immersed in a journey that will lead to the constitution of an identity on a neurotic basis (in the sense that it is based upon a pull of contradictory ideas). As the child learns to adapt to what surrounds it, so it tries to establish a sense of the familiar by which it can enjoy an illusion of security. But this does not satisfy us and we would like, to a lesser or greater degree, to break the bonds of such assurance. The individual is not a bounded entity free to act as it will, but an active element that is required to accept and participate in certain ways within a given culture. This process itself is also active: the culture seeks not to imprint the individual with its requirements, but to form an individual that will feed its own qualities back into the culture, enriching it with its own contribution. This requires that each individual needs to intervene in the lives of others, and it is this intervention that makes society possible.

This relation is crucial for understanding how as individuals we interact with our own culture, and conversely how we establish a relationship with that of others. When we travel out of our culture, we are at first disorientated. Everything seems strange in a way that replicates the initial strangeness we encounter when we enter the world. This strangeness may be called exoticism: it represents a projection of our own desires on to the person of others, just as the child projects itself onto the mirror. And just as the individual faces the danger of collapse into an embrace of narcissism that makes it difficult to respect or recognise the reality of others, so there is a tendency for our perceptions of other cultures to remain congealed in this relation: to view others as being nothing but projections of ourselves. As such, their difference is recognised only as a disembodied Echo, consigned to do no more than answer back the self in the terms that we, taking the role of Narcissus, have established as an incomplete form of relationship. The major challenge for the establishment of any society is to recognise the differences within it and to allow its different components to interact and communicate in such a way that retains internal coherence and allows respect and recognition.

Society is formed when an association of individuals consent to function according to a given set of values. No society can exist without this fundamental process of consent, which is nevertheless neither stable nor constant, and is always subject to tension. The formation of society also proceeds in a way that is analogous to the formation of self-identity by the child. A society is not formed by it own momentum as responding simply to an internally generated dynamic. It establishes itself precisely in dialectical relation with what surrounds it, in the face of the reality of alien others, which are a constant threat to its self-constitution.

Recognition of foreign cultures is not always desirable to society. Indeed, in many societies, the human Other is excluded from the category of human beings. To take an example at random: a Native American nation are today known most commonly as the Dakota; in the past they were more commonly called the Sioux. Yet neither of these words are names: Dakota is simply one of several descriptive terms used by particular tribes within the nation; Sioux is a French corruption of an Ojibway word meaning 'little snake'. Indeed, if they ever refer to themselves as a whole, it is apparently as '*Ikche-Wichasha*', which simply means 'real natural human beings'. For their own purposes they needed no name since they constituted the human race: other tribes represented different graduations of non-humans. This is a principle we find in most parts of the world. Nietzsche notes this, pointing out that Germans gained their name from their enemies: '*Deutschen*' originally meaning 'heathen'. This points to the way that engagement with others is not a straightforward process of communication. We choose our others in terms that give meaning to our own sense of identity. In this respect, other societies are often identified as being external not simply to one's own society, but to the human race as a whole; other people are, at best, enemies to be fought or with which to make an accommodation. In its essential form, society would like to be self-established and self-sustaining, but this is impossible: survival calls for interaction with other societies. Yet in its primitive form, such interaction is kept to a minimum. Striving to establish a bridge with the alien values of other societies is something of a recent phenomenon and has arisen only from the need in the modern world for increased interaction (most notably for trade). Understanding between cultures requires a conscious effort; it is not given and may at times seem unnatural, for all socialisation inscribes a world view that is fundamentally ethnocentric, even as it is formed in relation to what is other. In the same way as the self itself is culturally constructed rather than inherent, so, too, a society seeks to establish its identity in a denial of the Other. A society, just like an individual, is animated by a wish to perceive itself in its own integrality. This denial of the Other will only gradually be broken down as the self is forced into recognition of the Other's reality through its particular processes of interaction. This is why Hegel sees recognition as emerging from a struggle for mastery: the capacity to see the self from the point of view of the Other is not given but emerges as different groups are brought into intimate contact with one another and so forced to establish relations of either enmity or friendship.

In saying that societies are fundamentally ethnocentric, does this mean that some societies do not have a conception of otherness? Not at all: there is every reason to imagine that a conception of otherness is necessary for the establishment of society. However, the way in which this relationship is configured takes different forms in diverse societies. If it excludes the recognition of the otherness of neighbouring societies, it constitutes it elsewhere. In societies that exclude other societies from the domain of the human, the Other is precisely what exists beyond the human sphere. The Other against which most human societies measure themselves is given in the relationship it establishes with ancestors and supernatural deities. Marc Augé has shown how

> every identity is constructed through negotiation with diverse otherness and that consequently, upstream of phenomena presented as signalling an identity crisis, there is always a more profound crisis of otherness. Individuals or groups say they are in crisis when they no longer have a way of conceiving or 'thinking' the other, and we are indeed in an emergency situation today. (1999: 91)

This acutely presents a problem that affects culture as a whole in today's world in numerous ways.

We have a longing for community. Individual existence is insufficient to our species needs. As important as our sense of self is to us, we are also drawn to moments when this sense, this consciousness, dissolves into a greater whole. As aware as we are of our individuality, it is also an oppression. But so, too, is belonging to a group. Festivals strengthen the idea of group. These are the times when people as a whole express joy in the success of a harvest or a hunt. At such times they reaffirm their mutual dependence and perception of a common purpose, maintaining their coherence and honouring the Other that they respect.

What actually is a society, a culture? Marx gives us a very carefully formulated account of the dynamic that is at the heart of any constitution of a society in relation to its component parts:

> My *universal* consciousness is only the *theoretical* form of that whose *living* form is the *real* community, society, whereas at present *universal* consciousness is an abstraction from real life and as such in hostile opposition to it. Hence the *activity* of my universal consciousness – an activity – is my *theoretical* existence as a species being.
>
> It is above all necessary to avoid once more establishing 'society' as an abstraction over against the individual. The individual *is* the *social being*. His vital expression – even when it does not appear in the direct form of a *communal* expression, conceived in association with other men – is therefore an expression and confirmation of *social life*. Man's individual and species-life are not two *distinct things*, however much – and this is necessarily so – the mode of existence of individual life is a more *particular* or a more *general* mode of the species-life, or species-life a more *particular* or more *general* individual life.
>
> As *species-consciousness* man confirms his real *social life* and merely repeats in thought his actual existence; conversely, species-being confirms itself in species-consciousness and exists for itself in its universality, as a thinking being. (1974a: 350–1)

This provides us with a valuable insight into the way society takes its organic shape in the constant interplay of all its component parts. A society here can be seen as a body whose locus fixes certain values and concepts that are essential for its own functioning and survival. It is not an abstraction, but a particular cultural formation obeying the same sorts of exigencies faced by the individual in forming its own identity. Each cultural formation needs to struggle to establish its singularity and integrity, to define itself in itself and against others.

Yet cultural worlds do not exist in the singular; they most especially do not exist as distinct and bounded entities that can be separated one from the other. Each one exists in a nexus of relations with others. This communication with the others is essential to its cultural integrity. Even if it may be conceptualised as the enemy, or as outside the category of human beings as recognised by that particular culture, there is still a need to come to an accommodation with what exists external to the situation in which we find ourselves. No matter how much we may try to assert the singularity of our own cultural experience, the image of the Other necessarily impinges, even if often that image is distorted.

In this respect it is not, I think, going too far to say that the conceptualisation of otherness as a problem between cultures, as an issue that calls for philosophical reflection in the relation between societies, is a creation of colonial expansion. The establishment of a colony calls for a greater intimacy than is required of any society that does not seek to expand into the territory of others, and this reveals how difficult it is to admit difference and accept others on their rather than on our terms. A colonial power cannot dismiss the societies it has conquered as simply being comprised of aliens and enemies, but is forced to come to some accommodation with them. If the history of colonialism can be seen as an attempt to impose the reality of the self on that of other people, at the same time this gives rise to resistance and forces both societies to reformulate their sense of identity to deal with the new situation, establishing a form of dialogue that may not be equal but will affect both.

If recognition of otherness between societies is a concomitant of imperialism and successful colonisation requires some understanding of other cultures, Western colonialism has been of such a nature as to bring these issues into focus in ways that previous imperialist adventures did not. The essential difference seems to be that earlier empires conquered by means of culturally assimilating themselves into the indigenous culture and expecting the native culture to adapt itself to the colonisers. Perhaps the clearest example of this was the Manchu conquest of China, which founded the Ch'ing dynasty, giving the Manchus dominance, but without changing the essential features of Chinese society. The overriding concern of virtually all earlier conquest was prestige and it was conducted by heroic political and military leaders as an extension of military might. As such, the integrity of the other culture was not brought into question (although it may have been irrevocably changed). Western colonialism, on the other hand, was initiated and carried out neither by political nor by military leaders, but by adventurers in search of wealth and personal renown. It was conducted not primarily for political but for economic reasons.

Different societies have established highly complex and distinctive cultures, and this diversity remains considerable. However, one cultural conception – that of the West – is now dominant and demands that the diversity of cultures is conditioned by the relation it has established with Western hegemony. It is today legitimate to speak of an 'idea of the West' as a pattern within which all people, indeed all cultures, have a place, as a location to which all must belong or pass through. The expansion of the West through colonialism has been so successful that all people now exist as part of it, or at least have a relation to it that cannot be ignored.

In accordance with what we have said about the construction of identity, we can try to establish the constituents of this body, or this ideology, that we call the 'West'. From the Renaissance, we can see the 'idea of the West' being shaped not as a geographical description but as a cultural concept determined by historical contingency. Not a static or determined notion, but one that is protean and infinitely malleable.

The concept of the West is so ingrained in contemporary consciousness and discourse that there is a tendency to assume its identity as being self-evident, or, on the other hand, to dismiss it as a mystification. As with any cultural construction, however, its formation and constitution are extremely complex and are not at all a deliberated project on the part of the Western powers. As Jimmie Durham has said: 'Europe is a human project, it's not a European project, we have all contributed' (no date: 29). It is an entity in which all people living today have a stake. No one belongs to it wholly and the relations of the contemporary world turn on the different ways we interact with it.

In seeking to elucidate what this entity means, it is important first of all to make a clear distinction between the 'West' as a concept and 'Europe' as a geographical place. Indeed, the idea of the West may be separated from the idea of Europe, even though they mutually inform one another. The latter has continued as a parallel ideology, a part of the West, but differently configured. It differs in being centred in Europe itself rather than on its margins. 'Europe' is essentially a German concept, dating back to the time of the Holy Roman Empire and today embodied by the European Union. The idea of the West is a more amorphous concept, with a trajectory that is not so easy to trace, but which is intrinsically tied in with the development of Western colonialism and the spread of European values and culture by means of trade.

If we wish to seek the location of this idea, we have to consider many contingencies. We can trace its formation over a long historical period, in which it has gained different aspects that have added to its lustre. And over the centuries its centre of gravity has constantly changed. If its roots undoubtedly lie in ancient Greece and Rome, or more precisely in the way in which the Renaissance constituted them as part of its founding myth, its dynamic was established in Northern Italy during the fifteenth century and its core may be said to have been transposed to Spain during the sixteenth century, which itself ceded ascendancy to England and later France during the eighteenth and nineteenth centuries. In the twentieth century it moved out of Europe altogether to be embodied by the global culture of the United States. It is important to be aware of these shifting boundaries. When we are looking at the way culture functions, we need constantly to be alert to the fact that what we are considering is always in a state of flux and can never be tied down in any precise way. Conditioned by the activities of the various individual societies that comprise it, the West remains a cultural construction that is not determined by that activity. Rather, it is an individual entity that obeys its own exigences. Thus, Greek culture today has only marginal importance to what we are calling the 'idea of the West', even though ancient Greek culture planted its seed. Equally, perhaps the vast majority of European cultures (although they have rich cultural traditions) have had only a peripheral impact on its unfolding and in many ways are as marginal to its historical becoming as, say, Japanese culture. These cultures are largely excluded from its mainstream, which largely comprises the traditions of England and France and the United States, with other elements – of greater or lesser importance – taken at different times and in different ways from Spain, Portugal, Germany, Italy and Russia and many other cultures. The 'idea of the West' should therefore be seen as a hegemonic form in the way Gramsci understood it: it assumes those aspects that contribute to its hegemony, while excluding anything that does not. As a Romanian, E.M. Cioran can speak eloquently of how this hegemony acts in practice to exclude:

> I must confess, I once regarded it as a disgrace to belong to an ordinary nation, to a collectivity of victims about whose origin no illusion was permitted. I believed, and I was not mistaken, that we had sprung from the lees of the Barbarians, from the scum of the great Invasions, from those hordes which, unable to pursue their march West, collapsed along the Carpathians and the Danube, somnolently squatting there, a mass of deserters on the Empire's confines, daubed with a touch of Latinity. With that past, this present. And this future. What an ordeal for my young arrogance! 'How can one be a Romanian?' was a question I could answer only by a constant mortification. (1987: 70)

To some extent this mortification is one felt by all victims of Western hegemony.

The Renaissance as 'a new birth', a 'revival', gave Western culture the defining features that have sustained its historical development, and was itself established against the prevailing European culture, which it renounced, and indeed made Other, by characterising the medieval period that had preceded it as 'the dark ages'. Whether this period was in fact so 'dark' may be questioned, but it remains true that the Renaissance period effected a shift in consciousness that substantially conditioned if not determined the sensibility of the modern world. The most tangible element of this shift concerned what may be called 'spatial relationships' between people, but for the moment the aspect that concerns us is how it relates to cultural perception. Medieval European society was hierarchical and held in stasis. It was structured as an interlocking whole in which each element had its place. Hierarchical in all respects, movement was upwards, with the supreme deity of medieval Christian belief at the summit. The social fabric was maintained by mutual obligations and reflected a universal order: the peasantry provided the wealth for the clergy and the military aristocracy, which, in return, provided them with spiritual and military protection. This equilibrium was based on the assumption that capital accumulation was an evil, something encapsulated in the idea of usury – in other words the profit motive – as being sinful under canon law. The movement against this equilibrium was an essential founding feature of what we are calling the Western idea.

Brought into question with the rise of Venice as a trading centre and the consequent emergence of a merchant class reliant upon an accumulation of capital resources, the equilibrium of medieval society began to break down. Slowly, the profit motive was institutionalised and would ultimately come to be the determining economic feature of the social fabric. As Weber has shown, the schisms in the church and the rise of Protestantism made possible a break with the ideology of the medieval church and its notion of hierarchy, which had condemned capital accumulation and individual enterprise.

But it was the Renaissance that created the environment that made such a shift possible, above all making a radical transformation of relations between individual and society possible. Scope for individual initiative was massively increased. No longer did the individual need to feel entirely integrated into a pattern of culture, part of a collective whole whose components functioned in relation to one another. Instead the individual assumed a quality to itself. The responsibility the individual had to the larger society began to change away from the patterns of mutual obligation and security characteristic of feudalism. Instead, the individual was encouraged to act on his own initiative and, to some extent, to his own profit. The dynamic of capitalism required individual initiative and drive and thus gave the individual the power to determine his destiny in a way virtually unheard of in earlier periods.

This celebration of the individual led to humanism and a new conception of mankind. It may be said that the scientific discoveries of the West were predicated on this change in consciousness. Where man previously had a place in the nature of things and accepted that he lived in a symbiotic relationship with nature, the ideology of the Renaissance was to initiate (or to create the conditions that made possible) a view of man as superior to nature, and with the power to dominate it.

This heightening of the powers of mankind was manifested in every sphere of life, leading to the scientific achievements that have characterised Western society for the past five hundred years. It also provided the psychological bedrock for the exploration and conquest of new lands. In this it built upon the medieval spirit that had animated the Crusades. The conviction of Columbus was based on this fact, as Tzvetan Todorov put it:

> The profits which 'should be' found there interest Columbus only secondarily: what counts are the 'lands' and their discovery. This discovery seems in truth subject to a goal, which is the narrative of a voyage: one might say that Columbus has undertaken it all to be able to tell unheard-of stories, like Ulysses; but is not a travel narrative itself the point of departure, and not only the point of arrival, of a new voyage? (1984: 13)

Columbus was modern in the sense that, as an individual, he yearned to discover new lands, to open up horizons. While it may be that the profits that such adventures might bring only secondarily interested Columbus himself, without that secondary interest (which would soon predominate and become the primary concern) such discovery would have been impossible.

This widening of horizons is also to be perceived in the arts, and most notably in the invention of perspective, which deepened the image that could be created within a picture frame, a 'conquest of reality' that provided a window on the world reflecting the outward thrust of Western society. No longer was the drive upwards, it was outwards, ever more towards the horizon, which was constantly being pushed further away.

If these are its essential founding features, they did not develop sponta-neously from out of nothing to form once and for all what can be called the 'idea of the West'. Indeed, it was no doubt to be many centuries before any consciousness of 'Western culture' was established. Nor can it be said that the basis of such ideas was not already present within society prior to the Renaissance. Horkheimer and Adorno (1979) have traced the central ideas to ancient Greece, and specifically see them as being present in *The Odyssey*. When we speak about 'Western culture', therefore, we need to be aware of it as a slow development over the years, and as one possibility for the devel-opment of society among many. It can only be perceived as an entity as we look back upon it from our current vantage point. It has no concrete reality other than in the relations it has established and cannot be grasped as any-thing other than an amorphous line of development that contains innumerable contradictions within it. Certain trends may have been favourable to it at certain times, only to be rejected at others. Yet it is no less real for all that. It takes the form of an *égrégore*, as Pierre Mabille (1977) put it, that is, an aggregation of dialectical unity held together by its component parts but forming something that is not the sum of those parts. If it is sig-nificant, it is because it is the foundation of the modern attitude that continues to determine and provide a common heritage linking all cultures today.

A cultural entity like the 'West' requires something against which to mark itself in the same way as does an individual self: it does not exist in and of itself. Just as the Renaissance, providing the bedrock for the ideas that we can define today as the culture of the West, represented as a rebirth of classical consciousness, had to be charted in a way that set it against the supposed 'darkness' of the medieval age, so the very idea of the 'West' contains an assumption of a 'non-West': in geographical terms it is obvious that it is most especially defined against what is East, even as it also excludes the cor-responding geographical points of 'north' and 'south'. The 'East' is most significant because it is with Asia that Europe has established historically the most intimate relationship. As a contingent entity, indeed, the reality of the 'West' is defined most especially through the corresponding idea of the 'East'. This relationship has been historically established in much the same way as Lacan describes in relation to the construction of the individual: the West is clearly not internally generated, but forms itself by creating a desire that is projected from the Other as a will towards self-constitution and at the same time as a wish for recognition by that Other. The East becomes constituted correlatively only by a fluid projection from the Western self so that, while there is otherwise little to identify, say, Chinese and Arabic culture with one another in any meaningful sense, they gain an identity as 'Oriental' cultures by means of their relation to the West. Correlatively, too, the notion of the West is formed as an entity that exceeds its constituent parts so that, say, British and Spanish cultures become associated under its rubric. In this way, the 'idea of the West' gains form as a potent cultural entity with historical roots.

If there is no comparable 'idea of the East', it is because the peoples of Asia did not engage upon the sort of vast imperial adventure that began when Columbus set out from Spain to discover a western trade route to the Indies. The 'East' was negatively shaped as what was not Western, not by what was characteristic of the reality of the cultures of Asia. It is not a term of self-definition, but one that was refracted by means of the Other: the East is a reflection of the West, existing only as part of the construction of the former, and there are no defining features of it that can be accounted to identify it. If the idea of the West is amorphous, so, too, or perhaps even more so, are the ideas that constitute the 'East'.

As Edward Said has shown in his *Orientalism* (1978), the West constructed the 'East' in terms of its own negative representation as a means of cultural and imperial control. The Orient becomes a place desired by the West, a place of romance, remarkable events, mystical religions and mesmerising ideas, and as an escape from all the pressure of what was constituted as Western. Paradoxically, it also became the site of all that the West rejected: it was reactionary, primitive, decadent. It had to be what – and only what – the Occident was not. Such is the case for all cultural formations: each establishes what it is by means of a process of inclusion and exclusion. It follows a classic course of subject and object relations, establishing a hegemonic ideology that is congealed in a colonial relation. Said explains it as an all-pervasive discourse necessary for exercising power over the Orient. In his words, it is a '*distribution* of geopolitical awareness into aesthetic, scholarly, economic, sociological, historical, and philological texts; it is an *elaboration* not only of a basic geographical distinction (the world is made up of two unequal halves, Orient/Occident) but also of a whole series of "interests" . . . a certain *will* or *intention* to understand, in some cases to control, manipulate, even to incorporate what is a manifestly different (or alternative and novel) world' (1978: 12). It took shape as a discourse with no material reality but was 'a Western style for dominating, restructuring and having authority over the Orient' (1978: 3).

Said's book is not well argued, its methodology is suspect, its treatment of facts cavalier. At the same time, though, it hit a raw nerve and much of the criticism it has received has been motivated as much by emotion as by intellectual argument. For good or ill, it has served to define the nature and direction of the debate that has followed. It has also served to initiate us into the maze of post-colonial studies that have tended to establish the course of current debates about the relationship between cultures. While it is doubtless likely that the issues of post-colonialism would have developed in some form even if Said had not published *Orientalism*, they could not have taken the form they have without it. The book has served to form a closed discourse, which could itself be analysed in Foucault's terms of power and knowledge. The real weakness of the book is not methodological but philosophical: Said largely ignored the philosophical determinants of self/other relations to focus on Orientalism as a particular example of Western domination, without separating out what was particular about it. That is, he did not distinguish the general elements inevitably formed in the process of any cross-cultural contact from the particular elements that determined Western understandings of the East. He raised the problematic of subject and object relations without examining the mechanic of the relation itself, failing to recognise it as a material relation; therefore his analysis collapses into idealism. The conceptualisation that Said identifies as Orientalism was certainly a means of domination, but this was a secondary characteristic, not a primary one. That is, it was not consciously erected, as Said seems to believe, but emerged as part of a natural working of a phenomenological relation, in which master and slave interact in a way that conforms with Hegel's analysis of the development of the spirit. Yet Said ignores any such analysis, preferring to see Orientalism as something that was plucked out of the air to serve colonial authority. In the process, he vulgarises the relation, and his analysis consequently leads to a dead end in which perception becomes determined by Orientalism rather than the other way round. In so doing, he is forced to deny the undoubted elements of reciprocity and symbiosis that must be involved in any such relation as that between Western and Eastern cultures, so reducing the resulting discourse to the level of a crude annulment of communication: true statements become impossible, representation is always misrepresentation, and nothing exists outside power relations. This serves – against, it has to be admitted, his own intentions – to absolve the present and place blame on an abstract past. The global processes that have been set in motion since the publication of the book have served to emphasise the importance of these issues and have brought attention to the very serious problematic at the heart of the book.

Said's critique in *Orientalism* has led to the notion that we now live in a 'post-colonial' society. A current buzz-word, 'post-colonialism' gains currency along with the notion of globalisation and raises a problematic in implying that we are in a situation that is beyond colonialism. Can this genuinely be asserted when it is apparent that the power relations that pertained during the colonial era remain firmly in place and determine, arguably even more powerfully than during the colonial era, cultural forms in the world today? If direct colonialism was brought to an end because it was no longer sustainable in the post-war society, this failed to make an essential change in the relations between societies in the contemporary world. In addition, while the framework of the colonial empires established principally in the nineteenth century has certainly broken down, this was because the cultural centre of those empires, that is, Western Europe – primarily France and Britain – itself collapsed. The centre of Western culture, at least since the Second World War, and in many ways earlier, has not been a European power, but the United States, which never had a colonial empire in the formal sense. There seems something fundamentally anomalous, therefore, in speaking about post-colonialism unless one takes the view that the United States is itself a post-colonial society. In strict terms this is so; in reality it is risible, since the United States has long ago outstripped any colonial sensibility to become itself the repository of what we have called the 'idea of the West'.

Can this notion contain the reality of the world in which we exist today? It raises the question of what cultural identity means. Does it matter that we are English or Chinese or Argentinian? To what extent do we still belong to specific cultural groups? Or have we all become part of the same cultural system, sharing the same cultural values? If we have become part of one culture, does this satisfy us? In the past, the main human concern was to restrict difference. We lived in closed communities and only allowed contact outside their boundaries under certain conditions. The dynamic of society may have been founded in a fundamental difference at many levels, giving earlier societies a much greater heterogeneity at local level but at the cost of restricting external development. In our current situation, it is the other way round: the promotion of diversity and difference on a global stage acts to enact homogeneity in the general framework. This has led to the proliferation of identity politics that assert not so much the right to be different, but almost the duty to celebrate difference at the cost of cultural tradition and a fixity of values that allows genuine heterogeneity. The precise aim is clear: it serves the interests of a society devoted to the spread of consumption and the opening up of markets in a way that had always characterised capitalism and that has reached its apogee in the cosmopolitanism that dominates current discourse.

The anthropologist James Faris has said that our task should be 'to obliterate otherness while retaining difference'. This may perfectly define a post-colonialist catechism, but is not the real task for anyone concerned with cultural integrity the other way around: that is, that we should obliterate difference whilst retaining otherness? Because, in real terms, cultural difference does not exist. All cultures are essentially the same, and to be human involves a cultural involvement that is relatively constant: we all need love, beauty, knowledge. Yet, at the same time, constructions of otherness are essential to our sense of cultural singularity. We need to maintain heterogeneity in the cultural forms that lie at the root of human creativity. In order to do this, we need to remain alert to the fact that otherness is a construction that emerges from our lived needs and so should take multifarious shapes. It is not an essence. All constitution of the Other – where it is not devoted to congealed and narcissistic identification – is protean, subject to constant transformation and assuming a wide variety of different guises that can never be exhausted. This process should be viewed as a means of enrichment, devoted to the extension of communication and not serving the interests of control. But it does not mean accepting otherness as being merely what is different and accepted as such. The acceptance of difference as difference rather than as an aspect of what is the same is to deny communication and genuine variability.

A heterogeneous society entails confronting the nature of otherness itself, recognising that a society can exist as an entity and achieve a sense of self-identity only by means of a relation to the Other (not by a relation with what is different – this distinction is crucial, for what is different is undetermined and defies genuine communication). We can experience the Other only by means of an initial self-identification. The Other – in its dynamic relation with the self – presents a threat of cultural identity that must be met. The

Other is not essence as such; it is rather the negative essence of the self. The relation is coincident; it comes into existence and is maintained only as long as the relation continues. Self and other are mutually dependent and interlinked: they are separate and will always be separate, but their relation creates a third condition that must be encountered in order to subsist, but that retains lacunae and chasms that cannot be wholly breached. The most that can be done is to recognise how their separate necessities flow back and forth in a series of alternating currents. As such the Other may fundamentally be unknown and unknowable, but then so is the self.

The dynamic of self and other relations is central not because it enables us to know one another, not because there is something to be commended in such knowledge, but because our identity as human beings relies upon such a relation to give meaning and purpose to our lives in the recognition that we are each incomplete beings who are consigned by the very limits that life places upon us ultimately *not* to know. The Other is able to see those parts of us we cannot, as we are also able to see part of what is closed to the Other. It is by exploring this inexhaustible gap that there is in what is given to us by life a purpose and, indeed, a reason to live.

The politics of post-colonialism deny this dynamic. By reducing otherness to the level of mere difference, they dispel the ineffable and perpetuate the lie that existence is knowable by human means. This continues an Enlightenment belief in the knowableness of phenomena in general. In this respect, it may be argued that post-colonialism and the politics of identity are merely the emanation of a new global imperialism that acts in the cultural sphere in a way that is analogous to the mechanisms of political control that existed in the past. Far from confronting the colonialist legacy, they have a tendency to elide and continue it by positing that a fundamental break has occurred. In fact, it is difficult to see that this is the case. The collapse of colonial empires did little to undermine the power structures they had established and there is a suggestion that all that has happened since the Second World War has been that the frame of colonialism has been displaced from Western *political* control of the world economy to *cultural* control of it. Imperialism has changed its shape in a way that reflects the structural needs of US society, since the United States is unique in world history as a society that was shaped precisely in terms of an acceptance of difference and cultural plurality as bulwarks against a confrontation of Otherness (represented by the Native American Indians, the annihilation of whose culture was the prerequisite of the becoming of the United States, unlike elsewhere in the Americas, where the cultural otherness of the native population was accepted). Jimmie Durham, himself a Cherokee artist, notes how this necessity is continued today in the way US society regards Native American culture, the remnants of which it perceives as no longer containing a threat of otherness:

Alan Michelson, a Mohawk artist, reports that on a panel with white Americans a Christian minister said to him, 'You are the people who must now be our guides in how to live in this country.' Michelson thought, 'You've taken everything else and now you want to take our wisdom too.' (1993)

The taking of wisdom that Durham speaks of is the core of the cultural colonialism that remains the determining condition of cultural exchange today. In penning their text *How to Read Donald Duck* as the United States was preparing the overthrow of the Chilean government – revealing in the process the limits of cultural imperialism – Dorfman and Mattelart acutely set out the real issue at stake when they wrote: 'It is the manner in which the US dreams and redeems itself, and then imposes that dream upon others for its own salvation, which poses the danger for the dependent countries. It forces us . . . to see ourselves as they see us' (1975: 95). The American dream of life, as they call it, which has essentially been injected into the idea of the West, becoming its dominant feature in the modern world, contains this denial of otherness by which we are forced to see ourselves as the dominant culture sees us. This involves a psychic displacement by which instead of founding our self-identity in a denial of others that will be broken down by the processes of life, allowing a recognition of the Other, people increasingly today found their identity in a self-alienation by which the Other is seen as the self and only gradually can we gain a sense of self-recognition. What is lacking to us is any sense of the existence of a crossroads at which different realities can meet and exchange ideas before parting on their different ways. The gods of intersection – such as Legba in the voodoo tradition, Hermes in ancient Greece – have abandoned us and we are consigned all to follow the same direction. It is for this reason that Marc Augé has rightly perceived a crisis of Otherness to be central to contemporary debate, a crisis that is situated in the history of our colonial relations. The world as an international web of communications has not been a conscious design of colonialism, but is an inevitable consequence of it. The recognition of this was inscribed in the colonial people themselves. As Augé notes:

> Colonized peoples were the first to have this experience [of the internationalisation of the planet] because they were the first to suffer it. The colonizers, more or less impregnated with the evolutionist model and, before that, the belief that they were carriers of a universal civilization, saw in otherness only a primitive and deformed vision of their own identity. The fact of having come into relation with multiplicity and difference did not subvert their way of thinking or their relation to the world. (1999: 101)

This multiplicity and difference still had an effect on the colonisers, for they were still able to incorporate it without subverting their own world view, and this has become the core of the cultural colonialism that today dominates all relations between cultures, reducing other cultures to vessels of difference that serve the dominant paradigm. Multiple differences do not add up to an experience of otherness, but serve the disjunction at the heart of today's society, a society that founds itself in a pluralistic universe of diverse purposes rather than common aims and aspirations. This acceptance of difference, as opposed to otherness, has always been the condition of the society founded in the United States, the basis of its famed melting-pot sensibility, and today it is increasingly being imposed all over the world in the name of globalisation. The challenge here is to establish a frame of genuine dialogue, to reconstitute the crossroads, to reinvigorate the old gods of exchange and renewal and so allow for a heterogeneity of affect founded in a self-recognition that also recognises the Other within itself as well as outside itself and that can at the same time acknowledge and respect the ineffable quality that is the fundamental feature of any sense of otherness. In order to be able to see what this might involve, we need to understand something about how communication is established and maintained and what makes human communication distinctive.

4
CULTURE AS COMMUNICATION

In order to exist in the world, one of the first things we must learn is how to communicate. Communication is an essential quality of all life. If it is to survive in a material world, any life form must be able to communicate both with the world of matter and with other life forms. This is necessary in order for it to be able to feed and reproduce itself. For simple microbes this process may be very rudimentary, but it remains a necessary condition. As species evolve, so the means of communication take increasingly complex forms. Mating behaviour especially reveals this. In order to attract a mate, animals need to engage in an exchange of signs. This is so even for flowers and other vegetation, which use complex scents to attract insects to spread their pollen. Birds sing and dolphins and whales appear to engage in quite complex communicative forms. To affirm that language is exclusive to mankind is to deny that many features of speech are present in animal communication. Limited these may be, but they still represent a system of common signs, recognised as such by other members of the species. Clearly, whatever else it is, human language is a development of something that is present in all life forms.

There is therefore a mystery involved in why only humans have developed the symbolic system we recognise as language. No animal, as far as we know, can communicate anything other than a direct signal. Birds sing, but they do so within a fixed register of meanings. They are unable to vary the meanings of signs, but only convey a one-to-one correspondence between sign and meaning. Monkeys, it is true, appear to have the capability to recognise differentials between signs, but they can utilise this capability within a limited register and only at the instigation of humans, and then with difficulty. Human beings, on the other hand, substantially rely for their very existence on the ability to use language in complex ways. However one regards this, it represents a major difference between humans and other animals. All human beings must, if they are to exist in society, acquire skill in communicating through language. In this respect, language is as crucial to human existence as is culture, which it parallels and complements. Human culture begins at the moment we are able to create representations and the conditions to communicate them. In order to communicate effectively, we require the use of language of one sort or another. The relationship between culture and language is one of mutual dependence: each is the condition of the other. In speaking about language we are necessarily also speaking about culture.

Like culture, language in its essence is uniquely human. In what does the specificity of language lie? Humans share with other animals the fact that they communicate through signs, but the way humans use signs has served to extend them from having a single referent to having symbolic value. Being able to think in terms of symbols makes human communication distinctive and language possible. Language consists of signs, but signs that do not have a fixed meaning. A symbol is deceptive. It needs a greater perceptual alertness on the part of both user and recipient than a sign, even if this alertness is to be found deep within the unconscious structures of the mind rather than being something we are consciously aware of. To be understood, the symbol needs to be perceived in terms of its relationship with other symbols. It cannot be understood solely in relation to its referent, as a sign can. It becomes an object we can utilise for different functions. We can manipulate it for our own benefit, unlike a sign, which is fixed. The essential quality of a symbol is that its form is mutable. Realisation of this establishes the point at which society begins. In becoming part of a code, a symbol assumes a material form.

The origin of language is, like all origins, mysterious, and any attempt to reveal it leads only to contradictions. We can say that it is essentially human, that it provides one of the keys to understanding what we are as a species, but how it emerged remains a puzzle. Is language a necessary precondition of our existence as human beings? Certainly it helps to structure our thought and our perception of the world, but the extent to which it does so presents us with an unresolvable question: are thought and perception the result of our acquisition of language or an extension of it? Do we see the colour green only because we have a word for it? Or does language reflect reality? Do we see green and therefore find a name for it? This conundrum is just one of the many perplexing things about the situation of language within culture.

According to Lacan, language emerges as a bridge to help us to come to terms with the breach opened up by recognition of our insufficiency to the nature of the world. This breach, revealed to us during the mirror stage of infant development, reflects the transition from the imaginary realm, in which we perceive ourselves as coterminous with our surroundings, to the symbolic realm of representations. This symbolic realm is the one we must inhabit in order to participate in society, and it means that language becomes present within us. It is not simply a tool to aid our relation with the world, but an essential part of our cognitive structure.

In the Christian tradition, the word was present at the beginning of the world, a gift of God that perhaps became a remnant of our divine nature that was otherwise lost with the expulsion from Eden. As such, the word, *logos*, personifies God and acts as the guarantor of the law. In Lacan's terms, this is equated with the law of the father, which is imposed upon us as the condition of our entry into – and negotiation with – culture. If such terminology is overly patriarchal and may not apply in the same terms in other cultural contexts, the ideas contained within it still give us a starting point for considering in general the nature of language in relation to culture. What we can say with certainty about language is that, on the one hand, it provides us with a powerful tool for expression, and that, on the other, it limits us, reducing everything to the boundaries of linguistic utterance.

Language is a capability inherent in all human beings, but in order to be activated, it requires the intervention of culture, if it cannot be said itself to constitute culture. Language is formed from the distance that exists between the word and the object. This distance is the consequence of consciousness. In becoming aware of ourselves, we separate from the natural world and also create another world within us. Language may be an inherent capability but a child left alone will not learn a language by its own devices. The human world is one whose determinant feature is language. It means that the word is not identical to the reality it names because our self-consciousness intervenes between us and things. The distance this creates is an inevitable part of the reality of being human. We could not free ourselves from it and restore our immediate unity with the world except by renouncing the facility that language gives us. If we could do this, in fact, would words not become superfluous? Language is evidence of our alienation and silence is impossible.

Language opens up the world to us and brings with it the illusion of control. By naming things, we bring them within our frame of reference. This offers us a means by which to overcome our separation from what surrounds us. In using language to express meaning, we achieve a sudden mastery of the world and are enabled to communicate with others. This mastery is more in appearance than reality, however, for the experience we seek to communicate through language and the message received by the recipient are not the same. A gap exists between enunciation and reception that will never be entirely closed. It reveals to us that our world is not the unlimited one it seemed at first to be to the child but has become confined within certain limits. These limits are enshrined in language.

As noted earlier, language is also the guarantor of order. The connection between language and law is an intimate one. As Nietzsche observed, grammar has something in common with God: we tend to accept the authority of the written word. In the modern world, indeed, law is set by written statute. This is in keeping with the ascendancy of *logos* in the development of modern society. Customary law, so much the basis of our system of law, is only legitimate nowadays to the extent that it is enshrined in the written judgements of appointed judges. The community itself is no longer able to pronounce on legal issues; this has become the prerogative of lawyers and politicians and is given authority by the word, which in the process gains a transcendent quality. To undermine language is to undermine the legitimacy of law, but it is also to undermine the communicability of cognitive thought. We found our humanness in the fact of language. This tends to make us lose sight of its artificiality, the fact that, as a tool, it is extraordinarily imprecise and provisional. While language enables us to communicate with other people, it deludes us into thinking it is a primary means of communication, whereas in fact it also separates us from immediacy and acts as a reflection of our internal sense of alienation. What we understand through language are things not as they are but as language can represent them. Language is thus at the root of our tendency towards abstraction and towards making the world a thing separate from us. Because we can speak about the world, we see a distinction between ourselves and it. This is a limitation that restricts our thought, while giving us an enormous potential for communication.

Human life is based in a feeling of deficiency. We experience a lack at the heart of our beings, which we strive to overcome, turning things to our own advantage. It is language that gives us the means to do so. In this sense, language defines our existence. Through words we understand who and what we are. Yet these words do not belong to us. Rather, they pass through us and we become the provisional instruments of their transmission. Certainly we are not entirely in control of the use we make of words, as much as we might like to believe we are, for they are more than tools for us to express whatever it is we wish. In the way they may be used, words do not simply give shape to our thoughts; they also contain the life experiences of the myriad of people coming before us. Human existence as a whole is mediated through words, words that have been shaped by our ancestors and that only have meaning in relation to what human beings make of them. Yet at the same time they also have an autonomy that eludes our full grasp. In a sense, we live intoxicated by what words give us: they promise us the key to everything and yet keep us frustrated at the limits they impose on us. Words establish around us a maze from which there is no exit: we cannot deny the fact of language without denying our very human nature.

Wittgenstein famously stated that the 'limits of my language mean the limits of my world'. Without necessarily agreeing with what he believed this meant in practice, it would be difficult to deny that language itself does place a limit on what it is possible for us to achieve, something that has been an enduring issue in much contemporary thought about the way in which language and culture relate to one another.

While language is an inherent faculty of all human beings that even seems to be part of our very genetic make-up, the way we use language is affected in a powerful way by our cultural circumstances. We know that children up to the age of seven are able to learn any language, but that after that the learning of a new language becomes increasingly difficult. In this sense, culture prevails over linguistic possibility. It is this that opens the possibility of a linguistic relativism, the idea that different languages may inscribe different values and perceptions.

In proposing that language not only encodes our ideas and needs, but also shapes them, so constraining us to see the world in a certain way, Whorf's relativistic ideas have often been interpreted as leading to a determinism that was contrary to his expressed intention. Rather than showing the relative quality and integrity of each culture, the theory, taken to its logical conclusion, may lead to a linguistic determinism in which thought and behaviour are nothing but the emanations of language and cultural specificity is arbitrarily founded in the linguistic form that has developed in a particular culture. If this is so, can reality be the same for all of us, or is there an incommensurability at the heart of all communication? In a certain sense there is, but this incommensurability is present not only between cultures, but is also revealed in the gap that is present between all utterance and reception. A conclusive relativism between cultures is not therefore necessarily the conclusion if one accepts with Whorf that cultural peculiarity is inscribed in language in such a way that it affects what can be thought within that cultural configuration. In this respect, Whorf's explorations have been valuable in showing how important language use is in conditioning the particular cultural understanding of the world we acquire. Cultural identity is not established separately from language, but takes its particular shape by means of and in parallel to the development of language, perpetuating itself and reflecting the ideology of the group.

One cannot separate the cultural world view from the structures of language, but it would be misleading to read cultural determinism into this. Languages are no more bounded entities than are cultures. People borrow and manipulate words, transforming them in accordance with their immediate needs. There is no pure language; indeed language is infinitely flexible and adaptable. It needs to be in order to act as an effective instrument of communication. Cultures are not isolated and it is never possible to draw a circle around one particular conception of the world. Equally, though, each culture has its own integrity. While languages are instruments of thinking, as instruments they have their own very complex structure that is not commensurate with what we would expect of language as simply a means of communication. Language is not reducible to what we want of it, but imposes itself upon us. It not only serves thinking, but also tends to form and shape it in certain directions. As structures that are written into our unconscious and that we are forced to use in order to think, language has an impact upon our speaking and thinking and conditions our conception of the world. The relations between the cultural norms within a society and the structural character of the language are therefore significant. Cultural world view is certainly to some extent contained within the structure of the language.

We should not therefore underestimate the power of language within culture: it does, often forcefully, confine discourse to certain pre-established codes. In this respect, feminists like Dale Spender or Mary Daly are right to see in language a structure for the oppression of women. There can be little doubt that language has been a vehicle for the transmission of a male world view that has marginalised or even silenced women. But at the same time we should not overestimate such power. If men have effectively been able to use language to construct meaning and shape culture in ways that historically have been to women's disadvantage, the idea that men have 'made' language as an instrument of oppression seems to be based on a false understanding of the dynamic of language and culture attendant upon a more general tendency in modern cultural debates to overestimate the power of language.

Exaggeration of the importance of language is a feature of many trends in contemporary cultural debate, but is especially due to the dominating influence of structuralist and post-structuralist views of language as being a system of self-contained signs that have their own internal grammar and are bound together by consistent rules, an idea fashioned from Saussurian linguistics.

The concept of the sign in Saussure (1959) has been so influential because it connects up a lot of different ways in which culture is linked to language. Separating signifier from what it signifies, and showing how signifier and signified are united only through the linguistic code as it is constituted in the human mind, Saussure's theory has been instrumental in establishing the structure of language itself, rather than the context in which the particular language takes place, as the realm of legitimate linguistic inquiry.

In arguing that the sign is conventional or arbitrary, Saussure was opening up the way for the dominance of the sign, something that provides the structuralist tradition with its starting point and basic assumptions. If any word can theoretically be used for any object in the language, then identity becomes the result of linguistic relationships rather than something internally generated by a socio-cultural process. This has considerable cultural consequences.

In bringing into question basic nineteenth-century assumptions about the nature of language – that words stood for pre-existing ideas and represented things in a direct way – Saussure opened up the study of language. Instead of meaning being derived from universal ideas that became expressed in words given individual form by each speaker (that is, what I am now saying to you is my individual contribution to a universal truth), Saussure argued that meaning is inherent in language and does not exist prior to it. This means that what I am saying has a force that is independent of what I intend to communicate to you. The context giving rise to the utterance, not the content of the utterance itself, is what in the end determines meaning.

This way of thinking is at the root of the notion of discourse developed by Foucault. Foucault's idea of discourse has its basis in Saussurian linguistics: in distinguishing between signifier and signified, Saussure set them adrift from one another. As post-structuralism in particular developed these ideas, it came to be accepted that meaning inhered only in the signifier. This led to a concentration on the study of the signifier as having a meaning independent of the signified. In its most extreme form, in postmodernist debate, the signifier becomes the only reality, the signified having vanished into a web of representations, or simulations, to use Baudrillard's term.

This has had a far-reaching impact. Discourse has a wide range of meanings but, in simple terms, it can be described as the way in which meanings are constituted through language. To see discourse as the defining feature of culture requires that language use (considered in its widest sense) rather than cultural forms constitutes meaning and becomes the focus for investigation. It is also therefore related to another of Saussure's notions, being concerned with *parole* rather than *langue*. Under the influence of Foucault, discourse has tended to become the study of the way in which language constitutes meaning independently of the signified to which it refers.

Discourse is all around us. We are constantly engaged in different discourses that are differently configured in each social situation. The discourse we use reflects our own social class or situation and its expectations. In each different discourse certain ideas are put forward at the expense of others. The meaning of discourse is therefore contextual: it gains significance in its relation to other discourses. Meaning does not exist prior to the discourse, and the study of discourse relates to the significance of particular discourses.

Structuralism as a development of Saussure's ideas essentially analysed discourse in terms of universal patterns of human thought: an author does not express or reflect an immediate human experience but gives expression to something that can be understood purely through its deep structures and its semantic associations. This seems to assume that there is only one human discourse that is common for all peoples and all times. Reacting against structuralism, post-structuralist strategies introduce the idea of conflict between different discourses. Post-structuralism develops this further, arguing that meaning resides not actually within language itself but within the actual practices of languages, that is, in the social and political relations that emerge from such practice.

For Foucault there can be no general theory of language. There are only discursive practices. An object is named by a series of actions whose regularity establishes what it is in relation to other objects. By this means custom provides a context that limits the possibilities of what can and cannot be said. Such regularity provides a structure and a cultural pattern that can be analysed. Historically situated, this form of discourse serves to define the object and makes any criteria of truth external to the discourse inconceivable. Existing within the frame of the discourse, we accept its criteria because we have no other choice. Truth therefore is purely contingent, being nothing but a construction established by the internal requirements of the discourse. The mark of a successful discourse is the extent to which its structures are accepted as truth.

While this is undoubtedly legitimate as far as it goes, it is based upon the initial postulates about the nature of the world that structuralism takes for granted. This is the idea that reality is overwhelmingly discursive and founded in language. In particular, it relies on an acceptance of the arbitrariness of the sign. How justified is such an assumption?

All forms of discourse analysis raise the same difficulties. There is the initial problem of locating particular discourses and separating them from others. Each of us engages in many discourses in the course of a single day, many of which shade into one another. To locate one discourse is also to exclude other possibilities that would have been present if the discourse had not been located. Second, discourse is detached from the referents that give it existence. Since it is a signifier without a signified, it ultimately stands for the signified and it becomes impossible to locate any meaning other than what is imposed upon it by those establishing the discourse. This means that discourse represents an imprecise methodological tool since anything can be proved with it. It is true that Foucault sought, with his concepts of archaeology, epistemes and genealogy, to provide a means to evade such difficulties, and within his own framework he certainly succeeds to the extent of providing valuable analysis about particular discourses relating to discipline, madness, sexuality, and so on. However, as incisive as this social analysis is, it remains bound by methodological closures that its reliance upon language as a determining feature of reality will not allow it to go beyond.

Other thinkers like Derrida or Baudrillard recognise this, but, rather than address it as a problem, they compound it with their respective notions of text and simulations, both of which reduce our understanding of the world to textual configurations irrevocably cast adrift from their referents. Everything thereby becomes an image of everything else and only discourse has a – reflected – reality. Reliant on the presupposition that the structure of language is established by means of the arbitrary sign, the structuralist tradition that has given rise to this idea may be said to have willingly entered what Jameson has called the 'prison-house' of language.

To say that the word is arbitrary installs or reinforces a suspicion of language that can in many ways be said to be the modern attitude. Yet this view is recent and is doubtless connected to the development of the mass media, which have increasingly offered us access to greater and greater amounts of information without providing the means by which to process it effectively. People in earlier periods had more confidence in language itself as having a power to act on reality. Whether from a scientific point of view (language transparently represented the world) or from that of esoteric traditions (the word represented power in a positive sense), there was no conception that the sign and the object it represented could be separated. There were only true names and a correspondence existed between the thing and its evocation in language: far from there being an arbitrary connection between name and object, to name was to bring into life or to give identity.

According to Vygotsky, indeed, children still consider the name to be an integral part of the object it denotes. Asked in experiments whether the names of objects could be transposed, for instance by calling a cow 'ink' and ink 'cow', children will answer in the negative, 'because ink is used for writing, and the cow gives milk' (Vygotsky, 1962: 128–9). Such experiments are convincing, but I wonder if they are not too limited. Might not adults find it equally difficult to make a separation between word and thing signified on the same basis as the children in these experiments? Indeed, the charge of Magritte's various paintings, such as the one with the title *The Key of Dreams* – in which he misnames things, giving an image of an empty glass, for instance, a caption stating it is '*L'Orage*' (The Storm) – indicates a disorientation that is experienced if the word is displaced from its correct usage. While Magritte's sly humour contains many implications concerning the relation between word and image, it certainly suggests that the words given to objects cannot easily be said to be merely arbitrary.

Ernst Cassirer's explorations of symbolic meaning tend to support the conclusions of Vygotsky about the identity of name and object. In this context the separation Cassirer (1955) made between mythic and logical thought has some significance. According to this schema, mythic thought is centred in the emotions, while logical thought is proper to the intellect and is required for discursive, theoretical argument. These contrasting aspects of the sensibility are reflected in language. Mythic thought tends to attribute a concrete power to the word and assumes an identity between the word and what it represents. Mythic thought is still the motor behind art. Logical thought, on the other hand, treats the word purely as a symbol and vehicle to mediate between sense perceptions and ideas.

This separation between mythic and logical thought may on the face of it appear dubious insofar as it implies a qualitative distinction that devalues the former to the benefit of the latter. Certainly, it has little or no methodological value as a definitive classification. It can be shown, for example, as will be seen when we look at rationality, that mythic thought is not simply founded in an emotional response to the world, but is as logical as what Cassirer called 'logical' thought. However, to say this is not to undermine the central thread of Cassirer's argument. It remains legitimate to consider mythical thought as being more grounded in an affective relation to the world, which treats the word in terms of its concrete and material basis rather than as being a purely representational tool for understanding the world in a detached way. This concretisation of the word is something that underlies rituals and ceremonials and gives direct access to what can be represented not *in* language but only *as* language. Without denying the cognitive basis of all language, we can still assert that there is a language that directly expresses an experience of the world. This belongs to the realm of magic and divination.

To profess that language is purely conventional and that signs can be arbitrarily assigned to things is to deny to words any magical or sacred quality. It is, in fact, a form of profanation that refuses to language any sense of efficacy and renounces ancient beliefs in the word as an energy source. How justified can such profanation be?

The belief that the word has a sacred quality that, far from being arbitrary, is essential to the efficacy of ritual is bound to its exact pronunciation and respect for its integrity: one needs to listen to words, not simply to use them as instruments of meaning and messages. Speech itself speaks in the *Rig-Veda*:

> I am the queen, the confluence of riches, the skilful one who is first among those worthy of sacrifice. The gods divided me up into various parts, for I dwell in many places and enter into many forms.
> The one who eats food, who truly sees, who breathes, who hears what is said, does so through me. Though they do not realise it, they dwell in me. Listen, you whom they have heard: what I tell you should be heeded.
> I am the one who says, by myself, what gives joy to the gods and men. Whom I love I make awesome; I make him a sage, a wise man, a Brahmin. (*The Rig Veda*: 63)

Words in this understanding are not symbols that are forged into language by the conscious actions of people. Rather, they emerge from processes of recognition and mediation. To name the world is a part of knowledge construction: accurate naming – whether conducted by gods or man – brings into existence. It confers identity on what had been formless. By naming, what would otherwise be amorphous is given a shape that enables it to find a place in the world that surrounds it. To lack a name is more than a tragedy; within the frame that human culture sets up, it is not to exist at all. To refuse the magic power of language (at least its potential for magic) is to subsume language entirely and irrevocably to the law, to refuse its transmutability and thus its faculty to evade the limit that human thought in its infirmity would like to place on it.

Modern society as a whole places its faith in the law and so denies this exigency, whilst retaining its power. The result is that naming is transformed from mythology into ideology. This can be seen in the way in which we name our children. In appearance, the names we give them are arbitrary and purely associative: Peter could as well be called Paul. That he is called Peter is generally due to the name evoking something in the lives of the two parents. It is quite usual for people to have ready-prepared names for their child before birth; indeed this is expected by society: any parent to be will constantly be asked 'What are you going to call it?' The child only intervenes in this process through the uncertainty of its sex: we generally have needed to wait until birth before finally giving it one of the names we have chosen beforehand. This may be shocking to people in many cultures, who name children in accordance with what they perceive, or hope for, in the child, and this name may change at different stages of the life cycle as the child grows and changes. In Western society, however, the name is generally perceived as being given once and for all at birth and it confers identity. But this name is neither as arbitrary nor as innocent as it seems. Most parents spend hours deliberating over the name they should give to their child. The personal qualities of the child are almost always absent from such considerations. We choose names not for the sake of our children, but rather to tie them to us: we name them in order to prevent them from naming themselves by intervening in our choice. This is why we are expected to name the child very soon after birth: in order to make it part of ourselves. To delay naming a baby is almost a dereliction of duty, or a sign of emotional immaturity. In the Fritz Lang film *You Only Live Once* (1937), the innocent, yet criminal, couple, when asked the name of their newborn child, reply 'we just call her baby', attesting to their lack of adjustment to the symbolic universe we, as normal people, live in.

In fact, the names our parents give us are not fixed, indeed could be regarded as no more than provisional, for we have a legal right to be called whatever we like and we can easily change our names if we have a mind to do so. Yet, despite the fact that many people are dissatisfied with their given name, and it is hardly unusual to go through an adolescent phase of wanting to take another name, very few take advantage of this right, and even if they do, the decision is probably traumatic. Partly this is because to renounce one's birth name is to renounce one's heritage, and perhaps also one's parents (or at least it may be perceived that way). However, this does not seem to be the reason that so few young people do change their names (indeed, would not to do so be in keeping with the general rebellion of adolescence against parental authority?). Nicknames may serve as surrogates for our real names, but are rarely taken seriously and are often abusive: in general they tend not to be about naming, but are often about deflating the person's self-image or playing on their real name. The existence of nicknames is also part of a process of hiding or being reluctant to give one's true name. This is because our real name seems directly connected to our identity, and the reason it is so difficult to change it seems to be because to do so is to effect a change of identity that is disquieting. There is a sense in which, for most of us, *we are our name*: there is a direct bond between what our parents have called us and our perception of what we are that cannot be broken without having consequences for the psyche. To change name definitively is to change identity, and this would be something momentous in the life history of a person. Our personal names, therefore, seem to retain something of the magical quality they once had.

People often display a reluctance to share their name with strangers. This had often been observed by anthropologists. Iona and Peter Opie observed this among children:

Children attach an almost primitive significance to people's names, always wanting to find out a stranger's name, yet being correspondingly reluctant to reveal their own. They have ways of avoiding telling their name. They answer, 'Haven't got a name, only got a number.' They say, 'Same name as me Dad.' 'What's your dad's then? Same as mine.' (Opie and Opie, 1959: 176)

They also reveal fascinating ways in which children ritualise names, and how giving one's name too readily is regarded badly. As George Steiner has remarked: 'There was a time when the word was *Logos*, when a man would not readily deliver his true name into another man's keeping, when the name or numinous titles of the deity were left unspoken' (1976: 97–8).

The name is both secret and penetrating. It is a key that opens up the secret of the world: we only have to think of the use of passwords, of the 'Open Sesame' of magic, or more generally of the use of the names in magic spells. The purpose of magic words is always to issue a challenge to the authority of law, an equalising device that enables us to realise the fulfilment of the dream landscape as described by Ernst Bloch (1988). Imitating nature, the name refuses to be subordinated to the concept, from which, indeed, it must be protected. As such it escapes the snares of discourse. True naming is mimetic. It requires a precision of affiliation with the actual nature of things, so creating a unique form in conjunction with the referent that is not openly stated. It is for this reason that to call something by its true name is to expose it, to lay it bare. And this is why one's true name should not be spoken. The transparency that is the feature of contemporary society refuses such opacity, however, and so it reduces the giving of names to the level of discourse as it equates it with the law: as the mark of our identity we are given not a secret pass*word* but a pass*port* that contains our personal details and must be revealed on demand. What we are is required to conform with what is contained in this document, and we shall be in trouble if it does not.

This alerts us to the way in which naming in modern society is intimately tied in with ideology, an ideology founded in the profanation of the word that, no matter how imperfectly, seeks to deny the intimate relation existing between things and their names. Modern science is founded in the gap it opened between being and naming: the name, being arbitrarily given and thus separate from our identity, could not be held as secret as it did not belong integrally to us. Scientific autonomy, indeed, was based in an assumption of a lack of identity between sign and object, which it required for dispassionate inquiry. In this sense, Saussure did no more than elaborate – and problematise – this assumption: he showed how what was taken to be an accurate instrument of representation was nothing of the sort. The structuralist tradition has continued to elaborate upon this problematic, but is unable to question the assumption upon which it is based. It reinforces and in fact deepens the profanation of the word demanded by Enlightenment science.

Although not directed specifically against structuralist discourse, Adorno explicitly denied this reductionism: 'It is a sign of all reification resulting from idealist consciousness that the things can be named arbitrarily . . .' (quoted in Buck-Morss, 1977: 89). Against this reification, Walter Benjamin (1996) insisted that the view that the word is arbitrary results from falsely conflating language with mental being.

The structuralist error is to approach language from within the framework of language itself, failing to recognise that our experience of the world is not commensurate with language. In order to understand the nature of language, we need to be able to think about it from outside its own framework. It needs, therefore, to be separated from the nature of being. Language serves to communicate, but what does it communicate? Benjamin refutes the axiom that it communicates meaning. While it conveys the contents of the mind, it is itself not a mental but a linguistic entity: '[M]ental activity is identical with linguistic being only in so far as it is capable of communication' (Benjamin, 1996: 63). Nothing is communicated *through* language, only *in* it. It therefore follows that language communicates nothing but itself.

To say that language communicates nothing but itself may initially seem to be an even greater reductionism than saying that it is constituted as a system of arbitrarily assigned signs. The contrary, however, is the case. If language communicates nothing but itself, then it is relieved of the burden of existing for a purpose that is other than what it is. It can be restored to its own integrity: '[A]ll language contains its incommensurable, uniquely constituted infinity. Its linguistic being, not its verbal contents, defines its frontier' (Benjamin, 1996: 64). This linguistic being is the actual nature of language not as a verbal sign standing for something else, but as a reality that stands outside discourse, which it enters only by being appropriated to serve some purpose of representation. And it is such appropriation that denies to language its magical properties, which lie within its being as a linguistic fact.

To deny language magical status is also to deny our link with the divine. It is to deny the possibility of transmutation. Yet it is apparent that language is not some immutable form: the word is a symbol from which symbols develop; new words are constantly being created and new associations established. Language enables us to express our hopes and give tangible form to our dreams. Here we can see how conceptualisation, central to the modern attitude, serves to subordinate the link that language has to nature in order to codify it to serve purely human needs. When the name is given in complicity with magical forces, it serves to respect the provisional nature of the object's identity, identifying what makes it particular and unique without making it subservient to an external force. Being true to its own nature, it assumes a mimetic quality *vis-à-vis* the world and acts against a dominating classification.

Bearing this in mind, if we return to Saussure's contention that the word is arbitrary, we can see a fundamental problem. While it may be true that to define a concept, it is necessary to separate it and relate it to other concepts, this is a process of abstraction that is not necessary for the formation of language. A cat is a cat because it is so named, not because it is different from anything else. If it is true that we name it a cat partly to distinguish it from a dog, there is still no necessary relation between the words 'cat' and 'dog': any relation between the two words is as arbitrary as that between the signifier and the signified, in fact almost certainly more so.

If night is defined in relation to day, therefore, this is not a process inherent to language but to thought. There is no linguistic reason why we should not define each passing day concretely and give it a word that corresponds to each part of the twenty-four hours that pass between each rising of the sun. It is only when we wish to conceptualise the idea of night (which has no concrete reality) that we are forced into the binarism that requires using one word as the negation of another. In saying that this belongs to the realm of thought not language it might be objected that we cannot separate the two, that thought is dependent on language and vice versa. This is undoubtedly true, but a distinction must still be made in terms of their uses (otherwise why not say that language *is* thought, a proposition that would carry its own absurdity). The distinction in this respect is clear: language names and communicates while thought conceptualises. It is an inadequacy of the whole structuralist tradition to have failed to acknowledge this distinction sufficiently and often to have treated language and thought as if they are interchangeable.

A further problem raised at this point, in considering the nature of language as related to cultural formations, is that of translation. If reflection about the material – and at the same time magical – qualities of the word brings into question any attempt to reduce language to a code, the processes underlying translation suggest that discourses cannot be seen as discrete, but rather intermingle and interpenetrate and refuse a simple reduction. The problem of discourse here touches the difficulties raised by the relativism of the Whorfian hypothesis, for the possibility of translation challenges the incommensurability of communication across cultures (and equally across discourses).

Translation is integral to any process of communication, for communication, despite what we immediately assume, is not effected directly but involves the transmission of a message that may be interpreted in different ways at each moment of its passage. Even to order a message for transmission involves a translation of our ideas into linguistic form since language does not offer itself to us ready-made for the transmission of our thoughts. The mechanism of thought itself involves levels of translation simply in order to become coherent. This means that there is always a gap between our inner sensibility and the world that can never be bridged by means of language. Consciousness is incommensurate with the language by which we express our ideas, and no extension of linguistic proficiency will change this. Our experience of the world and what language will allow us to disclose do not coincide. As a tool, language is imprecise and does not allow exact communication. It divides us from others as much as it unites us with them. Expression is always difficult and eludes our grasp: the meaning of what I am saying is not one with what I want to say, and how you receive it will depend upon numerous factors over which I have no control. This is so for any communicative action, even within the same language. When we speak of communication across languages – and cultures – these difficulties are magnified.

Languages exist in dynamic relation with one another. They do not accept a static, purely descriptive role. We may express ourselves in our native language but we do not believe that what we are saying is applicable only within that context. While people may be indifferent to other cultures, there still remains a general expectation, or hope, that what we are saying could be understood, if not universally, at least by most other people who do not share our language. It would no doubt disconcert even the most insular person if one was to say that the words s/he is saying are only appropriate to their own language, that they have meaning only in that context and it would be impossible to translate them: to feel oneself a human being implies that we have something in common with, something which is communicable to, other people.

Translation therefore implies an anthropological relation: that communication is central to human beings and that there ought to be a means of conveying information and cultural values across cultural barriers. It is born in the belief that other societies have something of value that would enhance our own society; that all societies would be impoverished if they did not establish a means of communication that transcended their culturally specific languages. In the modern world, when the ease of communication is deceptively easy and world travel is taken for granted by many people, a common means of expression becomes a necessity. Yet cultural barriers still intervene to make translatability between different cultural worlds problematic. All communication is complex; that between cultures is especially so. The gap that exists between all expression and reception is accentuated when it is made across language boundaries, where the language conspires with cultural specificity to lay traps for the unwary who believe that meaning is always and everywhere the same.

In order to convey a message across cultures calls for recognition of certain values and responsibilities. Translation is a balancing act that brings cultural difference centrally into play: the translator must not simply take on the duty of learning an alien language code but must also understand the determinants of the cultural specificity expressed by that language. To translate, one must be intimate with what is Other in terms of language and culture and able to engage sensitively with the other culture, able to penetrate the secrets of its language in such a way as to render them effectively and appropriately in a different cultural context, retaining difference while making the message clear.

In learning to speak another language, one needs to some extent to live another way of life that brings into question (although we may often not be aware of this) our cultural identity. Even for those who take package holidays and expect everything to be clearly laid out in such a way that an encounter with Otherness is largely avoided, an element of strangeness cannot help but intrude to make us aware that we are out-of-place in the world we have entered. Simply trying to make oneself understood to a person who does not speak one's own language involves calling up resources that make us aware of how limited our normal frame of reference is. It cannot help but make us feel slightly inadequate, even if we respond to this feeling with aggression or shrug it aside.

For the translator such situations are central to the needs of translation and raise the question of whether it really is possible to communicate across cultures. What does a translation achieve? Is it simply a matter of transmitting a message, or does it convey something more elusive? There is an association of the translator as a 'traitor', contained in the fact that the words share a common Latin root. In Italian, for instance, the common pronunciation makes of the phrase *'tradittore-traditore'* an accusation. This is not simply a semantic peculiarity, for translation may indeed involve treachery in several different ways, the most obvious of which is by means of inaccuracy: to translate words erroneously, whether intentionally or not, can have extremely unfortunate consequences. But the correlation has wider implications: even a perfectly accurate translation can involve a betrayal not only of the language from which one is translating, but also of one's own.

All translation, in a sense, involves a double betrayal: by bringing the foreign element into the native language, the translator is striking at its purity and integrity; at the same time a translation is an abuse of hospitality, as it appropriates the values of the original to the profit of one's own language so the translator may be considered a thief who steals the other language's richness. Of course such 'betrayal' can equally be turned around and seen as representing an allegiance to both languages and translation as a process of enrichment for both the target and original languages. By bringing the foreign element into the new language, the translator allows both languages to grow and expand their respective frames of reference, so serving the needs of cultural exchange and allowing people of different cultural backgrounds to understand one another. These ambivalences are placed in relief by the legend of the Tower of Babel, which illustrates how an over-enthusiastic desire for communication may lead to its breakdown. The sin committed by humanity in constructing the Tower of Babel was precisely one of arrogance in a belief in the power of the word as containing a means to enable it to 'storm heaven', thus mistakenly making language itself the agent of transformation.

The translator in the role of traitor can be further highlighted by considering the role translation played in campaigns of conquest. Would the conquest of Mexico have been possible without the contribution of La Malinche, the Aztec mistress of Cortés? La Malinche undoubtedly did betray her own culture in a decisive way, and she provides a vivid example of what is at stake in all translation. Is La Malinche to be judged positively as a mediator between cultures, facilitating communication even at the cost of cultural conquest, or should she be unequivocally condemned for having undermined her own cultural values by consorting with the enemy?

The case of La Malinche also illustrates the different movement of societies, between those – pre-eminently Western culture since the Renaissance – that are devoted to geographical expansion and establishing a means of external communication, and those that are content to emphasise only forms of communication that serve the internal coherence of the society. For the latter, translation is a fundamental betrayal, one that opens up the society to external threats, while for the former, it is a necessary condition of development.

This is something that presents a dilemma for writers in the modern world who are faced with the difficulty of knowing how they can be true to their own cultures in their form of expression. It was perceived as an acute problem for the Peruvian anthropologist and novelist José María Arguedas. In his commitment to the lives of the Quechua Indians, with whom he had been brought up and had lived for much of his life, Arguedas was tormented by the problem of expression, perceiving a double bind involved in finding the means to express the reality of the Quechua people while exposing the way European languages acted to locate and establish power over the people. Arguedas saw that if Latin America was to advance, then its culture had to be able to find a way collectively to express the aspirations of whole communities in their varied and dynamic aspects. How to give expression to such realities without betraying them? How even to speak of Quechua reality in the Spanish language, a language that remains that of the coloniser? At times he uneasily accepted the idea of trying to discover a Spanish idiom that would accurately represent Quechua modes of thinking, which he called his 'Way of the Cross'. He explains:

> I solved the problem by creating for them a special Spanish language, which has since been used with horrible exaggeration in the work of others. But the Indians do not speak that Spanish, not with Spanish speakers, much less amongst themselves. It is a fiction. The Indians speak in Quechua. . . . So it is false and horrendous to present the Indians speaking the Spanish of Quechua servants who have become accustomed to living in the capital. (1985: xi)

His anguish over this dilemma was to lead him to write only poetry in Quechua during his last few years and was one of the reasons for his suicide in 1970. By translating Quechua reality into the Spanish language, Arguedas felt he was betraying it, but to write in Quechua was also in a sense a different sort of betrayal because it turned that reality inwards and reduced the possibility of communication with the external world.

Even if we accept the treacherous quality that is inherent in translation, it is difficult to deny its necessity, for without such cross-cultural communication progress is halted and languages and cultures become stagnant or inward-looking. Translation in this sense is not a luxury but a necessity, and, if it is a form of treachery, it is a doubled-edged one that has positive as well as negative characteristics. Indeed, our own initiation into culture is part of a process of translation and can itself be classed as a 'betrayal' – a betrayal of one's own self-singularity. In this sense, every act of communication – even one directed to oneself – involves a betrayal in a certain sense and language itself may even be said to betray the elemental solitude of existence. George Steiner brings attention to this in considering that the aim of translation should be to make

> tangible the implication of a third, active presence. It will show the lineaments of that 'pure speech' which proceeds and underlies both languages. A genuine translation evokes the shadowy yet unmistakable contours of the coherent design which, after Babel, the jagged fragments of human speech broke off. . . . That such fusion can exist, that it must, is proved by the fact that human beings *mean* the same things, that the human voice springs from the same hopes and fears, though different words are *said*. (1975: 67)

In order to achieve this, or even to establish the possibilities of it, it will also have to be recognised that languages do not exist in a symmetrical relation with one another: one language is always stronger than the other, and this obscures and may even obliterate the glimpse that the translator seeks to establish of this third presence.

The paradox of all language indeed lies in the breach with a self-sufficient world that life *qua* life represents, accompanied by the will to overcome that breach: by naming a stone we give it an identity, but this identity is provided by the one doing the naming. Stones become stones only by being translated into processes of human communication. In this sense, even the very process by which we name things is not so arbitrary as Saussure asserted, for what is named becomes fixed in a particular language, which, at the very least, provides an inescapable cultural context. '*Une pierre*' is not the same thing as 'a stone', even if the referent is identical. To translate the French word '*pierre*' as 'stone' is to effect a displacement, no matter how slight: the name does not simply describe, it also adds something to what it is describing. '*Une pierre*' can exist only in the French language. As we have seen, language not only represents, it also expresses what Benjamin (1996) called the 'linguistic being of things'. But this also implies that by translating what exists into language we are bringing the world within the frame of our will, subjecting it to human control. This process cannot be renounced: it is inscribed in the very state of being human, for language is the primary means given to us to enable us to situate ourselves in and develop communication with the world.

If the origin of language itself is shrouded in mystery, so too is the fact that humans speak such a diversity of languages. We cannot ascribe this to genetic factors for, if language were a cognitive faculty, biologically given, then it should surely follow that all humans would speak the same language. Yet it is estimated that something like 5000 different languages are spoken in the world today, and that possibly a similar number have been lost. Does the disappearance of languages matter? Will the future see a rapid reduction of wealth of world languages as communication improves and people learn to speak across cultural boundaries in a common tongue?

We have become used to the idea that English is becoming a universal language, but this idea should be resisted. As much as it may be welcome to have the possibility of communicating ideas with people globally, there is something reductive about the process. For if language and culture are inseparable, the English language is not simply a neutral means of communication; it is also a repository for the cultures of the English-speaking world as they have developed over the past eight hundred or so years. It contains not only an enormous richness that has accumulated since English became an intelligible language, but also the memory of what formed that language: the heritage of the Indo-Germanic people is also contained not only in the words used in the English language but in its very structure. As rich as it may be, the English language represents but a small proportion of the cultural experience of humanity and must by its very nature exclude the experience of the vast body of other cultures. More than this, it also contains within it the experience by which the English language has become dominant, that is, the experience of British (and American) imperialism. As such the English language itself is necessarily imperialist, independently of any intention of those who speak it. It cannot encompass the experience of those who have suffered under the weight of that process other than in translated form, that is displaced. In any event, any notion of a universal language has the danger for the human spirit of reducing diversity and the communicative and experiential possibilities that lie in the expression of difference: cultural specificity loses its meaning and all thinking would be in danger of being reduced to a single register. If this may have advantages for an immediate sense of communicability, its long-term losses may be much greater and are likely to contribute to a decline in genuine communicability. In this respect the adoption of English as an international means of communication may represent a kind of rebuilding of the Tower of Babel, one that is carried out on equally shaky foundations and, indeed, with as little concern for the consequences.

For the past century, the loss of the variety of languages has been one part of a process of progressive degeneration of language. For Karl Kraus, who, more than anyone at the beginning of the twentieth century, recognised the general symptoms of this process, the degeneration of language was a mark of the degeneration of civilisation itself. Mastery of language, he was at pains to point out, serves only the basest commercial interests. In our century we have seen language being abused by totalitarian politics for a variety of purposes, the most recent of which consists of the development of advertising techniques to control what the word may say, the aim being to institute the free use of language in support of the spread of falsification and dehumanisation. In such a world we live lies, awash in the millions of words served up by the media. A politics of terror bears down on the individual, reducing what may be said to a level in which, paradoxically, it appears that everything can be said. But to say that people can say everything is to say that they can say nothing: reducing everything to the status of enunciation – that is, to discourse – is a way of controlling the word, of framing it within a context that we command. Against this will to control, 'an artist,' as Kraus maintained, 'is a servant of the word.'

Mastery of language arises from a loss of faith in the efficacy of the word and breaks the intimate link between objects and words. The profanation of the word that has characterised our age – whether in its commercialisation or in the reductionism of the structuralist tradition – is marked by the decline of imaginative procedures of communication. It is only, as Kraus says, by recognising ourselves as the servants rather than masters of language, recognising that language has been given to us as a privilege and not as a tool of domination, that we will be able to begin to restore a sense of universal meaning to it.

Words are a powerful aspect of reality, bearing testimony to our presence in the world and giving us the means to act on it. Thought and language are inseparable and define the limits of what can be known: we verify knowledge most effectively in human terms by the use of language. We learn by means of words and we cannot escape them. But we should not delude ourselves into believing that we control words: they will always elude our grasp. We often use words as our nets but frequently all we catch are other words, and these words become increasingly abstract and unable to express our innermost feelings. Language is an organism, it is not an object of study or a passive receptacle for the communication of what we want to say. In order to study language, we must at the same time use language: the theory of language, more than any other realm of study, is a praxis. Invested with the authority of *logos* generally in the Western tradition, the power the word has gained in the twentieth century has had significant cultural implications. It means that, more than ever, criticism of language is also a criticism of culture.

5

EXPERIENCE OF THE SENSES

Christian tradition may extol the word as being at the beginning of the world, and there may be no denying its importance for the development of culture. As we have seen, the acquisition of language is an undoubted necessity for the process of becoming human. However, the word is not at our origin. The child in the womb may or may not be able to hear the words spoken around it, but even if it can it is unable, without any interaction, to distinguish the special quality of words from any other sounds. Its formation is far more connected to the rhythms of its own heartbeat and to the movements of the mother's body. Its world, prior to birth, is one of the pulsing of the natural motions of the body. The world it experiences upon birth, too, is above all a sensual one of physical contact. For the first months of our existence, it is the sense of touch that is most crucial for our experience of the world, and it remains the most elemental of the senses. Sound, at first, is experienced as a cacophony of disconnected noises, while sight, taste and smell are very underdeveloped. In this respect, again, we differ from most other animals, whose sense of touch is limited by the fact of having either thick skin or fur covering their bodies and insulating them from the surrounding world. Even if animals had the mental capacity for tool-making and the creation of culture, they would face physical limitations in being able to construct complex cultural forms. Being human, therefore, is not simply a matter of developing our mental faculties; it also involves a particular experience of the body. And yet, especially in Western culture, the body is considered in ambivalent ways and is distrusted in relation to the mind; it is, indeed, often denied to the realm of culture as indicative of what remains of our animal nature.

Yet it can hardly be denied that experience of the body is fundamental to the way we construct culture, an experience that, in Christian tradition, is both revered as the realm of original innocence before we were taken with a sense of shame at our nakedness and, simultaneously, loathed as the evidence of our fall. Our senses are distrusted in their immediacy; faith is to be placed in the evidence of the mind (either human – as in rational or empirical conceptualisations of experience – or that of God) as revealed through the concretisation of the word.

In other cultural traditions, it is more likely to be the dance than the word that is at the heart of existence. Some myths speak of the creation of the world as the dance of God. For instance, Siva Nataraja, the lord of the dance, dancing on the demon the sages had hurled at him, sent waves of sound through matter, awakening it from lethargy, threatening to spin the world into chaos, but at the same time holding it in tension, so making life possible. As such he is the source of all movement in the universe. Dancing maintains the stability of life, not as something static (as the pre-eminence of the word would indicate) but as emanative of energy. A pose of perfect harmony is therefore needed to maintain a pulse that keeps at bay the flames that would otherwise devour the world. This cosmic drama takes place both within the centre of the universe and in the heart of humanity. Becoming manifest in the dance, the god closes the gap between existence and the world in a way that is unavailable to language. The dance, in this sense, implies that it is mankind that has responsibility for the stability of the world, not an external force like the Christian God.

The movement encapsulated in the dance is communication with the divine, something that can never be achieved in language (for language, even as it is a remnant of our divine nature, escapes us and does not submit to our will, whereas in dance we become one with the movement generated and our will ceases to be significant). In the dance, paradise is re-created by ritual means. Connected to the breath, the rhythm of the dance is what maintains the link between us and our divine origins. There is a purity in our first movements that provides a link with our primeval being. We see here a fundamentally different sensibility to that which has motivated Western culture by means of Christianity and is centred in the primacy of *logos*.

Learning to walk itself is a process of dancing for it relies on a sense of balance and co-ordination – at least the desire to walk is a desire to dance, co-ordinating the body to the rhythm of the world.

Maya Deren captures this quality in observing the movements of Haitian people:

> [T]he grace of the bodies' bearing is so manifest that it imparts elegance to even the most poorly cut dress and the most patched and baggy overalls. In the backyard, the women cooking, tending the children, carrying water, forever doing laundry or braiding each other's hair, possess, also, this same grace of the body, which, since so much is demanded of it, has discovered how to achieve by balance what might otherwise require muscular force. [. . .] It is even as if this way of moving, which the visitor's eyes drink in so constantly, were accumulating in his own limbs and muscles; so that even the total stranger may, one day, discover with surprise, in his own posture, this very stylization. It is a natural grace, in that it is a necessary grace for the Haitian way of living; but it is natural also in the sense that the infant spectator, riding its mother's shoulder or hip continually, and even often cradled to the beats of the ceremonial drum, could not but learn this as the way the body's movement, could not but come to know the drums' beat as its own, blood-familiar pulse. (1970: 225–6)

In this passage, Deren, herself a dancer, demonstrates the mimetic yet natural quality that dance assumes and how it is centred in natural movement. Dance asserts our presence in the world; the dancer is no longer a passive onlooker in the process of creation but an active participant.

For the child, communication begins as a performative act: it attracts the mother's attention by mimicking the actions of those around it. Communication takes place through movement. As much as it is a natural capacity within us, the specific form of language comes later and must be learned. Communication by means of movement is a more immediate experience: dance is about co-ordinating the body with the rhythm of the world. Culture, therefore, is not primarily founded in the intellect, but in its initial articulation is a development of a sensual response to the world. Touch is the exploratory sense and is what opens the world up for us, providing our real initiation into culture, and touch, in this sense, is never static: alone of all the senses, it does not simply accept the stimuli it receives, but engages with them as it makes us an active participant in the world. Life, conceived in this way, is constant movement linked by universal sympathy.

We know the world through our senses. We establish the features of space, the awareness of what is nearby and what is distant, through the co-ordination of the different senses. It is through movement, from the way our body responds to the rhythms it perceives and experiences in harmony with our sense of touch, that space takes a shape and a texture and so allows us to develop a sensitivity to the subtle modulations present within the life that exists around us. We need to feel comfortable in our body in order to respond effectively to external reality.

The aesthetic sensibility and the principles of art are equally founded in sensual expression. Mimicry is a feature of many life forms. In mankind, this becomes a complex capacity touching on our identity: not content with our own limits, we have a will to become other, to experience what the other feels. Mimesis is thus based in a sense of union of all the senses with the object. As Walter Benjamin noted, this is decisive for human becoming, and it is legitimate to see this wish as lying at the foundation of the urge towards artistic creation.

This faculty is centred in play. Children everywhere use mimesis as the basis of their games, and this is founded in the theory of correspondences that once ruled ideas about the nature of the world. There seems to be every reason to believe that the essence of art lies in the human propensity for play. Huizinga also notes this primacy: '[E]very form of poetic utterance [was] so utterly bound up with the structure of play that the bond between them was seen to be indissoluble' (1955: 158)

As play is centred in the pleasure of the body, so what we call art and the aesthetic response are founded in play. Huizinga has shown how our sense of play is tied in with aesthetic questions: we expect the game to be beautiful,[1] and beauty is connected with movement and with what Huizinga calls a temporary and limited perfection: 'Play demands order absolute and supreme. The least deviation "spoils the game", robs it of its character and makes it worthless' (1955: 10). It is also part of a magical operation connected to power. Michael Taussig emphasises this point: '[W]hat I call the magic of mimesis is the same – namely that "in some way or another" the making and existence of the artifact that portrays something gives one power over that which is portrayed' (1993: 13). This mimetic quality is at the heart of the impulse towards art, which is undoubtedly shaped by the elemental aspect of play.

The decline of mimesis is connected with the rise of scientific inquiry and the loss of the magical understanding of the word that we explored in the previous chapter. 'If the mimetic genius was really a life-determining force for the ancients,' as Benjamin stated, 'it is not difficult to imagine that the newborn child was thought to be in full possession of this gift, and in particular to be perfectly adapted to the form of cosmic being' (1999: 721). It is this childhood faculty, a form of 'knowledge' that is inherent in becoming and yet unformed, or not conscious, or, perhaps more accurately, undirected and unrepresentable, that is at the root of the human personality as potentiality unlimited and yet unable to realise itself because it is still to be integrated with social being. And this integration will serve, inevitably, to reduce it, leaving only a residue. It is this residue that will form the basis for the creative impulse that results in art. To this extent, the process that we are describing may be equated with Lacan's notion of the imaginary. It would be wrong, however, to reduce the mimetic quality to a developmental stage of human becoming. It is a faculty from out of which all forms of expression take shape. Yet we need to be aware that such expression cannot be limited to linguistic form. Expression has other needs that escape such contingency and it has to become productive in other areas of human experience. Words cannot capture the sense of reality in its totality; they can do no more than establish linguistic being, as Benjamin put it. Therefore we need means of expression that leave open the possibility of a concrete language that has an active quality.

Theories of art tend to intellectualise the process of creation. The two traditional views that art is either imitation or expression both fail to do justice to the essence of what art is. Or, at least, while it can rightly be said that art is both imitation *and* expression, it is reducible to neither. The essence of art is not that it either imitates or expresses anything, but that it uses imitation to express something specific that can be expressed in no other way. In this respect, and since both language and art are concerned directly with communication, the comparison with language is worth pursuing.

In considering art as language, the work of Ernst Cassirer remains crucial, both in itself, and because it was instrumental in enabling thinkers like Susanne Langer and Nelson Goodman to argue strongly for art to be considered in terms of its symbolic relations rather than as a representational form (that is, as imitation or expression of pure feeling). In Cassirer, language itself can be divided into a propositional, scientific language, which expresses logical statements that can be verified in relation to everyday reality, and an emotive language, proper to art or poetry, in which signs are used for the expression of emotional states that defy the logic of consciousness. The first is created by means of a subject, a predicate and a relation between them. If the language of discursive thought introduces us to abstract concepts, emotional language refers to the symbolic realm that cannot be captured by direct language. This is the realm of the arts – music, poetry, painting, dance, sculpture and architecture.

According to Cassirer, language gives us the possibility of objectification, but the price to be paid for this is that the concrete experience of life fades. We create a world of constructed symbols by means of a mental operation rather than as a response to immediate experience. In contrast, art provides us with a means by which we can preserve a more direct, an immediate, approach to life. It presents another symbolic universe that is beyond the universe of speech. Human culture as a whole takes shape as a progressive objectification of human experience. We strive for a means by which to express emotions, desires, impressions, intuitions, thoughts, ideas. Language is a tool for communication that can take many forms, but can be separated into two fundamental usages. Propositional language is predicated on the fact that we have a need to establish a fixed empirical world in which we feel comfortable, something that requires that we have a means to grasp and make sense of that world. However, this codified language is not sufficient for our emotional, inner needs. There is therefore also a need for an emotional language to connect us with that world in an affective, sensual way. As such, symbolic associations and myths, as well as artistic creativity, establish a realm distinct from the world of propositional language, obeying their own rules, which are different from but analogous to linguistic ones, and responsive to particular forms that may be identified and placed in relation to one another in the same way as can be done with propositional language.

Cassirer seems to conceive of art as emerging as a reaction to spoken language, as being its complement. As he sees it, the inherent quality of language is to become abstract. Therefore if we rely too much on spoken language, we lose a sense of concrete life. If this is allowed to continue unchecked, the world we inhabit will be transformed into a world of intellectual symbols in which immediate experience is lost. What we now call the arts therefore develop as a response to this increasing abstraction. The aim of art is to restore a balance between our emotional and intellectual life, so as not to allow conceptual language to dominate our sensibility and so force us to make an abstraction of our sense of existence. This sounds plausible, but to what extent can art, or creative expression in general, genuinely be considered a language, or even a symbolic system? Can it not be described more accurately as what escapes – or strives to escape – from the snare of language (or, depending on one's point of view, that doesn't need to escape from it because not subject to its exigencies)?

We know nothing, of course, of how language came into the world, and the earliest peoples have left us with no trace of their language. We know no more about the origins of art. The earliest peoples have, however, left us a trace of their art work in the images found painted on rocks and in caves. Although this tells us little about how they saw the world, there is no suggestion in their art that their need for visual expression came about in any way that compensated for the loss of an emotional response to the world in language. As little as it is, the evidence suggests that art work was an essential element of our becoming as humans, certainly as elemental and essential to our nature as language, rather than being simply a reaction to the limits of language.

Even if it is true that art can be considered as a language, this neither explains nor describes it. It may be true that art needs to obey certain rules of construction (in accordance with its quality as play). Yet such rules are necessary for nothing more than the internal coherence of the activity and frequently take a culturally specific shape: art is not reducible to its laws of composition in the way language is. This can be seen generally in modern art, which establishes fresh perspectives that constantly serve to establish criteria for judgement that need to be learned anew. If it is a language, therefore, it is one that is unstable and provisional. A language that was subject to as much variation as we expect in art would soon become incoherent. That art in its essence is a product of the same cognitive or emotional faculties as language seems doubtful, therefore, because it escapes the strict rules that are characteristic of what we define as a language: I can, if I wish, learn the Chinese language and, though I shall never speak as well as a native Chinese speaker, I have the certainty that I am making myself understood by following the same principles of language construction as the Chinese. In seeking to understand Chinese music or painting, however, I have no such certainty. If it is true that I can learn the scales of Chinese music or the principles of Chinese painting, I will never be able to replicate the emotional response with which it will be imbued for a Chinese person. This emotional residue is not reducible to language; it springs rather from an elemental, physical response to the world that surrounds us. In particular, far from ordering the world in the way that language attempts, art is often at ease with a certain formlessness, concerned less with explaining the world than with participating in it. Insofar as art is a language, does this not, as Kleist (1972) shows in his extraordinary essay on the marionette theatre, indicate a degeneration of affective response to the world that actually weakens its foundation, which is to maintain our link with the elemental processes of our being? The foundation of real art, in contrast, contains – imperfectly – this residue that cannot be reduced to language.

There may be little doubting that language is an essential ingredient in the development of culture, and it may be difficult to see how human culture could ever have emerged without the simultaneous development of language ability. To say this, however, does not mean that language is the only, or even the primary, means of human expression, or that it alone determined human becoming. The myth of Original Sin, according to which language was the one divine part of our beings that escaped the expulsion from Paradise, does not satisfy us. There is also a powerful impulse within us to engage directly with the world, to recover the lost Paradise that we find it so difficult as a species to renounce entirely. This impulse lies at the heart of the construction of images and the foundations of art and, conversely, founds the contrary movement of Western religious and philosophical thought towards distrust of the image, to which we shall return in a moment.

Cassirer admittedly does recognise an essential distinction between linguistic and emotional forms of expression:

> There is an unmistakable difference between the symbols of art and the linguistic terms of ordinary speech or writing. These two activities agree neither in character nor purpose; they do not employ the same means, nor do they tend toward the same ends. Neither language nor art gives us mere imitation of things

or actions; both are representations. But a representation in the medium of sensuous forms differs widely from a verbal or conceptual representation. The description of a landscape by a painter or poet and that by a geographer or geologist have scarcely anything in common. (1972: 168–70)

Yet this distinction seems inadequate to the extent that it reduces art to the status of representation. If art is undoubtedly a representation at a certain level, is this all that it is? And if it is, is its status comparable to that of a language?

While the distinction drawn is legitimate, to give it as central a role in the function of art as Cassirer does is to fail to do justice to what is fundamental about the creative action. If art is to be distinguished from language, is it not also because art goes beyond limits of language and refuses to accept the sort of framework that language relies upon? The aim of art is often impossible: it strives to express what cannot be expressed. As such it cannot be classed simply as a symbolic form.

In this respect, and if, as we have argued, the essence of art lies in play, it may be argued that there is a convenient consonance about seeing propositional language as belonging to the reality principle while emotional language belongs to the pleasure principle: the first serves the needs of work, the latter that of play. This is provisionally acceptable. However, we should also question such a neat separation of tasks.

A clear distinction between work and play is of course difficult to maintain and is founded in the division of labour and class differentiation in advanced societies. Huizinga (1955) gives a resonant example: can we really say that a gambler in Las Vegas is playing, while a stockbroker trading shares is working? We can extend this example back and forth in numerous ways to problematise the relation between work and play. The activity of neither gambler nor stockbroker is productive or contributes anything useful to society and so both might be classed together as play. Yet both involve high stakes with the possibility of high rewards, even if the former may be more risky than the latter (or at least most gamblers have an overall expectation they will lose while stockbrokers expect to win). What distinguishes both gambling and stock-market speculation is that – whether seen to be work or play – both are contained within the structure of a capitalist division of labour founded in a strict demarcation of tasks that privilege certain activities against others.

If culture is founded in the need to work, the task of work does not have to be onerous and may frequently be pleasurable. Even when it is physically demanding, there may be a pleasure in it, a purely carnal enjoyment that belongs, properly, to the realm of play. This is retained even today, but we consign such physical enjoyment to the realm of distraction; it is a hobby rather than 'work'. Work is characterised not so much by what the activity itself actually is, as by where it fits within the productive process. We need here to explore how work and play are separated and what the essential difference between them is.

Of course, Marx long ago brought attention to the way that 'productive life is species life. It is life-producing life. The whole character of a species, its species-character, resides in the nature of its life activity, and free conscious activity constitutes the species-character of man. Life appears only as a *means of life*' (1974: 328). This life-producing life constitutes both work and play. Do we, then, have to make a separation between them? There is a sense in which all productive activity belongs to the realm of play, as part of the aesthetic sensibility that is essential to the functioning of society at a basic level.

Joanna Overing has powerfully described how among the Piaroa, an Amazonian tribe, art and work are inseparably inscribed in the way in which socialisation takes place. Work, she tells us, was

> to be pleasurable, and a product of desire; it was not a realm set apart from either the personal or the social. Rather, both intensely personal and social, work was both a product of pleasurable social relationships and a creator of them. It was action that fulfilled the desire to provide for self and the desires and lives of others. Without the tranquil relationships of good community life, one could not work; and without work, one had no community. (1989: 164)

Notions of aesthetics are, she argues, tied in precisely with the productive quality of life and the development of community. What is beautiful is what constitutes the creative skills by which, on the one hand, production is effected or, on the other, tranquil relationships are facilitated. The obligation for the individual is to achieve a proper balance of forces within the self, for 'the social and productive world could neither maintain nor regenerate itself without human beings constantly recreating it through will and cultural capability' (Overing, 1989: 172). The final phrase is significant here. We do not assume in today's society that such will to create and renew through cultural capability is necessary: the world exists independently of us. In modern society work itself is necessary neither for social harmony nor for production; rather, it is utilised as a means of social control and discipline. And it is this that makes the social division of labour so essential a part of our lives.

In a society such as that of the Piaroa, the view of the social as an achievement that has to be constantly extended and each day has to be re-created anew is fundamental. Here the social is a process of daily negotiation that admits of no aesthetics of revolt. In the culture of accumulation and consumption in which we live today, on the other hand, such social concerns seem to be a luxury touching not on the essential, but rather standing for a certain utopianism. We live under the rule of a reality principle that structures our activities in terms of their usefulness in one way or another: every activity has to find a place within a scheme of exchange-value, even hobbies or supposed 'pleasure' activities. In this respect, propositional language, as defined by Cassirer, represents a form of initiation into the reality principle, having a task to perform that allies it with work or, in Lacan's terms, establishes the symbolic realm that defines our condition in the modern world. Art, on the other hand, is essentially defined by retaining a link with the Lacanian imaginary and refusing to adapt itself entirely to the realm of symbolic meaning.

The primary repression that language entails does not – on this point we can be grateful to psychoanalysis for having revealed this – eliminate the will there is still within us to go beyond our limits and touch the ineffable. This can never be entirely subsumed to the rules of society. Violent exuberance and excess are necessary aspects of the human personality that need to be given an outlet. Feasts and festivals provide the domain for the expression of these needs, while work, dedicated to the needs of efficiency, represses them.

In no other realm, perhaps, can the tension existing between the reality and pleasure principles (a tension that exists in all levels of society) be seen as clearly as in the arts. This is one of the reasons for the arts having been seen since the nineteenth century as the repository of the recalcitrant and the impractical. Indeed, the dynamic of the arts in Western society, at least since romanticism, has undoubtedly been founded precisely in the aesthetics of revolt that Joanna Overing sees as being absent in Piaroa society. This dynamic is one that can only emerge in the emphatic form that is characteristic of modern culture in societies in which the tension between the reality and pleasure principles becomes acute. However, it is a tension that is to some extent present, no doubt, in all societies, although there may be very different ways of resolving it.

There is a tension between conscious and unconscious urges that is crucial to all artistic endeavour. This is probably true in all social contexts and is the reason for art – or at least aesthetic design – being an essential element of shamanistic practice, or indeed of the effectiveness of any ritual. In all societies, then, art may be considered to represent partly a struggle with the reality principle. In this respect, as Georges Bataille (1986) has argued, it is part of the transgressive moment that validates the taboo upon which society is founded. In no society, however, do repressed instincts, seen as restoring primary pleasures that have been condemned by society, give to art the particular qualities it assumes in the contemporary world, in which its role in activating play and striving towards being an elemental activity is trenchantly denied by the dominating ideologies of that world. And yet there remains a determination, perhaps a primal need – manifest in all human activities but most predominantly in what we call artistic endeavour – that refuses incorporation into the dominant order of reality. The artist is someone who is not afraid to get embroiled in the labyrinths of being, and to this extent art remains as a token of primal striving, an achieving of consciousness, that is connected to fertility and the flowering of the earth.

This is more than mere nostalgia. As Agnes Heller states:

> Art is the self-consciousness of mankind, and works of art are always bearers of species-essence 'for itself': and this in more than one respect. The work of art is always immanent: it depicts the world as man's world, as the world created by man. Its scale of values reflects mankind's axiological development: at the summit of art's scale of values we find those individuals (individual affections, individual attitudes) which have entered most fully into the process of species-essential efflorescence. To put it another way: 'survival' of a work of art will depend on its success or failure in reflecting mankind's memory; and if we can enjoy artistic masterpieces generated by the conflicts of bygone ages, it is because we recognise in these conflicts the pre-history of our own lives and our own conflicts.

> In the process of creating a work of art, suspension of particularity is complete and without residue; the homogeneous medium of the particular art elevates the creating agent to the sphere of species-essence: his particularity has to be superseded, and the imprint of his personality has to be placed on the world of the artefact. (1984: 107)

Art does not therefore represent a reproduction of something given but strives to be the 'infinite represented in finite form' (Schelling). As such it plays on sound and colour, melody and harmony, the accord and concordance of words and images in such a way as to enter into communion with what exists, not content with what is mere appearance, but seeking out the hidden unity of the world. It is in this way that art incarnates itself by means of mimetic play as a process of harmonisation with the world.

Although to some extent the separation between work and play must be universal (in all societies, one imagines, there are tasks that are regarded as unpleasant and involve an element of compulsion in order to be performed), only modern society has institutionalised this distinction to such an extent that it attempts to make both serve the needs of work, and in so doing reduces both work and play to arenas of consciousness. Yet the mentality informing such a separation is not recent but is inscribed in the very earliest moments of Christianity, being one of the features of the myth of the fall, which not only instituted the idea of a separation between mind and body but also laid the principles for the division of labour that would found the reality principle as the feature that has come to dominate modern society. Against the cultivation of the faculties of mind that has been the determining feature of Enlightenment ideology as inflected with Christian morality, the genesis of art lies in the retention of fundamental needs that all humans have to express themselves through the body, something the central tradition of Christianity has tended to deny.

If the foundation of art is a physical one, centred in the experience of the body, this is not to deny that cognition also plays its part, for thought and action cannot so easily be separated. There is indeed no such thing as the natural body for the body itself is a social construction, formed as much from mental activity as from physical action and responding to cultural needs. Nevertheless, a distinction needs to be made between the development of the cognitive faculties through language and the physical expression of creative energies. This argument turns on the distinction between representation and embodiment. In ancient religions embodiment rather than representation was the essential element of human life, based in animist beliefs that assume that the world is held in tension and it is mankind's duty constantly to recreate it. From ancient Egyptian beliefs to those of a contemporary society like that of the Piaroa, rekindling the energy of the world is a daily task essential to the vital principle of the world.

This idea has come to be less important in the monotheistic religions, although Judaism has the myth of the Golem, the creature brought alive from dead matter by the recital of a magical act through use of the word of God. In Christianity and even more in Islam, the image must reflect only the glory of God. To worship or embody images is contrary to the First Commandment as an offence against the virtue of religion. The scripture is worth quoting:

> You shall have no other gods before me.
>   You shall not make for yourself an idol in the form of anything in heaven above or on the earth beneath or in the waters below. You shall not bow down to them or worship them; for I, the Lord your God, am a jealous God, punishing the children for the sin of the fathers to the third and fourth generation of those who hate me, but showing love to the faithful who love me and keep my commandments. (Deut. 5: 7–10)

This is quite unequivocal, providing as it does the legitimation for the Christian condemnation of the image, which is, at the same time, a condemnation of the body. It was encapsulated by what in particular characterised Christian dogmatism: its condemnation of idolatry.

In the Western tradition, the Christian attitude towards the image has conjoined with Plato's denunciation of art on the ground that it is nothing but a deceptive process of imitation of ideal forms. As being capable of stirring the emotions, Plato considered art to be dangerous, leading to mystification and deception: the artist tried to deceive us into thinking that what was really an empty form was actually real. As such, art did not strive towards truth but undermined its investigation. Artistic creations were thus mere idols (the symmetry with Christianity is surprisingly striking, at least in terms of how Plato's thinking in this respect has been understood within the Western tradition[2]). Plato's demand was that we should not succumb to the lure, or seduction, of images, but seek the reality hidden by the image, something that retains great resonance in contemporary debates about the use of images.

We can see in Western culture this double exigency, which dominates – if uneasily and not without great tension – the history of Western art. Painting indeed gained legitimacy from the fact that it *merely* represented. It did not contain truth within it but was based in a notion of empty mimesis: not the will to be other (which would have contradicted the idea of inherent identity) but to copy the form of something existent.

In general in Western discourse the condemnation of the image has pertained only to the image that brings attention to itself. This was the reason not only for Plato notoriously to bar the poet and painter from his ideal Republic or for Christians to destroy idols and graven images, but also why scientific research has sought to deny the problematic of representation, treating its own representations as transparent and direct. Hence the view that the act of writing is purely an objective act of recording reality. Reality exists out there. All I as a researcher have to do is to interpret it: 'I tell you what I have witnessed.' In this lies the authority of the word.

The embodiment of the world in Christianity has always been through the word, not through the image. The word is given to mankind directly by God. The New Testament states: 'In the beginning was the Word, and the Word was with God, and the Word was God. He was with God in the beginning. . . . The Word became flesh, and lived for a while among us. We have seen his glory, the glory of the one and only Son . . . (John 1: 1–3, 14). As transparency, therefore, the word is the unmediated truth of God and as such it eludes the snares of representation.

This is the basis for a separation of mind and body that is crucial for understanding how Western culture has taken shape and established its identity, which is based in the idea of non-contradiction, which we shall examine in more detail later. Boundaries are clearly defined: I always equals I. From this proposition all of our ideas about the structure of the world are formed: cause and effect, free will and determinism, whether the world is structured by material presence or by the perception our minds have of it, are measured by an assumption of a separation between body and soul or mind (this may be said to respond consistently to Christian tradition, which equates body with the fall, the soul with what was left to us that was divine). We will examine some of these points in detail later. Let us here, though, concentrate on the nature of images.

The image is what embodies, in other words it gives body to what exists. In contrast to the word, it does not – indeed cannot – merely represent. Octavio Paz defines it in these terms: 'The image does not explain: it invites one to re-create and, literally, to relive it' (1973: 97). The basis of the image lies in movement: it fixes an unstable impression at a moment of revelation without giving it a permanent shape.

The problematic of vision is a central theme in our contemporary world when we are so saturated with images that vigilance is required if they are not to overwhelm us. The 'power of the image' has assumed a centrality that we can interpret in several ways. Indeed it might be said that in modern discourse sight has replaced the body as the locus of shame and censure.

If we consider mind and body to be separate, the eye holds a curious position as being both an extension of the brain and the organ of the sense of sight. We perceive sight as the most important of the senses, fearing its loss more than that of the others. In many ways this is an illusion: touch and taste are more elemental senses. To lose them may be even more terrible because the world loses any sense of contour and we become disembodied from it (this is what makes leprosy such a debilitating illness). A child born without a sense of touch or taste would be unable to survive because it would be unable to learn to nourish itself or distinguish itself from the world. A blind person may be debilitated, but can still function in human society. And sight itself is less self-sufficient than other senses, requiring a greater collaboration between the brain and the other senses, especially with touch. If this collaboration breaks down at any point, sight will be affected. Sight is therefore simultaneously part of the cognitive and sensual relations to the world. Since the institution of literacy, in particular, the cognitive faculty has increasingly overwhelmed the sensual response to the extent that visual appreciation, detached from its tactile basis, is appended to cognition. The anthropologist Edmund Carpenter noted this: 'Literate people experience sound as if it were visible; they listen *to* music. Non-literates merge *with* music. Far from becoming detached, they become involved participants, immersing themselves totally within it' (1976: 41).

The image, when fully realised, draws upon all senses and maintains, in a way that language cannot, the elementary spontaneity of our relation with our surroundings. As an emanation of the imagination, the image retains a direct link with the divine in a way the word cannot. This implies that the transformation of the world cannot be the result of a Promethean act of will; it also requires the complicity of the world itself. If our relation to the world is a spontaneous one in which the sensual rhythms of the body participate in reality, then, as Paz noted, it invites us to reinvent the world.

This sense of the image as positive emanation is, however, subordinate within Western culture. It is common today to see the image as being associated with power and – in a curious reassertion of the Platonic condemnation – to consider sight itself to be the sense of deception and mystification. The use of the image in advertising, in particular, reveals the extent to which the image can be used to elude conscious intent and deceive us into accepting what we would otherwise reject.

The main trends of postmodernism have taken the distrust of the image to fresh heights. The critiques Foucault made of surveillance, Derrida of logocentrism or Baudrillard of simulation share a doubt about visual meaning and imagery that provides something of a reformulation of warnings about the dangerous quality of the visual and represents an almost visceral return to the Platonic condemnation of the image as the realm of deception and control.

As Martin Jay (1988) has shown, by raising the notion of 'scopic regimes of modernity', ways of seeing are more complex than is allowed by the various postmodernist critiques of the visual. In particular, they take for granted a 'Cartesian perspectivism' that may have been the dominant way of constructing visual space in Western discourse, but it is by no means the only one, and there are many 'regimes of vision' based upon different ways of conceptualising images. Jay's exploration is certainly valuable, bringing attention to the fact that the debate about the hegemony of vision in postmodernism is faintly absurd. For the fact is that sight is a hegemonic sense. This is the reality of seeing. In other words it is in the very nature of sight itself to be hegemonic; it has not become so through historical determinisms of modern society. Sight may not be the most important sense, but it certainly has the most powerful emanation. In this sense Plotinus was right to assert that the eye is itself a sun.

Sight is hegemonic because it depends on the other senses and must to an extent override them in order to establish itself effectively. In contrast, the other four senses are largely autonomous. What is characteristic of sight is its complexity and the possibility it has to develop in different ways, on the one hand, and its fragility, on the other. We can see this if we think about the loss of the senses: if we lose sight, our other senses become more acute in order to compensate. Yet if we lose any of our other senses, our sight does not become more acute: the deaf do not see better for being deaf, while the blind do become more sensitive to sound. This is well conveyed in a remarkable story by H.G. Wells, *The Country of the Blind* (1911) in which he shows how in a land in which everyone is blind the one-eyed man, far from being king, would be regarded as a dangerous deviant or madman and as strangely crippled (although in the story, the man is normally sighted and the people intend to cure the stranger's malady by surgically removing his eyes). In such a land, the perception of the world would be wholly different, with a set of values incommensurate with those of a sighted world. It would not be a world of deprivation, but one enriched by the opening up of the possibilities of the other senses. The peculiar puritanism that sees sight itself as a problem to be corrected has deep roots in our culture and has become acute in postmodernism, which continues this prevalent distrust of the image and has made it almost all-encompassing. Baudrillard's notion that there is an 'evil demon of images' reflects a tension that is not really a distrust of sight itself so much as a doubt about the way that sight is constructed in an ambivalent way, something that disturbs the principle of identity that postmodernism in general – protestations notwithstanding – is sanctioned to uphold. The fear of sight is a fear of vision and the powers of the imagination. It would surely be more accurate to say that what characterises Western discourse is not control *by* the visual, as Foucault claims, but rather control *of* the visual (albeit, often by visual means). In lacking cognitive authority, the image connects us with our physicality, and distrust of it seems to be linked to the fact that it thereby escapes the control of mind and can only participate in our overcoming of bodily limitations by being divested of this physicality. Hence the need for it to be controlled by *logos*, which enables the celebration of pure mind, free from bodily concerns. This is how the image tends to be controlled in modern society: by being subsumed into the word. The visual thus comes to be conceived as an extension of speech. Increasingly it becomes necessary for us to learn to read images not visually but *linguistically*, so that the image itself becomes subsumed into the productive capacity represented by *logos*.

This linguistic encoding of images is a feature of the contemporary media, and gives rise to a need for a corresponding visual literacy that will enable us to uncode – or at least not be dominated by – the messages given to us by the media, but in the process it also tends to disable us from appreciation of the visual image in its own terms. We are told that we live in a world increasingly permeated with images, but this is only partly true. We really live in a world in which the empty image – the image reduced to a seductive accoutrement (to be read in a certain way to hide its own emptiness) – is dominant, but in which the full image, the one that embodies change while always remaining the same, that is replete and yet expansive, concrete and yet ungraspable, is marginalised. It is doubtless vain to think one can challenge this dominance; the most that can be done is to broaden the margin, to bring awareness to the fact that dominant images do not exhaust, or even begin to engage with, the possibilities the image contains.

And what is significant here is that the ambivalence of sight also reflects the way the body has traditionally been considered in Western culture, being both celebrated as the noblest sense and yet denigrated as the realm of deceit. 'Seeing is believing,' we say. We may speak of the nobility of vision. And yet at the same time we distrust it and need to control it. This ambivalence is imprinted in language: the eye is associated with being *visionary* or *clairvoyant*, able to penetrate the nature of things and see beyond immediate appearance, but it is also associated with the *voyeur* or the *snoop*, with surveillance and seduction. If the latter is characteristic of the way in which modern society endeavours to control visual meaning, reducing it to serving its own power structures, it can do so only by denying the integrality of sight as the sense of vision and insight.

This returns us to further consideration of the image of the body as being the essence of art, as providing us with the indissoluble core of what art is, founded in the propensity of the human body towards movement and the pleasure it takes in sensual movement and play, emphasising visionary and clairvoyant qualities that threaten a stable sense of identity. Here we need to question what art itself actually is. We have to this point taken the concept of art for granted as something that really exists. Is it legitimate to do so? According to Jimmie Durham, for instance, art is nothing but 'a European invention'. Is this a fair description, and if so, how does it fit with our discussion thus far?

Certainly it is true that what we habitually speak of as art is a creation of nineteenth-century ideology, formulated against a backdrop of a capitalist society developing a system of values that would have a significant impact upon the ways in which art would be appreciated. In particular the growth of an art market and the public display of art in museums were to establish a public consciousness of what 'art' is. Yet such a conception of art was anathema to most artists at the beginning of the twentieth century, so that the most radical movements, such as Dadaism and Surrealism, denied that their activity – whether of painting or writing or whatever – had anything to do with art: art, as Francis Picabia insisted, 'is a pharmaceutical product for morons'. Art in the sense that Jimmie Durham says is a European invention was what European artists at the beginning of the twentieth century reacted violently against. Whether they succeeded in reinstalling a universal sense of creative expression is another question, however, and we need to consider whether it is possible to go beyond the idea of art that is prevalent in modern society and responds precisely to the needs of European society.

Is it then still legitimate to speak in terms of a universal propensity for creating art, or is it something peculiar to the development of a complex modern society? Much sociological and anthropological literature of recent years inclines one towards the latter point of view. Pierre Bourdieu (1984) in particular has demystified the notion of art of its aura of significance and has shown how in practice what we call art is no more than a means for establishing 'cultural capital' that shores up our sense of personal and social standing; consequently our tastes in art are determined by our social status and class. Appreciation of art is therefore learned and responds to certain expectations of society and of our own identity: we like certain things because they conform either to our own self-image, or to the image we want to convey to other people. It does not respond to any inner core of necessity.

The implication here is that appreciation of art is a fully learned process, not – as we have thus far argued – an elemental part of the human personality emerging from an affective response to the world. Yet, if it is undoubtedly true that particular tastes are conditioned, and sometimes determined, by social processes, it is difficult to see how this can represent the whole story.

The argument can be seen in microcosm in an article by anthropologist Signe Howell (1991) criticising universalist assumptions of art. Insisting that social facts only have meaning in social context, she denies any universality to the production of art. Arguing against art critic Peter Fuller for his assumption of such universality, she tries to show that all art is culturally specific and can only be understood within the context in which it is created. Perhaps this is so, but she seems oblivious to the fact that cultural contexts are themselves constantly shifting and meanings are no more determined by their particular configurations of time and space than they are by any inherent universal human urge. If the importance of cultural context must be recognised, this does not of itself mean that there is no such universal impulse or that art cannot be appreciated across cultural borders. She looks at an exhibition of Henry Moore sculptures in Hong Kong, citing the horrified reaction of a Chinese woman. Howell argues from this that Henry Moore sculptures are only comprehensible to a Western audience with Christian baggage, who are able to relate Moore's work as playing upon understandings of the body as founded in Western discourse. While it is undoubtedly true that Moore's work gains resonances from the Western tradition, to state that this exhausts its possibilities is absurd. Do all Westerners respond to Moore's work with those associations in mind? Are all Chinese unable to relate to it? She doesn't tell us how typical of the Chinese women who saw the exhibition this was. 'Why they have holes where their stomachs should be?', as the woman is quoted as saying (in Howell, 1991: 219), surely might just as easily be the response of a Western woman who comes upon Moore's work for the first time. Meaning may be relative to context, but this does not mean that it cannot be understood outside that context, or that the intentions of the artist are not the same cross-culturally. It cannot be assumed that either intent or meaning is merely constructed by the collective representations within particular societies. Understanding responds to processes of affinity and aversion that are themselves culturally formed, but may not be culturally specific. Can it be said that the work of any artist can be reduced simply to the status of a social fact of a particular context?

The central issue may be not so much whether other cultures have a concept that approximates to 'our' concept of art but rather whether there is a concept of art that is even generally accepted in the West. Definitions of art are vague. It is generally defined as what is created by human skill as opposed to being a creation of nature. More specifically, it is the skill to create something beautiful. But what does this tell us? Does it not mean everything that is created by humans? If it means something specific, then what is meant by 'skill' or by 'beauty'?

Rationales of art work and the act of creativity by which it is brought into being are many and varied: it may be due to a will to imitate what we see in the perceptual world; it may result from a need to use the skill of our hands to render what we see with our eyes; it may be due to a demiurge, a will to bring into creation something that did not previously exist, to assume the mantle of God; it may bear witness to a will towards religious devotion, the artist using skill to give honour to particular beliefs; it may be from a will towards healing, something that can especially be seen in relation to shamanism; it may be from a will towards knowledge, to capture the essential purity of the state of existence, as in the work of Mondrian; it may simply be due to a wish for a career and for money (which for a long time was considered anathema, but has gained increasing respectability in recent years). In fact, the motivations of most artists are no doubt a combination of these factors. However, we already perceive a further problem. All of these reasons take the creation of the work as the motive point, and assume that the work itself emerges from within the consciousness of the individual artist. They do not take into account of the role of art and the artist in a given society.

The nature of the creative act and the role of the imagination are key elements in the creation of a work of art, yet where do these capacities emerge from? Do we accept the commonly proposed idea that creativity and the imagination are capacities of the individual genius, that certain people are born with a gift that enables them to capture this essence that we call 'art'?

Janet Wolff dismisses the idea of the individual genius as 'inadmissible'

[T]he concept of the artist as some kind of asocial being, blessed with genius, waiting for divine inspiration and exempt from all normal rules of social intercourse is very much an ahistorical and limited one. Its kernel of truth lies in the fact that the development of our society *has* marginalised artists. . . . (1981: 12)

This may be true, as far as it goes, but there is a lot more to this issue. The idea of inspiration as an individual gift is clearly an ideological construction that underwrites capitalism through the supposition that the motor of society is not collective participation but the free activity of individuals acting for themselves. This myth is undoubtedly resonant and provides the rationale simultaneously to disparage and exalt art. Yet its kernel of truth lies not in the fact that art has marginalised artists (something that is by no means self-evident: Goethe, after all, perhaps the archetype of the idea of the genius, was socially well adjusted and respected), but in the fact that there is such a thing as inspiration that is mysterious and is ultimately not containable by the capitalist means of production. If everything is socially constructed, as Wolff, like Bourdieu and Howell, appears to believe, how do we explain the particular qualities of Goethe – or indeed of anyone? We would all be embedded within social structures and unable to transcend – or even comment on – social practices. Such sociological reductionism simply leads us into a meaningless determinism founded in the positivist world view that rejects metaphysical explanation. While it may be the case that the 'genius' is socially created, this does nothing to explain the source of creativity and the imagination; nor does it allow us to conceive of how excellence in any sphere becomes possible. Indeed, the critical faculty Janet Wolff displays in writing her book contradicts her very argument: if she really believed that everything was socially determined, there would be little point in her writing her book since all it could then do is reproduce the very structures it criticises. To reduce the notion of genius to an empty social construction is to capitulate to the values of consumer society just as surely as does its elevation to a principle.

We can turn to Adorno for illumination on this point. He writes:

> If the category of genius is to be retained, it must be divorced from the crude identification with the creative subject. This equation tends to diminish the status of the work, glorifying instead its author out of a false sense of enthusiasm. The objectivity of art works is a thorn in the side of people living in a commodity society because they falsely expect art to act as a palliative for alienation, provided only art is translated back into the person standing behind it. In reality this person is little more than a character mask trumped up by those who try to sell art as an article of consumption. (1984: 243–4)

In separating out genius from the individual in this way, Adorno reveals the error of sociological determinism in relation to the creative act. Individual genius is an untenable notion not because inspiration does not exist at an individual level, but because the individual, quite simply, does not exist isolated from social processes. Creativity itself flows through an individual as a concentration of energies of all that surrounds that person. It is in this sense that Ducasse's injunction – which we should perhaps give in full here – takes its real force: 'Poetry must be made by all. Not by one. Poor Hugo! Poor Racine! Poor Coppée! Poor Corneille! Poor Boileau! Poor Scarron! tics, tics and tics.' For Ducasse, everyone participates in the creation of poetry, not simply the person who writes or appreciates it. From such a point of view, it is difficult to see how the impulse by which the creative activity is initiated is not a universal possibility.

This view that everyone participates in poetry supports Adorno's view by undermining the notion of genius without destroying it: genius claimed in and of itself is revealed to be nothing but a nervous spasm embedded in capitalist relations and having nothing to do with the deeper function of art. In order to elucidate this point we need to look further at the constituents of the creative act as such.

It has, of course, become fashionable in today's criticism to decry the role of the author. In proclaiming the 'death of the author', Barthes and Foucault transferred the focus of attention both from the author to the reader and from creation to reception. However, in contrast to Ducasse, such a critique does not undermine the notion of individual genius, but rather turns it away from the process of creation to the process of interpretation: the reader (or, more accurately, the critic) rather than the author becomes the centre of gravity. (Signe Howell, too, participates in this movement: her critique explicitly asserts that only the anthropologist or sociologist who has studied the context of the original art work is entitled to make a pronouncement on it.) If this means that creativity is no longer to be seen as inherent in the gifted individual and is not the expression of emotions and ideas that are unique to that person, so asserting that art is no longer a process of personal expression or of self-realisation but part of a process of relations, it tends to exalt secondary characteristics, so that what matter it is the situation within which the art work is established rather than its content. To be accepted as a leading artist or writer one needs not to be a good painter or writer, but to take control of the discourse in which one is working: one must become a personality, so that the shading of art into life becomes complete. This inverts the aim of artists at the beginning of the twentieth century, who sought to make life one with the practice of art. What this means is that to be successful as an artist in modern society one should make one's life an adjunct to one's art: this is the reason aspiring artists today must go to art school or writers take a creative writing programme, from which they learn not so much the techniques of painting or writing as ways to present themselves and to interpret and criticise other art and writing, something that was anathema or at best a necessary evil for writers and artists of earlier eras. The discourse itself becomes its own rationale, dispersing the subject and making all meaning contingent. Yet if we accept such a definition, then what goes out of the window, along with the concept of genius, is any idea of universal creative expression. Art becomes simply the result of effective self-publicity available to anyone with the means to avail themselves of the machinery of such publicity that is offered by the contemporary media.

Curiously, a contrary movement to this breakdown of the notion of authorship is advocated by anthropologist Sally Price in relation to the art works of non-Western societies. In a book that is in many ways hopelessly confused and poorly argued, Price (1989) nevertheless raises a key issue that especially brings into question the 'death of the author' thesis. She argues that the idea that art in traditional societies was the product of cultural tradition and not the creation of the individual artist is itself a false construction of the West that served the interests of collectors, who had an interest in constructing an idea of 'primitive art' as the product of anonymous artisans who were unable to appreciate its real value as 'art'; the real creators of primitive art, therefore, are the collectors who recognised it and brought this art to the West.

This chimes in an interesting way with the 'death of the author' thesis and provides a critique of it, because Price essentially seems to be saying that the refusal of authorship here is a process of domination representing a will to deny creation where it really belongs and to displace it on to those doing interpretation of it. It is difficult to deny that this is so, and it should be pointed out that, to be consistent, such a view (which unites her with the postmodernist stance as well as with Howell and Wolff) would have to applaud these collectors who were responsible for the recognition of the value of this 'primitive' art, whose qualities had hitherto not been appreciated. Rather than draw this conclusion, however, she reverts to acceptance of the idea of individual creation, asserting that we need to recognise its primacy in non-Western cultures.

It is difficult to deny that Sally Price is right to raise this issue, and there has to be sympathy with her view that we need to recognise what is at stake and try to restore agency to these anonymous works as a process of repairing the crime that has undoubtedly occurred whereby such works have been taken into the Western canon without proper acknowledgement of their sources. Elementary justice implies this. However, her solution to this problem – that we should actively seek the names of the individuals who were responsible for making these products, giving them the acknowledgement due to them – seems as fully a product of Western ideology as the process she is attacking.

It is one thing to say that traditional societies respect the individual skill that goes into an 'art work'; quite another to say that this means the 'art work' is regarded as the creation or the property of the person who fabricated it. It should go without saying that there is enormous variation in the way in which artists are regarded in different cultural settings. It therefore seems highly dubious from a theoretical point of view to assert that the individual artist should be recognised in the way in which Sally Price advocates. By making such a plea, she is doing the same sort of violence to native categories as the collectors and art historians she attacks so fervidly. The fact that all non-Western societies almost certainly place greater emphasis on social and communal values than on those of individual becoming is not a myth conjured up by Western art collectors: there is plenty of anthropological evidence to support it. To impose authorship on objects that in their native setting are seen as collective products may be extremely dangerous and risk upsetting a fragile social equilibrium. Indeed it seems to be accepting the fact that only the criteria of art laid down by the Western art market are operative. That an anthropologist should not be alert to this risk seems extraordinary.

Creativity has always seemed a mysterious thing. Yet while it may be true that art cannot communicate a specific meaning cross-culturally, there seems no reason to believe that it cannot *embody* a universal meaning. Such at least seems to have been the postulate of most Western artists prior to the introduction of the relativism that postmodernism has initiated as the primary assumption of modern discourse (that such universalism was not present to non-Western artists was due simply to the fact that their societies had no universal conception). Is it therefore still legitimate to assert universal aspirations as a focus of creative expression?

We can here return to Cassirer's separation of language and say that there are indeed different ways of communication, but these are not reducible to language. As we have seen, communication is a fundamental feature of all life forms, which may be manifested in multifarious ways. In humans, the will to communicate with our fellows has led to the establishment of complex language forms, but it is also part of a will towards communication – to communicate with the infinite, with what is beyond us, with the world, and this aspiration is one art responds to in all cultural environments, whether conceptualised as such or not.

We all structure an aesthetic response to the world in the way we move, the way we dress, the ways we prepare our food, indeed in all the ways in which we construct our culture. Art is merely one manifestation of this process, taken to its greatest level of intensity. In all contexts the artist must establish the common meanings and purposes by which the art work may be recognised and appreciated. Most artists would probably say that they saw their relation with their public as ideally being an unmediated one: the artist directly creates something to be directly perceived by the viewer in reality. It is never so simple. All art is mediated by innumerable factors. The production of any art work is part of a process in which it is never entirely possible to separate out the different elements that have made it possible. Who is the agent? The person who commissions the art? The person who paints it? The person who makes it available? The person who receives it? In some societies a mask may be created when it is seen by a shaman in a vision. He will ask a craftsman to make the mask for him. The craftsman makes the mask in accordance with both the tradition of the society and the instructions given by the shaman. Yet to what extent can it be said that the final mask is the vision of either the shaman or the craftsman? For no matter how 'beautiful' it may be, it will be unacceptable if it fails to convince the community that it is the embodiment of the spirit that has given rise to it. Is this process really substantially different in Western society? All artists are constrained by the perception within society of what is acceptable as art work and must work within such constraints, even if the lack of constraint is touted as the condition of art itself, as tends to be the case today. The question of what art actually communicates haunts contemporary art practices. Modern artists may rejoice in their freedom, or lament the loss of anything resembling a collective purpose. Despite all the freedom to create they have, however, no artist transcends the social conditions in place and all are forced to work within the framework these set.

What is of course very different in contemporary art is that the nexus of relations is mediated by the incorporation of a market economy into the process, which now provides the only recognised means of judging the value of the resulting art work. The mask created by a modern artist cannot satisfy society in the way that a shamanistic mask could. This does not, however, prevent many contemporary artists from working towards a reconciliation of social praxis. Despite everything, art retains a will to act as a mediation between the visible and the invisible, to restore to us a direct relation to the world that holds in balance the energy forces of existence to maintain a relative stability of human life.

That art is now imbued with an aesthetics of revolt that is our modern condition does not negate the fact that it can still act as a guardian of human memory and sanctity. Against the flow of modern society, hostile as it is to any spontaneous movement of restoration, there remain artists committed to a vision of art as responding to primal needs as a perpetual re-creation in a form of play that, like Siva's dance, keeps the world in harmony. In this it surely joins in a universal movement that retains a vital link with those unknown Palaeolithic peoples who first began to paint on the walls of caves in their native land and whose art, whatever else it might be, reminds us of our transience and the fact that we are creatures of flesh and blood living in dynamic relation with the natural forces that exist all around us.

Notes

1. This can be seen, for instance, in the fact that football in the present day, as much as it may have succumbed to commercial crassness, is still described as 'the beautiful game'. The resurgence of football during the nineties, and even its possibilities for commercial exploitation, came about in reaction to the dreadful 1990 World Cup final between West Germany and Argentina, which finally forced the authorities to address the cynicism that had engulfed the game and was threatening to destroy its beauty.
2. Although Plato also put forward another idea of art that seems to contradict this. It asserted that the artist is directly inspired by the gods to express what is beyond appearance. The artist imitates not nature's products, but nature's productive activity. This is undeveloped in Plato's own philosophy but is a view that is more associated with Neo-Platonism and also ties in with aspects of Gnosticism that saw philosophy as having the aim of reaching union with God. In this, art becomes a demiurge.

6

CULTURE AND THE NATURAL WORLD

Whether man is seeking . . . to make himself ultimately larger than life or finally to diminish the stature of life itself remains the enigma of self-proportion.

Wilson Harris

We have seen how the child needs to differentiate itself from what surrounds it. As it does so, it confirms itself in time and space and establishes nature as something distinct from culture. To this extent, culture is negatively defined: it is what is not nature. In some ways it could be said that our whole understanding of culture is based upon this fundamental distinction, which is nevertheless perplexing, because we are natural beings, we belong to the realm of nature. But if this is so, then how can this mysterious thing called culture, as something distinct from nature, arise? If culture is what has been humanly created rather than what naturally exists, and yet humans are natural beings, how can there be culture? In defining it as opposed to nature, as what nature is not, we are faced with a paradox with many implications. Our relation with nature thus lies at the heart of the enigma of what we are.

Nature not only exists externally to us; it is also retained within us, being both what is most alien to us, what is other, and yet at the same time what is most intimate and familiar. Bodily functions, the mechanical operation of the body, even aspects of the psyche, such as unconscious drives and desires, dreams and longings, may be said to belong more to nature than to culture. Although such separations may be culturally specific and grounded in the separation of mind and body that underwrites much of Western discourse, they still bring attention to the mystery that surrounds our relation with the natural world.

If culture defines our humanness and establishes our complex relationship with the surrounding world, then how do we relate to the fact that nature also exists within us? We recognise ourselves as animals and yet, at the same time, separate ourselves from all other animals in a conclusive way. In general we do not define ourselves as one species among many others having particular characteristics. We don't make classifications in terms of the particular qualities of human beings on the same level as the particular qualities of the tiger or the dog. Rather, we conceive of ourselves as a species distinct from all other animals, but pinpointing something we have that other animals lack. This may be language, the ability to think or feel, to associate socially, to create tools and work, to act freely, and so on. All of these elements serve our definition of culture. Marx gives a most lucid statement of the essence of our differentiation from animals:

> The animal is immediately one with its life activity. It is not distinct from that activity; it *is* that activity. Man makes his life activity itself an object of his will and consciousness. He has conscious life activity. It is not a determination with which he directly merges. Conscious life activity directly distinguishes man from animal life activity. Only because of that is he a species-being. (1974: p. 328)

In this respect, the human uniqueness of culture is crucial, for if other animals have culture, then the divide between nature and culture breaks down. Some – especially vegetarians or those connected with ecology movements, on the one hand, and proponents of socio-biological and eugenics movements, on the other – may wish to argue the latter point, saying that it is an artificial divide that falsifies what we are, that we are fundamentally no different from other animals. Ironically, though, if we deny the division, we are faced with a serious moral problem that actually undermines the rationale of ecological and vegetarian movements as it brings into question eugenics and genetic experimentation. (It is interesting that as opposed as ecologists and geneticists may be ideologically, they share one point of departure: that human nature is essentially one with animal nature.) For if culture does not exist and everything is nature, then all we do is natural and in accord with universal structuring. In this case, there is no need to regulate our behaviour: we can pollute the earth, kill other animals unrestrainedly, experiment with nuclear weapons and destroy whole populations. In so doing, we are merely acting in accordance with our natural sensibility and we can have no moral responsibility for what we do, any more than the shark can have when it swallows smaller fish or the lion when it kills an antelope. We can have no relationship *with* and no responsibility *for* nature because we *are* nature. It is only if culture exists as a definable human characteristic, distinguishing it in some way from what we are, that we can have a relationship *with* nature that affects our behaviour and provides the basis for our having a responsibility in the way we act towards it. That we have culture, while other animals – as purely natural beings – do not, is a fundamental element in our own identity. When we talk about ecology, what we are really talking about is the relationship between nature and culture; ecology itself becomes meaningless if we obliterate the distinction. Indeed, any idea of moral responsibility can only emerge from a concept of culture. In the same way, from the opposite perspective, genetic experimentation is based upon the idea that life is homogeneously structured: by experimenting on rats, therefore, we can learn something that will apply also to humans. The refusal of moral responsibility for animals by geneticists is based upon exactly the same assumption that ecologists make for such responsibility. It just changes the frame of reference: such experiments are justified in the name of a universal good, and in the fact that the human being, although fundamentally the same as other animals, is more highly evolved, something that confers a licence to make choices about the general improvement of life, even at the expense of pain or suffering to other animals.

It should here be understood that nature is not an object; it has no existence separate from our relation to it. If we are to understand it, therefore, we must examine it as a construction and how it relates to our consciousness. From this point of view, the essential feature of nature is that it is lacking in form. According to Lefebvre, it 'designates cosmic reality without implying an ontology or a cosmology' (1995: 133). It is therefore something that escapes our ability to conceptualise: nature, almost by definition, is limited to cultural categories that, in its essential characteristic, it must exceed. In other words, theories about nature are interlinked with those of what is understood by society and culture. Nature has no reality in itself but attains one only as a projection of human perceptions. In other words, it is itself a cultural category. It exists only by the fact that humans have created culture, which itself assumes meaning only by being what nature is not. Nature therefore comes to gain a reality as that which is not culture. The newborn child does not come into the world informed with the means to engage with culture. On the contrary, it does not distinguish itself from nature: the surrounding world is part of itself. This is why the process of socialisation is also a process of defining oneself against nature, of becoming 'cultured', hence enculturation. Other animals do not live in nature: they belong to it only through human conceptualisation. Animals know neither time nor space, but exist in an extended duration that is continuous with their existence. They know nothing of death, because in order to be able to conceive of one's own death requires a way of measuring past and future activity. Humans live in the assumption that they will die. Actually, there is nothing natural in this assumption. It is born of cultural constructions: we assume we shall die because we have learned that this is in the nature of all living forms. We perceive the existence of death and we have the means to bring it about: we have the power to kill anything that lives, even a thousand-year-old sequoia. What cannot die we perceive as not being alive. Death, indeed, is for us the condition of life.

Other animals may perceive the existence of death, but they cannot conceptualise its effect on themselves as an element of time and space: a dog cannot contemplate the idea that in a few decades it will be dead. It has no way to imagine the time frame this involves or to engage with the process of rationalisation such a thought implies. The same thing is true for space: a tiger in Tanzania cannot conceive the idea: 'I wish I lived in China.' It is, as Marx's quotation above emphasises, fundamentally one with its life activity and has no conceptual means by which to transcend it, whether in time or space. To conceptualise nature, death, time or space – all related concepts – requires a cultural framework that is alien to the lives of any other animal but the human.

It is through establishing cultural categories by means of an exploration of the surrounding world that we, as humans, are able to locate ourselves within a framework of an era and a place. Like nature, space and time are cultural categories that do not exist naturally in the world. We experience them only because we are enculturated beings. The world for dogs and tigers alike is one in which the depth of space is differently configured.

It is important to recognise that as human beings we are structured in a way that is fundamentally different from other creatures. Other animals, including those that are most close to us, primarily rely on the senses of smell and hearing to establish their relation to the world. In contrast, we rely most especially on those of touch and sight. This is not to say that we have a more acute sense of sight. Indeed, it may be that other animals have a sharper visual sense. What they lack, however, is the delicate tactility of humans; it is this that enables us to perceive the world by means of direct contact with it. All other animals are protected from tactile intimacy with the world: fur, feathers and padded paws or hoofs place a barrier between most animals and the world that prevents them from developing a sense of touch with the nuance of human touch.

We return here to understanding of the human body and its relation to what surrounds it. In this respect, the modern sensibility is unusual in human history: we not only make a distinction between culture and nature, but also see culture as being triumphant – whether for good or ill – over nature. This is also, as we have seen, a triumph of the mind over the body.

It is almost certain that all societies make some distinction between nature and culture, but the terms by which this distinction is conceptualised vary enormously and the distinction is rarely made in a distinct way. Indeed, even in many modern societies people find it difficult to conceptualise such a distinction clearly. Almost never in cultures of which we are aware outside the modern West is mankind elevated above the natural world.

In medieval European society the world was part of an organic unity. Its hierarchical structure was based upon the assumption of a heavenly order that was imprinted upon both the social and the human body. This supported the view

> that all things were permeated by life, there being no adequate method by which to designate the inanimate from the animate. It was difficult to differentiate between living and non-living things, because of the resemblance in structures. Like plants and animals, minerals and gems were filled with small pores. . . . By virtue of the vegetative soul, minerals and stones grew in the human body, in animal bodies, within trees, in the air and water, and on the earth's surface in the open country. (Merchant, 1980: 27–8)

Some variation of such a relation with nature seems to be present in most societies prior to the Enlightenment in Western culture and can be loosely defined as 'animism', that is, the belief that everything – whether animate or inanimate – possesses a vital spirit that is essential to its nature.

Today few support the old idea that the earliest religious forms emerged from the fact that people had to engage in a constant struggle against the forces of nature, and that animistic beliefs were a kind of 'faulty science'. Animism, in one form or another, may be said to be a constant in much of human culture and remains central to supposedly 'higher' religions like Buddhism and Hinduism. However, the idea that the whole of nature is 'alive' and that we are part of nature rather than separate from it remains alien to our modern temperament, despite an often pervasive sense of longing within the West for the recovery of such a relation, as can be seen in the allure that pagan and witchcraft ideas, as well as Eastern religions, retain.

In the West, animist beliefs continued well into the Renaissance, perpetuated in the curious and well-documented cases of animal trials conducted by the church, in which we see the power of the non-human world as still being alive and recognised as a significant element within the dynamic of society. Luc Ferry (1995) raises animal trials to highlight dangers of irrationalism that the contemporary ecology movement may be subject to. Yet can we not see animal trials, far from being irrational, rather as a significant moment of transition from an animist sensibility to a modern, human-centred one, representing a necessary accommodation between Christian and pagan belief systems? If they represented something irrational, it was only because they were attempting to reconcile what was irreconcilable, and it was precisely because Christianity and paganism could not, in the long run, be reconciled that an Enlightenment sensibility was able to take root that sought a scientific way of explaining our relationship with the natural world. It was undoubtedly the case that the development of science demanded the annihilation of old animist ideas (which Christianity opposed but was unable to eradicate) for it could only establish itself within the framework of a different understanding of the relationship between humans and nature.

Until the Enlightenment, it is clear that natural objects were not seen as things that human beings could act upon at will (whether for good or ill). They contained their own powers and forces that acted in sympathy or antipathy with what surrounded them. One therefore meddled with them at one's own peril. This was not monolithic: Carolyn Merchant has traced three different ways of relating to the world in medieval and Renaissance Europe. Nor was it absolute: we can see that the urge to exploit the world was already present, but kept in check. As Merchant says:

> The image of the earth as a living organism and nurturing mother had served as a cultural constraint restricting the actions of human beings. One does not readily slay a mother, dig her entrails for gold or mutilate her body. . . . As long as the earth was considered to be alive and sensitive, it could be considered a breach of human ethical behavior to carry out destructive acts against it. (1980: 3)

This contains an essential point. The cultural determinants of a given society are all of a piece and cannot be abstracted out. The medieval perception of the world spirit was not based on a faulty understanding of the nature of the world, any more than the Enlightenment perception is based upon accurate understanding. Both are centred in certain moral and metaphysical assumptions that respond to the dynamic of society itself. Merchant explains this well:

> While the organic framework was for centuries sufficiently integrative to override commercial development and technological innovation, the acceleration of such changes throughout western Europe during the sixteenth and seventeenth centuries began to undermine the organic unity of the cosmos and society. Because the needs and purposes of society as a whole were changing with the commercial revolution, the values associated with the organic view of nature were no longer applicable; hence the plausibility of the conceptual framework itself was slowly, but continuously, threatened. (1980: 5)

This 'death of nature' that Merchant sees as being a product of Enlightenment remains with us as an essential aspect of our sensibility and is at the root of the environmental crisis that today threatens to undermine human culture entirely. The disappearance of the organic model of the world was a result of an increasing mechanisation of society. This involved not simply the use of machines to improve human life, but also the disestablishment of earlier views and the resetting of human values in terms of mercantile and technological values. To achieve this required the transformation of the world itself from something living into a mechanism that could be abstracted and studied. Enlightenment ideas of a consistent and coherent world were a metaphysical assumption that – irrespective of its 'objective' truth – was necessary for the imposition of scientific methodology, but this also chimed with other elements at work within society. Enlightenment needed a nature that was dead, because it could not justify the investigation and control of what was alive. As Horkheimer and Adorno argued, 'In the anticipatory identification of the wholly conceived and mathematized world with truth, enlightenment intends to secure itself against the return of the mythic' (1979: 25). The force of such a doctrine was such as to underwrite a shift in the perception of the nature of the world.

Today's ecology movement has been at the forefront of re-examinations of our relationship with nature, and the extent of contemporary environmental problems is undoubtedly such that this re-examination is long overdue. Yet the assumptions of the ecological movement have been brought into question by French philosopher Luc Ferry, who sees in it a pernicious refiguration of authoritarian ideas, especially of fascism. He argues that the particular ways in which much recent concern for the environment has been manifested reveal an anti-humanist nostalgia that threatens to undermine democratic processes. Ferry argues that ecology fills the vacuum created by the collapse of belief in an alternative society, a consequence of the fall of Stalinism. He ties this in with a whole range of phenomena that have seen the emergence, in various spheres, of what he calls an 'ethics of authenticity':

> This ethics consists, on the one hand, of rejecting *aristocratic* values, of combating hierarchies in the name of the *egalitarian* and . . . democratic idea that *all practices are equally valid*, that each of us possesses the right to live out his difference, to be himself. . . . the 'sexual liberation' movement would reject the traditional discrimination between 'normal' and 'deviant', attempting to destigmatise homosexuality and, more generally all behavior previously condemned in the name of a normative ideal that arranged all forms of life within a *hierarchy*.
>
> On the other hand, the ethics of authenticity endeavors to disqualify the moral notions of *duty* and *merit*: If it is now 'forbidden to forbid', it is because the transcendent norms, the 'ascetic ideal' Nietzsche denounced in Christianity and in Protestant rigor, no longer carry weight. If we have any duty, it is to 'be ourselves'; if there is a new norm, it says that *each of us must invent his own norm*. Previously ethics consisted in *endeavoring* to achieve, most often against the grain of one's penchants, the attainment of *standards* external to ourselves. It supposed an effort of the will impelled by *imperatives* expressed in the form of a

'must'. Now its goal is the realization of the self in the idea that the law, rather than being imposed upon us from without, is immanent within each individual. (1995: 144)

Ferry is not entirely mistaken and his warning should be taken seriously. He is certainly right to caution against the reduction of human culture to the status of nature; against the tendency to deny the very real differences that exist between humans and other animals in the name of a deep ecology that would restore the balance between humans and the rest of nature by giving rights to nature against the activity of humans. This does raises the spectre, which was briefly realised by the Nazi regime, of an anti-humanist authoritarianism. Nevertheless, Ferry's argument is fundamentally flawed in many respects and lies in exactly what Horkheimer and Adorno saw as one of the articles of bad faith of Enlightenment: the will to secure itself against the return of the mythic.

This seems misguided to the extent that, arguably, the impulse of much of the ecology movement Ferry sees as being so dangerous is founded not in a return to the mythic, but rather precisely in a humanistic sensibility. As much is announced in the organisations he castigates: *Greenpeace* and *Friends of the Earth*, their very names indicate how strongly they are grounded in an Enlightenment sensibility, even as they protest against its triumphalism. Indeed, they probably need to be so grounded in order to be able to act effectively as pressure groups in the modern world.

Is not the real danger here, as Ferry himself (almost as an aside) raises, that such movements still assume a human arrogance that sees itself as superior to nature, whilst merely reversing the terms: the will is no longer to exploit nature, but to protect it? The rationale is entirely installed in human agency and assumes nature to be merely passive matter whose only reality lies as the destination, or the victim, of human activity. Without seeming to realise the implications, Ferry locates the real problem this raises: 'Ecosystems are better designed than most human constructions. As a result, any intervention on our part most often turns out to be extremely damaging. . . . Even when his intentions are good, man is constantly bringing about unexpected results . . .' (1995: 142). Precisely. And how did such ecosystems come to be so well designed if they do not contain their own internal logic that surpasses human understanding? Does this not take us back to some form of 'animism', or at least to a view that nature cannot be reduced to a passive form that is irrevocably subject to human manipulation?

This returns us to the argument made by Carolyn Merchant (whose well-argued and meticulously supported thesis is dismissed by Ferry simply as a 'model of the genre', while he devotes considerable space to dismissing some of the more fanciful arguments of eco-feminists in a rather tendentious way). The significance of her book *The Death of Nature* (1980) is to show how the difficulty raised by ecological concerns relates to contemporary human mentality as much as to our relation with the environment itself. Is it possible to develop a more satisfactory relation with nature given our current mentality? Ferry himself can do no more than posit science as able to solve the problems, even though many of them are things it has itself created.

If Ferry is right to signify the importance of the distinction between nature and culture, it should be remembered that Enlightenment does not always retain this distinction. By establishing the mind as the motivating feature and condition of human existence, so reducing matter to the inanimate and separating humans irrevocably from animals, Enlightenment established a realm of humanistic consciousness but also paradoxically encouraged a contrary movement in the theory of evolution that reduced humans to the realm of the animal. What unites both humanism and evolutionism within the frame of Enlightenment is the will to separate the knowing subject from the nature of the object under study. Nature therefore becomes an object of contemplation rather than defining an Otherness with which we need to make an accommodation. Therefore, where an ancient form of knowledge of the world like totemism establishes a relation with nature in which humans are both continuous with and differentiated from animals, Western cosmology, dominated by the Cartesian *cogito*, classifies animals as mechanical beings that do not participate in the cosmic drama of human consciousness. Paradoxically, though, evolutionism brings this into question, reconnecting us with the natural world by the discovery of genetic structuring and processes of natural selection that feed back into and re-emphasise humanistic ideas. Equally, and almost contemporaneously with evolutionism, psychological research, especially the 'discovery' of the unconscious, also re-legitimised the idea of our continuity with nature by highlighting nature as a repressed force contained within us, as the 'beast within us' that provides evidence for our savage beginnings. That such paradoxical ideas can be generated from within the rubric of Enlightenment brings attention to the complexity of our relationship with nature.

This is inscribed in Enlightenment in its beginnings. For it is curious how, for all that Copernicus and Galileo were displacing the earth from its centrality in the universe and showing how the human itself was not the centre of creation but a minuscule part of a vast universe that in its totality is far beyond our understanding, the human was to be reinscribed as the centre and measure of everything. It is as though by extending the field of human endeavour to infinite (or unimaginable) dimensions, the Scientific Revolution needed to compensate by making the human subject the centre of the phenomenology of being. Another paradox: by showing how insignificant we are in the grand scheme of things, we managed, in our own eyes, to inflate the significance of our own subjectivity almost in proportion to the way in which the physical limits of the universe were being extended. The consequences of this have remained with us and are fundamental to contemporary cultural concerns; it is, after all, our own skill, our own genius (not to say our own self-importance), that has enabled us to reveal our universal insignificance. Bizarrely, too, it often seems that the more we think we know, the less certainty we have about the nature of what we actually know.

Of course, the mentality to which the Enlightenment gave form and legitimacy was not something it invented or created from nothing but, as Carolyn Merchant makes clear, had been present within humanity for a long time. We can see its roots in many areas of culture. In particular, there is a sense in which humans slip in and out of nature, and in all cultures there is a tension between the urge towards dominance of or integration with it. It is because this tension exists that belief systems – from totemism to the higher religions – seek to establish codes of proper conduct in relation to the surrounding world. The dominant Western idea of a paradoxical separation from and yet continuity between nature and culture is one that has provided the motor for modern society, but it did not emerge from nothing and has complex roots that are present, no doubt, in all cultures, if only in nascent form.

Horkheimer and Adorno, for instance, have seen the principle of Enlightenment as prefigured in *The Odyssey*. And they saw the paradox we have noted in this sensibility as already being clearly defined: 'The very spirit that dominates nature repeatedly vindicates the superiority of nature in competition. . . . The formula for the cunning of Odysseus is that the redeemed and instrumental spirit, by resigning itself to yield to nature, renders to nature what is nature's, and yet betrays it in the process' (1979: 57). Cultural forms marked by this simultaneous rendering and betrayal to which they have succumbed with a rapaciousness that is difficult to control and is central to the ecological problems we face today, are present in many different aspects.

One of the significant features of what we may call the Enlightenment surge to deny animistic identification with nature was to conceptualise this in gender terms and use it as a means for disciplining feminine knowledge: culture becomes associated with the male, nature with the female. This is prefigured in the earliest Christian myths, especially that of the legend of Adam and Eve. Let us remind ourselves of its essential features: after creating Adam from the dust of the ground, God planted a garden, which he named Eden, and appointed Adam to live there and look after it, with the injunction that he must not eat the fruit of the tree of knowledge. God then created Eve, the primeval woman, as a helper for Adam, fashioned from his rib. The serpent tempted Eve by telling her that if she ate the apple from the tree of knowledge, she would become like God. She did so and gave some to Adam. They became ashamed of their nakedness and God punished them with death and work, expelling them from the Garden of Eden. The Christian myth is significant in representing a fall into nature caused through the folly of the woman. Previously we were the guardians of nature and quite separate from it. After the fall, we gain an animal nature that separates us from the divine, making us incomplete, tainted beings: this is the meaning of the Original Sin that characterises Christianity.

This myth founds the dualism of masculine and feminine. Male being connected with culture, female with nature, nature also comes to be what we need to control. It is not really until the Enlightenment that we see this taking a definitive form. Celebrating light, and associating it with control of nature, Enlightenment became manifest in unexpected ways so that the witchcraft trials and the struggle against magical practices become not a feature of Enlightenment itself, but an essential preliminary to its becoming, centred in the will to control and master nature. There is a clear correlation between everyday and intellectual suppressions of the idea of nature as living reality. By defining being in terms of the *cogito* (I think therefore I am), Descartes was denying being to animals, let alone inanimate objects, in the same way that witchcraft accusers were denying the inner reality of magical practices. As much as these two movements in many ways were pulling against one another, they were essential to each other in fundamentally altering the way human beings related to the world that surrounded them.

Linked to the renunciation Horkheimer and Adorno observed in the mentality of Odysseus, this was perhaps the moment when a male sensibility finally came to prevail definitively over the female spirit. In this process,

> Mechanism took over from the magical tradition the concept of the manipulation of matter but divested it of life and vital action. The passivity of matter, externality of motion, and elimination of the female world soul altered the character of cosmology and its associated normative constraints. In the mechanical philosophy, the manipulation of nature ceased to be a matter of individual efforts. . . . (Merchant, 1980: 111)

It should here be borne in mind that myths do not found the way people actually forge a world around them. What matters is how these myths are culturally interpreted and applied in historical practice, and it is important to remember that there is no inevitability about the process by which this occurs. The Genesis myth itself may be interpreted in different ways. In some gnostic sects, for instance, it is the woman who is the founder of culture: formed from Adam as Adam was formed from the earth, Eve is the superior of Adam, being the quintessence of the male. And it was by tasting the fruit of the tree of knowledge that she opened up the possibility of liberation from the cruel God by introducing culture. Such an interpretation leads to a fundamentally different way of conceiving human history, a path that humanity could – and perhaps still might – take. The Greek myth of Pandora – freed from misogynist interpretations – can be read similarly. The myth of Melusine, which we have earlier looked at, contains the ambivalences involved in the association of women and nature in perhaps their most complex form.

In this context it is important to open up possibilities of an inter-relationship between humanity and nature so that ecological problems can be addressed not simply mechanically through science, but also culturally through understandings of the sensibility. In a rich ethnography of the Trio, a tribe living in the rainforests on the Brazil/Surinam border, Peter Rivière (1969) demonstrates the complex inter-relation between nature and culture. Men and women here are both of culture and of nature, having elements of each in particular circumstances and belonging to both but in different ways. This separation may be conceptualised by relations between inside and outside, between home and wild, or raw and cooked even if a clear distinction between human and animal and nature is not focused as it is in Western culture. We need to understand such distinctions in terms of a complex of continuities and interpenetration.

In this respect, the great value of Lévi-Strauss's interpretation of totemic identification is to show how totemism is not simply a form of logical classification, but also a means established within society to maintain a continuity with nature while simultaneously upholding a separation between what is naturally formed and what is culturally developed. As Lévi-Strauss (1963b) shows, totemic classification imposes order and stability on the world by means of making distinctions and contrasts of a consistent character that structure culture and nature as contingent in relation to one another rather than as existing as stable states of being.

At this point, it is perhaps worth returning to the importance of mimesis. We have already seen how mimesis – the will to imitate in order to become other, to reveal oneself by disguising oneself – has a fundamental part to play in the process of human development. As differentiation from nature is an elemental part of the process of becoming human, so this leaves a residue that impels a desire to return to it. Mimesis in this sense is related to the death instinct as explored by Freud, as a will not simply to become other, but also to collapse back into the nature of things, to become undifferentiated. Freud relates this to the childhood pleasure in repetition:

> *It seems, then, that an instinct is an urge inherent in organic life to restore to an earlier state of things* which the living entity has been obliged to abandon under the pressure of external disturbing forces; that is, it is a kind of organic elasticity, or, to put it another way, the expression of the inertia inherent in organic life. (1984: 308–9)

This enables Freud to assert that the aim of all life is death.

It seems that here we see one of the roots of the urge towards sacrificial practices, which, whatever else they may have been, were certainly a manifestation of a will to copy the cosmos, and to regulate our relationship with nature. Bruce Lincoln argues this point explicitly, saying that sacrifice is 'a ritual which effectively repeats the cosmos, shifting matter from a victim's body to the alloformic parts of the universe in order to sustain the latter against decay and ultimate collapse' (1991: 170).

Sacrifice is centred in loss and its practice seems to be connected to this moment of collapse that Freud identifies as the death drive, which involves a wish not so much to die as to merge into the nature of the world, to lose the burden of social demands and the requirement to assume a cultural identity. Sacrifice dramatises this moment, providing a vicarious and limited experience of death that enables the community to satisfy both the life impulse and the death drive.

To what extent does sacrifice respond to an elementary human need? Widespread as it is, sacrifice as such does not appear to be universal, and seems to be more associated with agricultural societies that are dependent upon a harmonious relation with the natural world to protect the harvest, which is crucial to the reproduction of the social order. Sacrificial practices in general thus seem to represent a release of energy that is connected with fertility: the divine principle of life comes into contact with the elementary urge towards death; it this energy that makes the fields fertile, expels sickness and sanctifies human culture. Whatever else sacrifice is (and one needs to be careful about generalising specific sacrificial practices), there does seem to be little doubt that at its heart is some form of communication between humanity and the greater cosmos. Sacrificial rites were performed to balance the fact of our being in the world with universal fact, represented by our mortality. Sacrifice as a practice seems to arise from consciousness of the reality of death as a creative principle: only through death is life brought to fruition, death being the condition and principle of life.

It is undoubtedly the case that death and communication lie at the heart of the sacrificial impulse in other complex ways. By offering up something of value, a community strives to create an obligation by which the society can achieve its aims through a gift. This unilateral giving, generous and yet interested, represents an inherent part of all human relationships, as Mauss was able to show in his seminal study. It is this that alerts us to the fact that if sacrifice as a practice is confined to particular types of society and is today obsolete, it still contains an echo within us that is enormously important to the foundation of what we are and how we relate to the society and the natural world that surround us.

All sacrifice is a disruption of nature, a sign of the disequilibrium brought to mankind by the foundation of culture. It is also, at the same time, an attempt to restore equilibrium and heal the breach this causes. Sacrifice responds to a sense of human guilt, founded in primal loss, that is experienced at both the individual and the collective level. It involves a highly complicated relation that bears upon the very construction of our identity and reality. In order to understand this significance, we need to look at how sacrifice relates to individual psychic reality. The violence that is an essential part of sacrifice emulates the violence that is at the heart of creation itself – experienced within us overwhelmingly as anguish – while confronting it with the further violence of death. All death, to this extent, can be said to affect us as a sacrificial moment. In this sense, the association made between the moment of orgasm and the moment of death is founded within the idea of sacrifice, to the extent that it may be said that erotic activity – in its intense form – enacts an experience of sacrifice.

For in the mingling of otherness in the sexual act, we see at the individual level something of what was at stake at the collective level in sacrificial rituals. Sexual attraction is a sign both of our incompleteness and of its potential remedy. As Georges Bataille put it,

> Only the beloved, so it seems to the lover – because of affinities evading definition which match the union of bodies with that of souls – only the beloved can in this world bring about what our human limitations deny, a total blending of two beings, a continuity between two discontinuous creatures. (1986: 20)

This desire to be *other*, to mingle – one might say to immolate – one's being with that of another is a desire to transcend what our individual beings are. This seems also to be the essential characteristic of sacrifice, and such an eroticism shares with sacrifice the fact that it is experienced within us as a loss, a loss that is welcomed as such. The erotic impulse tears us away from ourselves, dissolving our personality and propelling us into a realm of terror and disassociation. It offers a glimpse of what surpasses us and promises profusion in an act of generosity. It affirms, as sacrificial practices once did for societies, the continuity of life against the practical everyday concerns of human activity as such. Instead of being integrative, as sacrifice once was, this movement is, however, essentially asocial in the modern world.

Indeed, such integration with the continuity of existence, such generosity, is alien to our contemporary sensibility and may only fleetingly be appreciated at an individual level. Its denial at a collective level is centred precisely in the will to conquer nature and make all things our measure, so denying the complex bonds that tie life as a whole together. In this respect the will to conquer nature and the will to conquer death correspond. This will also represents a denial of the impulse that lies behind sacrifice.

For where once sacrifice was a means of seeking accommodation with the forces of life and death, today we try to outwit death not by means of communication with it, but by conquering its effects. Through understanding the structure of life we gain the knowledge and the power to prevail against death. This may seem rational, and the achievements of science are undeniably impressive, to the extent that it can seriously claim to have gained ascendency over nature and has the potential to be master of all that exists, but the ecological problems we see in modern society are not simply residual difficulties that science can solve in time. They are difficulties inherent in scientific procedures and emerge as a corresponding aspect of these very achievements, being essentially inscribed in its very impulse. Horkheimer and Adorno perceive this: 'The history of civilisation is the history of the introversion of sacrifice. In other words: the history of renunciation. Everyone who practices renunciation gives away more of his life than is given back to him: and more than the life that he vindicates' (1979: 55).

It is in this process of giving away more than is given back to us that the real risk lies. The mentality of conquest – tied in as it is with the imperialist impetus of the societies in which it was born – contains a danger much more potent than that which Luc Ferry perceives in ecological movements, and this is here clearly laid open:

In class history, the enmity of the self to sacrifice implied a sacrifice of the self, inasmuch as it was paid for by a denial of nature in man for the sake of domination over non-human nature and over other men. This very denial, the nucleus of all civilizing rationality, is the germ cell of a proliferating mythic irrationality: with the denial of nature in man not merely the *telos* of the outward control of nature but the *telos* of man's own life is distorted and befogged. As soon as man discards his awareness that he himself is nature, all the aims for which he keeps himself alive – social progress, the intensification of all his material and spiritual powers, even consciousness itself – are nullified, and the enthronement of the means as an end, which under late capitalism is tantamount to open insanity, is already perceptible in the prehistory of subjectivity. (Horkheimer and Adorno, 1979: 54)

It may be said that it is precisely such 'open insanity' that results in the crisis in our relations with the natural world. In the process of sacrifice, on the other hand, we affirm our existence, not as isolated beings whose reality begins and ends with ourselves, but as belonging to a greater whole constituted by existence. A society that engages with sacrifice is one that lacks the arrogance to believe it is above nature, but is able to recognise the extent to which the integration of the world requires engagement with a contagious and violent transgressive moment that serves social solidarity. The disappearance of such a sensibility in contemporary society is a denial of such integration in favour of control. What is at issue in sacrifice is the character of our relationship both with the world of death and with the world of nature. Sacrifice, as a gift offered to death and to nature, implies that this relation is one that involves complex obligations that are central to the fate of culture. For if there is a need for human action to prevent a collapse into nature as a feature of our existence, this also creates reciprocal ties. Today we are unable to speak to nature. Rather it has become silent; it no longer says anything we can hear and, even in radical ecology movements, the overriding urge is to save it, not to listen to what it has to say.

This means that it is we who construct nature in terms of how we can appropriate it into a shape that satisfies us. We can gain further insight into this process by inquiring into how we relate to – and create – notions of time and space. Like nature, these are not naturally existing categories but constructions we make about what surrounds us.

Human society, in order to take shape as such, needs to establish a sense of time and space to protect itself against formlessness and the chaos of infinity (in which limits do not exist). This is given shape by means of the realm of the sacred, which society needs as a mediation that maintains the tension between temporal order and infinite disorder. The sacred is an acknowledgement that such a tension is real, which is denied by a profane everyday life that would like to dissemble it and pretend that the world exists in an inert form. This tension is a fundamental one and if it is interrupted in either direction it brings dangers: if the sacred gains the upper hand, there is a sense of paralysis, overwhelming with chaos; if the profane is ascendant, (as in today's society), reductionism may follow. Control of time and space is fundamental to the way any society founds itself, for this relates to this process of mediation between sacred and profane spheres, allowing the motion of the universe to appear harmonious and intelligible to us.

Time and space presuppose one another and raise similar issues. It is now clear that, against Euclidean geometry, which asserted that space is three-dimensional and independent of the material it contains, space is not only interdependent with time, it is also reliant upon energy, which moves in every direction. The significance of this is to reveal that time and space have no absolute existence in themselves but can take shape only as human categories. And these categories are differently conceptualised according to context: we establish the features of time and space at a physical level, relating to our situation within nature and the cosmos; at the mental level, relating to logical and formal abstractions; at the social level, relating to how we construct our everyday relationships; and at the affective level, relating to how we respond to the time and space of the other.

In our daily lives we are constantly creating different frameworks of time and space. We seek to control time through historical or mythical narratives that regulate it and situate us within it, while we project ourselves onto space to provide a place for ourselves that is coterminous with our sense of reality. According to the nature of our lives, we orientate objects so they will respond to our conception of what we are. This is relative to our interaction with other people, with our perception of internal and external, with distance and nearness. We need to orientate ourselves to exist in time and space in a way that forms a permanent structure that belongs to us alone. This is necessary for us to feel at home in the world and comfortable in our relationship with what surrounds us. At the same time we project ourselves outwards: this may be vertically – towards the sacred realm – or horizontally – into the social world. The fall into an alien nature that is part of the anguish of being is also a fall into time and space.

We become individuated by means of a response to what has come before us through collective memory. What our ancestors experienced is retained within us and augmented. We can, to some degree, 'tame' time, or at least give ourselves the illusion that we have tamed it. We may remain fully aware of the illusory nature of this conquest, and that it may be subject to sudden collapse, that ultimately destruction awaits us, and regard time as a relentless process. To this extent, history represents a will towards mastery over time. As Walter Benjamin observed: 'The past can be seized only as an image which flashes up at the instant when it can be recognised and is never seen again. . . . [E]very image of the past that is not recognised by the present as one of its own concerns threatens to disappear irretrievably' (1970: 257).

In this way, we experience time as cultured beings, which requires that we recognise our life as a process that will continue within a limited framework defined by our birth and death. In actual fact, we know nothing of time or space: we know only what we can measure of it. The temporal and spatial world we inhabit is a construct, mentally and physically experienced, that in effect is a compromise between pure being and what exists beyond being which we can only define, even while we are unable to conceptualise it, as infinity.

The way we conceptualise time in particular affects the structure of our life. Identified with the periodic movements of sun, moon and planets, it is measured in all societies as both linear and cyclical, although there may be wide variations in how this is emphasised. All such measurements are attempts to reduce it to the measure of the human context.

In Western culture, the linear pattern dominates in a way that we take to be natural. We bemoan time passing, and the fact that there is not enough of it available for us to do all we set ourselves, but we accept that events occur only once. This means that, as we are urged to save time, so it becomes a commodity, to be earned, managed and spent, or wasted. 'Time', we say, 'is money.' It is also something to be fought against and this related to the sense of speed and progress that characterises the cultural flow of our society. Time can be added up and is a hard taskmaster that is constantly watching over us. We are forced to schedule our lives to fit its needs and are engaged in a relentless struggle to avoid the loss of time or to make it go further. Time becomes defined by its present immediacy. This implies a disavowal of the past, or rather the requirement to re-create it in the present; we can change our past, become 'born again', but we cannot repeat it. The present, in the same way, is transient and ungraspable, while the future is infinite and exploitable. These are symptoms of a disposable culture based upon maximum exploitation of available resources. As such, the time that the clock documents predominates, ordering and patterning our lives in a way that is difficult to avoid, even as we recognise other forms of time whose necessity, although perceptible, has to be shaped to fit in with this predominant need. Like most else within contemporary society, time is an object.

If the theories of relativity and non-Euclidean geometry may have been accepted at an intellectual level, this has done little to displace the everyday idea of time as an absolute category that defines the passing of events and is marked by the clock. And even though science has established the relativity of time and space, it still assumes that they are absolute in relation to social actions and take shape as constructs of the mind. Our lives, in the modern world, are constructed on the basis that we are engaged on a path that leads inexorably to the grave.

It seems significant that whereas in most religious traditions God is associated with time, in the Judaeo-Christian tradition God creates time and space and stands outside of them. Although cyclical elements are present within Christianity, these are seen to be patterns *within* time rather than part of the structure of time itself. As God created the world, so he sent his son to redeem our sins as a unique event that changed the condition of mankind, and therefore everything starts again with Jesus' birth.

The linear view of time is that as the world had a beginning, created by God, so it will have an end, on the Day of Judgement, when our sins will be judged. The world will then be destroyed. This view gained credibility from the scientific findings of the seventeenth century especially Newtonian physics, which asserted that the geometrical line provided the model for time, and was reinforced in the nineteenth century by the discovery of the Second Law of Thermodynamics, which states that in every physical process a certain amount of energy is irretrievably lost in the form of heat, something that will lead to the death of the universe. Time was therefore like an arrow directed in an irreversible direction. In addition, the theory of evolution also gave evidence for the progress of life on earth. The theory of evolution only makes sense if time is a continuous and irreversible process.

Christianity was partly shaped by a will to be taken out of time. It set up the idea that time is nothing but history: a passing from one point to another made of a past, a present and a future. Jesus Christ existed once in history as the saviour of mankind, a promise that will only be finally fulfilled with the destruction of the world and, along with it, time. For it was God who has created time as an aspect of his creation of the world. This differentiates the Christian God from those of most other traditions, in which the deities *are* time. Since the Christian God creates time in Christianity we have no possible escape from time until it is destroyed at the Day of Judgement: events happen once and for all and we are responsible for our actions. They are never repeatable. The straight line rather than the wheel symbolises this point of view. It is within this notion of time, abstracted from any cosmic ordering, that the frame of reference is established for our being in the world. Time is experienced as a solid reality that informs our way of life as something inexorable from which we can never escape, and with which we are forced to come to an accommodation, making the most of it; a one-dimensional entity that we 'kill' when we are not 'saving' it. Time is thereby transformed into a belief contained entirely by the frame of a single human life, whose segment of years pass in a way that has no other significance outside its own immediate necessity.

Yet, as noted, time was once a deity, rising and dying each day like the Egyptian sun god Ra, who changed form as he passed through the day, emerging as a scarab and setting as a crocodile. This implies a fundamentally cyclical notion of the foundation of time. Against a purely linear view of time, cyclical time implies a greater integration with natural forms, as Hannah Arendt explains:

> Cyclical, too is the movement of the living organism, the human body not excluded, as long as it can withstand the process that permeates its being and makes it alive. Life is a process that everywhere uses up durability, wears it down, makes it disappear, until eventually dead matter, the result of small, single, cyclical, life processes, returns into the gigantic cycle of life itself, where no beginning and no end exist and where all natural things swing in changeless, deathless repetition. (1958: 96)

This gives substance to the idea of recurrence: just as the sun rises and sets each day, so time constantly repeats itself in an endless rhythm. Or, like a river, time flows from a spring into the sea before being transformed again by the action of the clouds into spring water again. Life is thus seen to be a continuous cycle, possibly with no beginning or end. It is symbolised by the wheel, or by the snake devouring itself.

Recognition of this cyclical movement is important because it brings back into focus the idea of value and ties us with the rest of nature in a way that is denied by a strictly linear time-frame, which situates us *in* time rather than as *part* of it, with the implication that life is no more than a period of constant duration between the time of our birth and that of our death. In this schema, all endeavour becomes aimed at the alleviation of the difficulties of this time-span, to which everything else is sacrificed. Our way of conceptualising time therefore has significant implications for our mode of cultural being.

In making a distinction between linear and cyclical time, we are inevitably reifying what, within social context, is far more complex. Anthropologists and social historians have brought attention to the complex ways in which time is conceived in different societies depending on social structuring and particular cultural configurations. Ancient American civilisations like the Maya or the Zapotec are known to have had extremely complicated ways of measuring time founded in the fact that it was not an impersonal condition of the world, but rather a dynamic element in which human activity itself participated actively. Similarly, in many African societies, the dominant time is not what can be measured against the clock but what responds to the natural rhythms of the society. Even in a modernised society, sociologists too have located many different ways in which time exists in terms of our everyday activities and we frequently respond not to the duration marked by the clock but to periodic rhythms marked by the tides or the heartbeat, or to particular social requirements which may override the time marked on the clock (for instance the fact that, when invited to a party, we are generally expected to be slightly late, whereas when we go to a job interview we are expected to be early). Therefore, if clock time may dominate, it does not entirely exhaust the way we respond to processes of duration. Time, inseparable as it is from space, is also dependent upon what are perceived as social necessities within particular contexts. The forward movement of time, giving linearity its perceived inevitablility has only come to be present in modern industrialised society. In medieval times or the Renaissance, we were still close to eternity and time was simply a manifestation of the eternal in temporal form that could take various shapes.

In the present day, on the other hand, eternity is remote and hardly to be conceived. Time has become manifest and present in itself. Instead of relating ourselves to eternity, we mark our passage through life against the past, elevating a concern with history and archaeology to the status of an obsession. Time becomes an important resource that has to be documented accurately and kept alive. Cultures based upon a cyclical idea of time are concerned less with what actually happened in the past, and more with how it affects the present. They are concerned with appeasing the needs of their ancestors and integrating their world into the world of the living. The past is seen as a mythical realm. In contrast we are dominated by a form of history Walter Benjamin identified as 'a triumphal index by which it is referred to redemption' (1970: 256). This redemption lies in fidelity to a past we mythologise by claiming it to be accurate to what once happened and not to a 'mere' mythology that legitimates the present. Yet in such documentation, it remains the present that is at stake.

'How can we grant more importance to the hour which is than to the one which was or which will be?' asks Cioran (1975: 53) in a typically acerbic comment that brings attention to the way that, in contemporary culture, we are dominated by an internal vacancy in which time and space remain empty forms devoid of affectivity, leaving us only the future as offering the possibility of the resolution of our immediate problems, but a future that is no more than a realisation of the present. In having dispensed with the idea of eternity – or recurrence – as a presence within life, our only reality is founded in the here and now, which it is assumed will continue into the future marked by the idea of progress and scientific development.

'Nature', Katharine Hepburn tells Humphrey Bogart in *The African Queen* (1951), 'is what we are put in this world to rise above.' This Enlightenment conviction remains central and dominates ecological discussion, as much as we may wish to restore agency to nature through the idea of rights. Yet it is a conviction that is finally unsatisfying and, more importantly, leads to a dead end. We still dream of what exceeds us and remain haunted by what we have lost.

In establishing a sense of personal identity founded in overcoming our animal nature, we have at the same time widened our alienation from what we actually are. This means that having individualised itself, the self has ceased to be the measure of all things. It stands outside of everything that is not itself and so it becomes foreign to everything. It can understand nothing unless it establishes a distance from itself. It is this that impels us to see nature as a hostile force to be conquered, which means equally a conquest of that aspect of the self that is seen as still being linked with nature, in other words the internal world of desire and instinct. This means that it can understand nothing from within, but must externalise everything and analyse everything in a void.

Furthermore, this process assumes its own dynamic, following the path of technical innovation at the cost of human needs. We are unable to measure things in terms of their use-value, but only in terms of their exchange-value: everything has its price and can be bought. The idea of Enlightenment is tied in with gaining dominance over nature, but in the process it has provided a means by which our dominance of ourselves has been increased.

This is the real ecological issue that faces us: not to save the world of nature by protecting animals and vegetation from the damage caused to them by human activity, but to examine anew the way human existence can maintain an affective relation with the rest of life. Any apparent resolution that does not involve a reconfiguration of the human sensibility can only succeed in deferring this predicament. No doubt there can be no going back to a conception of the world as a living organism, at least not in the same terms as our forebears. Enlightenment has done its task too thoroughly for that to be possible. What is required is to be able to find a way of reconceiving the world in terms that displace human-centredness without denying it. We have no right to act on behalf of nature, since to do so is to impose a false category on it (one imbued with human perceptions of what nature should be). It is only by divesting ourselves of preconceptions about what nature is, by giving it room to act for itself, that ecological balance can be restored. This requires a rigorous acceptance both of our separation from and of our intimacy with nature. We need to be able to merge ourselves into the patterns and forces of nature in order to allow the things of the world to assume a spontaneous course. This requires deference to the way of the world and a recognition that nature is greater than us: we are indeed, as Friedrich Schlegel put it, no more than 'nature creatively looking back at itself'. In the process, we do not have to deny human nature or our need to act as humans in accordance with our own interests. Equally, it is a mistake to see nature either as a benevolent or malevolent force to be nurtured or subdued. Whatever else it is, nature responds to its own singularity.

In this respect, genetic manipulation of the environment and new scientific evidence about the structure of life are hardly going to be enough to restore fertility to a ravaged panorama. An objective consideration immediately reveals that to conquer natural forces is impossible. Nature will tolerate a certain amount of abuse, but if this goes too far it will destroy us. The real danger here lies in the fact that we have established a society in which humanity has become the measure of humanity: we are answerable to nothing but ourselves. In so doing we have deprived ourselves of any possibility for renewal because nothing exists beyond us (other than the burlesque idea that we shall discover more advanced civilisations in outer space). With no external point of reference against which to judge ourselves, we are doomed simply to continue to exemplify our own mistakes. In this respect, it is the exaltation of thought as the essence of what makes us human that provides the means by which we subdue our animal nature. Culture is therefore not simply a material manifestation of human activity but also involves a process of mental activity, something that will be examined in the next chapter.

7

THE PLACE OF REASON IN CULTURE

No reasoning person believes what is contrary to his reason.

Isidore Ducasse

Humans, as sensate beings, belong to the world they share with other living creatures. Encultured, we enter a world that is marked by reason and restraint. Descartes, of course, posited this as the essential feature of human existence: 'I think, therefore I am.' The Cartesian *cogito* has inserted itself as an Enlightenment catechism that retains its power to the present day, despite the inherent problems that surround it as an explanation of the essence of what we are. As such it has reinforced the emphasis on reason that unites the Christian and Greek philosophical traditions through the concept of *logos*.

No matter how we respond to the Cartesian *cogito*, it provides us with a starting point for a consideration of the rational within culture. Whether thought determines our existence or not, it is an undeniable fact that we do think and that consciousness affects our sensibility in significant ways. Yet what is thought? What mechanisms allow us to have ideas and to act upon them? Do different cultures have different ways of thinking about and conceptualising the world?

Rationality means 'the possession of reason', and there can be little doubt that this is a further factor distinguishing us from all other creatures: we are able to reflect upon the world and such reflection affects our actions. All humans are imbued with rationality; if they were not, the organisation of human society would be impossible, and we know that humans only exist as part of a society. There can similarly be little doubt that all human beings think and that they act in accordance with thought. However, when we look closely at the question we see that we really know very little about how this takes place and about the role that thought really has in human consciousness. What rationality actually means in practice remains a difficult concept to address.

The problem lies in the fact that the notion of the rational has been appropriated to the flow of Western ideas. From this point of view, it is perhaps essential to make an initial – if provisional – distinction between 'rationality' and 'rationalism'. The former is an inherent quality of human beings, while the latter is an ideological formulation, a concretisation of a particular form of rationality that has been especially connected with the development of Western society since the time of the Enlightenment. As an ideology it emphasises particular thought processes as being appropriate for the correct apprehension of the world. It is 'reason', as opposed to religion, faith or myth, that provides us with the proper way to proceed to making an accurate examination of the nature of life and the world. Yet to what extent is reason itself the measure of all thought?

What are the characteristics of what we call 'thought'? In essence it may be said to be – or aspire to be – logical. Rationality proceeds from an assumption that precise conclusions can be drawn from given inferences that can be agreed by anyone who looks at the data. This is as true for the stereotypical image of the sorcerer seeking to conjure up magical forces as it is for the nuclear physicist examining the properties of the atom. Logic, by this criterion, is not necessarily rational, at least not by the standards established by the propositions of Western science. Of course, thought may be illogical: it may draw faulty conclusions from given data. But thinking that leads to illogical conclusions may still be rational. Conversely, what may be called irrational thought can be logical: its conclusions may be shown to have been arrived at by a process of thought that, at least for the thinker, follows a logical sequence.[1]

Are logical thought patterns inherent or the result of learning? There can be little doubt that the former must be the case. If it were not, language, culture and the construction of society would be impossible, for they require some form of logical arrangement of possibilities if they are to be accepted by a human collective. Instinct and genetic inheritance may explain the society of bees or ants, they cannot explain that of humans. If the means for such logic was not an inherent characteristic of human beings, it is difficult to see how it could be instilled through teaching. Children are not born illogical and learn to see the world correctly; they are born with a potential for logic as they are born with a potential for language. What is learned is not logic but its refinement. A doubt nevertheless persists, because if we are inherently logical, how are illogical behaviour and thought to be explained?

Can human beings be illogical? The question seems inane. Can we not all easily identify examples of such behaviour and thought from our everyday experiences? Nazism or extreme forms of religious belief would seem to be obvious examples. And yet, if we examine the basis upon which such ideas are founded, it is clear they are centred in logically constructed argument. We may think that this logic is faulty, but it still proceeds from a demonstrable process of logical inference: it is not illogical, certainly not for the person who holds such beliefs. The most we can say is that that person is drawing faulty or perverse conclusions from the data s/he is presenting. Indeed, the Nazi 'Final Solution' was impeccable in its logic, if not in its morality, and the notion itself could never have been conceived other than by people convinced by the lineaments of logical argument: the very fact that they could perceive it as definitively solving a 'problem' reveals the fact. However crazy this may appear, it was still 'logic': satisfying the logical criteria of the person in question.[2] Fascism itself, 'reason revealing itself as unreason', as Max Horkheimer (1973: 46) appositely defined it, marks the limits within which reason as an ideology encloses itself.

In Western culture, we have been brought up to place logical thought within a context of rationality that is determined by Enlightenment ideas of mind and founded in a scientific and philosophical tradition that tends to use a methodology based on the rational principles of induction and deduction. These principles – respectively taking paths from particular to universal or universal to particular – posit the notion of empirical proof as a criterion for the judgement of the effectiveness of the logic. The requirement for such empirical proof gives a powerful tool for the dominance of particular ways of constructing a logical argument. It also creates considerable problems, placing limitations on what may be thought and channelling debate into particular directions. An assumption of reason in such terms – which necessarily requires the exclusion of other logical forms of explanation – brings into play, as Foucault among others has amply demonstrated, the categories of 'unreason' or the 'irrational'. Yet the latter are moral, not logical, categories: to describe someone as mad or irrational is to say not that they are lacking logic, but that they are placing themselves outside criteria culturally considered to be acceptable as reasonable.

'Enlightenment' is the cultural form taken by the ideology of the rational. It assumed a triumph of light over darkness, the notion of which emerged in the form of a conquest by the illumination of culture over the 'darkness' of nature (the idea of Hell in fact assumes its fearsome characteristics as the Enlightenment is beginning to dawn). It involved a deliverance of humanity from the throes of superstition. At different times and in different ways, such superstition, such darkness, was projected outwards: it could encompass the medieval period of Western history, women, the Orient, the primitive or, in more general terms, the notion of the Other; or indeed it could be extended to cover any concept that could be shown to reveal the existence of a different, more primitive, more elemental, sensibility that existed and could threaten but also could be used to legitimate the form of rationality the Enlightenment embodied.

This involves a curious paradox. At the heart of a rational view is the assertion that nature is rational and that the human mind of itself has the power to penetrate its secrets. Functioning like a machine, the natural world obeys laws that can be observed, and, by means of such observation, we are able to act on that world. At the same time, however, nature is viewed as being irrational, as what we must rise above.

Bounded by the Cartesian *cogito*, Enlightenment elevates thought at the expense of sensual and inherent (or intuitive) understanding: what is valued is what can be proved and tested, what can be externalised as an object of knowledge. Based on three key precepts – that reasoning alone provides the means to obtain knowledge about existence; that knowledge constitutes a single system that is deductive in character; and that everything is explainable, contained by a universal standard of truth – Enlightenment is a feature of a particular cultural formation that emerged within a Europe of the seventeenth and eighteenth centuries that was faced with particular social problems.

Deductive logic, as we know, is confined to assumptions the mind makes about the nature of reality and is unable to engage with anything that is not already implicit in its initial proposition. In addition, the exclusion of sensual experience from the process of thought presented deductive reasoning with an intractable problem. From an empirical point of view, as Francis Bacon stated, deductivists were like 'spiders spinning webs from out of their own bodies'. Empiricism was shaped as a reaction to the problems inherent within deduction basing its examination not on the primary processes of thought but on experience of the material world. Here it is the senses rather than the mind that provide the fundamental criteria for examination. But induction as a method faces a problem as intractable as deduction: if deductivists spin webs based on their initial hypotheses, inductionists are faced with the difficulty of how to evaluate – and determine the significance of – the mass of data that is provided to our sense impressions. In order to establish a methodology, empiricists, as limited to the senses as deductivists are to the mind, also need to confine their investigations to a particular framework if they are to be of value. To extend the metaphor, the danger they face is that they may be seen less as spiders spinning webs into infinity than as ants busily building to no purpose.[3]

The foundation of Western science required the exactitude made possible by the deductive and inductive methods. They were, however, particular methods for ordering data to produce worthwhile results within a particular framework; they did not, as claimed by Enlightenment ideology, provide a superior logic or a means to discovering incontrovertible truths. Rather, as has been shown by Thomas Kuhn (1970) and Paul Feyerabend (1975 and 1987), they established particular paradigms that opened up certain possibilities for knowledge but closed down others.

Deductive and inductive methods were directed against a mode of logic that dominated medieval thought and is the foundation for the ideas found in many other cultures. This may be called the 'theory of correspondences' or logic by analogy. Analogical thinking is not characterised by a movement from universal to particular or vice versa, as in deduction and induction, but proceeds by means of making comparisons between particular and particular. This form of logic is not necessarily rational. Notoriously, according to Lévy-Bruhl, it is even 'pre-logical'. Yet it can easily be demonstrated that analogical argument is not at all illogical. The difficulty for science is that analogy provides no empirically testable means to judge the value of its findings. As such, the rational tradition has seen it as a faulty form of reasoning that has no place in scientific argument: it is the preserve of the poet, the madman and the primitive. The sciences of alchemy and astrology – supposedly 'primitive' forms of chemistry and astronomy – are both based upon analogical principles and are thus suspect to the scientific mind. Yet this does not prevent the latter thinking analogically: we might point out that Francis Bacon, in the quotation above, revealed the problems of deductive logic not by means of subjecting it to an empirical examination, but precisely by use of analogy.

Apart from its methodological problems, the rational attitude – whether deductive or inductive – has more substantial ontological difficulties.

Founded in the principle of identity and the supposed 'law' of non-contradiction, it makes a fundamental assumption that everything is identical to itself: that a thing can only be what it is and not something else. Thus if two ideas contradict one another, one must be false.

This seems at first a self-evident argument. I am me and cannot be you; your experience of the world is incommensurate with mine. I can never know what you are thinking or experiencing and vice versa: the formula $P = P$ is constant. However, things are not so simple because, as any cultural analysis will soon reveal, the non-P always intrudes on the P. I cannot determine what exactly I am. It is impossible to say where my body begins and ends. If I lose a limb, am I losing something of myself, or merely an appendage that was only coincidentally part of me? What is the I that constitutes my irreducible identity? Quite clearly, we are not independent beings existing separately from everything else. We must eat to survive. When I consume an apple, part of that apple is transformed into me: it is no longer an apple but part of me. Similarly, as we have seen, social interaction determines our very being. While it may be true that I can never know your experience of the world, our different experiences of the world determine what we respectively are. When we speak together we transform our respective sensibilities. We are not what we were before we spoke together. Our communication means that we take a little of the other into ourselves. In reading this text, your sensibility will be changed, no matter how slightly, even if you find it uninteresting or if you disagree with it. The very fact of having read it will have some effect upon you: you are not the person you were before you read it. We can never unlearn any experience, each and every one of which has some impact on our sense of self-identity. How, then, can such identity be identical with itself?

Neither induction nor deduction can engage with this sort of dynamic. Both types of reasoning assume that the identity of things is stable. They are practical types of logic directed towards some pre-established aim. As such they are present in all humans: the invention and use of tools alone prove it. Yet the dominant Western philosophical tradition has tended to be based on the assumption that these two forms of reasoning are the only legitimate ones, that they assume an ontological status that supersedes other forms of logic.

It was indeed this ontological principle that Lévy-Bruhl saw being contravened in what was then called 'primitive thought', which he identified as being based on what he called the principle of participation. In defining this as a 'pre-logical' form of reasoning, Lévy-Bruhl was in essence saying that it was not bounded by deductive and inductive norms. By the end of his life he had come to realise that this form of thinking could not be parcelled up so easily. Supposed 'primitive' thought, indeed, was nothing but analogical thought applied in contexts that were alien to those of modern Western society. As much was made apparent when the anthropologist E.E. Evans-Pritchard, much influenced by Lévy-Bruhl, published *Witchcraft, Oracles and Magic Among the Azande* in 1937, which was to initiate a significant debate about the nature of rationality when the philosopher Peter Winch wrote a critique of it in 1963 (in Wilson, 1970. See also Borofsky et al., 1997; Finnegan and Horton, 1973; Hollis and Lukes, 1982; Obeyesekere, 1997; Overing, 1985; Sahlins, 1995).

Examining witchcraft beliefs among the Azande, a people in the Sudan, Evans-Pritchard clearly showed how the basis of their thought, although it did not conform to Western ideas of rationality, made sense in the context of Zande society and was logically constituted. Nevertheless, while logically and intellectually consistent, it was still irrational because, as Evans-Pritchard believed, it was based upon faulty propositions.

Evans-Pritchard's study, as anthropologically cogent as it is, could never-theless not escape the rationalist assumptions in which its author was brought up. This was seized upon by Peter Winch, who argued that the issue of truth or falsity of Zande belief was irrelevant since it could not be judged accord-ing to criteria established by Western methodology. The Azande were interested not in establishing a theoretical system to gain scientific under-standing of the world, but in solving problems in a way that was effective in their own context. It was therefore unfair to judge them by any other stan-dard, and to say that their beliefs were effective but irrational made no sense: within their own terms they were acting rationally. All human actions, he argued, could be judged only by the standards applied by the actors them-selves; they were relative to the situation of the actor.

The positions put forward by Evans-Pritchard and Winch remain essen-tially the two poles around which debates about rationality continue to revolve. Is there a standard of rationality that can be applied cross-culturally and that provides a starting point for consideration of the different concep-tual categories used in different cultures? Or is such a standard a chimera, a fundamentally ethnocentric imposition of the observer's categories of thought onto those of the other culture? Both positions contain fundamen-tal difficulties. The first makes certain universal assumptions that may be unwarranted. The second leads to an extreme relativism in which all meaning dissolves and understanding across different cultures becomes impossible: if there is no universal standard of judgement, then all behaviour can be morally justified. These problems are unresolvable within their own terms because both are based upon acceptance of a particular concept of rational-ity that has its root in Enlightenment thinking.

The project of Enlightenment does not come all of a piece. It is not some-thing established once and for all in the eighteenth century, but is as much a creation of the nineteenth century, which had different concerns, some of which are at odds with, or give a quite different orientation to, the way Enlightenment has unfolded historically. In particular, Enlightenment think-ing itself had little of the optimistic and positive faith in progress and the triumph of rationality that we now associate with it. It was directed against the world in which Enlightenment thinkers lived. They regarded reason as a corrective to the ills of that world, not a universal palliative leading to the possibility of limitless progress. Indeed, for many of the Enlightenment thinkers, the ideas of other cultures might be superior to those of the West, as we can see from Montesquieu's *Persian Letters* or the ideas about the 'noble' savage. To some extent, indeed, reason in the Enlightenment was seen as the means to restore a primitive sense of human decency that had been destroyed by the process of civilisation. Reason as a constituent of Western thought to the exclusion of that of other, supposedly more backward, cultures is not a strictly Enlightenment notion but part of its positivist overlay.

Indeed, the period from the Renaissance to the French Revolution, considered as a whole, was far from being a refuge of light, and indeed may be said to have been far darker than the preceding medieval period. In that time the devastating effects of European colonialism on other peoples, especially the destruction of native American culture, had become apparent and religious and racial persecution in Europe took place on a scale never before witnessed. Throughout Europe persecution was directed against anyone perceived as an outsider, especially women (who were denied all legal rights and often condemned as witches), Slavic peoples and Jews. In Spain the Moorish kingdom of Arabs and Jews was suppressed and both races were expelled, as the Inquisition, in the guise of fighting heresy, spread religious terror throughout Spain and Italy. The slave trade was also established, degrading Africans for the sole purpose of increasing European wealth. These terrible events were unprecedented in human history in their brutality and especially in the cultural intolerance they bear witness to, and this cannot be detached from the flow of Enlightenment ideas.

We tend to think of the terror of the French Revolution as a culmination and negation of Enlightenment progress through reason, and it certainly cast doubt on the ideas of the inherent goodness of humans, but it should be remembered that the period prior to 1789 was itself a dark one in which many of the most terrible crimes of humanity against itself were committed, and in this context the darkness within people could hardly have been ignored.

These ambiguities are well conveyed by Goya's lithograph with its resonant title *The Sleep of Reason Produces Monsters* (1797–9). In this, Reason, in the shape of a sleeping figure, is assailed by animal figures whose features indefinitely emerge from the surrounding darkness to invade the world that reason inhabits. Are these figures a threat to reason, or its complement? Is Reason in danger because of having fallen asleep, or because it has tired itself out trying to deny the reality of sleep? The legend reads: 'Fantasy abandoned by reason produces impossible monsters; united with reason, fantasy is the mother of the arts and the source of their wonders', a clear warning to reason not to abandon its need for the dark heart that would, with romanticism, become a central theme of Western art during the early part of the nineteenth century.

Peter Gay sets up the fundamental frame of Enlightenment ideology: the world, he says, 'was being emptied of mystery. Pseudo science was giving way to science, credence in the miraculous intervention of divine forces was being corroded by the acid of scepticism and overpowered by scientific cosmology' (1969: 27). From one perspective, this was certainly true. But other considerations need to be taken into account to understand the way in which science established itself by means of reason. If the influence of magical thinking declined during the seventeenth and eighteenth centuries, this is not adequately explained by Enlightenment and by the findings of science disproving the epistemological premises of magic and revealing it to be ineffective.

The point to be made about rationality here is that it is not possible to impute irrational beliefs to magical operations. To do so requires a distortion of the aims of such operations. It assumes that the aim is to produce a given effect in the same way as in a scientific operation. Yet anthropological evidence makes it plain that this is inaccurate. In performing a rain dance, people do not believe that their actions will cause rain to come. They perform such dances for a complex of reasons that are principally about maintaining the cohesion of the society: at times of crisis, such as drought, it is obviously necessary not to allow people to become demoralised. As Lévi-Strauss has demonstrated, the use of magic is only irrational if we judge it according to the terms of the explanatory framework of modern science. The practitioners of magic may be just as sceptical about the causative effectiveness of their methods as are modern scientists; they persist in them not due to some irrational faith or blind belief, but because they are effective in practice. This effectiveness relies upon a whole range of socio-psychological factors that are not reducible to proof by scientific methodology (see Lévi-Strauss, 1963a). What Lévi-Strauss calls '*la pensée sauvage*' does not bring rationality into question, but widens its frame of reference.

In this respect, we might note that Western science did not set itself up against magic. Many of the great innovative scientists of the Renaissance (even up to and including Newton) continued to believe in the efficacy of alchemy and astrology and other magical practices. Indeed such ideas were often instrumental in achieving the great breakthroughs of science. It wasn't that scientists proved magical views false or even that they perceived science to be in an inevitable conflict with their ideas. There is every reason to believe that magic declined not because it was seen to be false, but because wider changes in society were making its aims obsolete. People's mentality was changing, causing them to place a value in different things. If Copernicus and Galileo were instrumental, through their findings, in promoting this, it was because they instituted a different way of thinking about the world. It is almost certainly an error to impute the fact that people in medieval times falsely believed that the world was flat and that the sun went around it: not so much because they *did not* believe this, as because it was not important to their view of the world.

What science did require, in order to develop its modern form, was a reliable methodology containing a means of verifiability that could establish its firm foundations. Analogical thinking, in this respect, is insufficient, since it cannot provide the exactitude required to allow scientific development. We can see this with alchemy. Alchemy may be regarded as a pseudo science to the extent that it is seen as a process of turning base metals into gold: it uses both inductive and deductive methods to achieve this end but without drawing proper rational inferences due to its reliance upon the theory of correspondences as its fundamental framework. However, alchemy was a process not for making gold, but for achieving the Great Work, of which the transmutation of base metal into gold was but the symbol. Alchemists were not interested in scientific understanding of the world and their quest was not to prove that gold could be made from base metals. As a form of knowledge, alchemy was concerned with the interaction between human existence and the cosmos in order to effect transmutation (symbolised by the forming of gold from metal). Alchemy was not a pseudo-science but an activity that has few parallels in the mainstream of present-day society, being based in a quite different view of the structure of the world that is reliant upon and can only be understood in terms of analogical principles.[4]

To state that analogy is not sufficient to the condition of the culture we currently inhabit – which requires as its foundation a solid, rationally conceivable world – is not to imply that it is lacking in either logic or rationality. As we have seen, what it defies is the principle of identity based upon an assumption of non-contradiction. In the theory of correspondences, there is no need to account for the co-existence of contradictory ideas because this is seen as the condition of life. It is therefore vain to look for ultimate causes because these must, of necessity, remain outside the grasp of human endeavour. The aim of the quest for the Great Work of the alchemists was not to explain anything but to give access to a realm in which the contradictions of the world are resolved. Like the people of many cultures, medieval alchemists took the framework of the world itself to be opaque and beyond human understanding. It has been the genius of modern Western science to refuse this opaqueness, and in doing so it has opened up new areas of exploration that have had an enormous impact on modern life, although it has to be doubted whether modern science has actually done anything to dispel the essential opacity of the world, and the belief that it has is perhaps the greatest danger that currently faces us. However one views this, the achievements of Enlightenment have clearly not been the result of people becoming more rational than in earlier or other cultures.

To identify the limitations of medieval or other analogical systems of thought as a weakness is to reveal a prejudice in our own ways of thinking and a failure on our part to appreciate the inadequacy of our own conception of the world. It is also to fail to recognise the extent to which a particular notion of rationality is a product of our world view (which is based upon what we prioritise within the cultural framework we inhabit). It is a fundamental error to see this as co-extensive with the nature of the world. For, as noted above, all deductivist and inductivist thinking is unable to account for the existence of contradiction and the dynamic by which contrary ideas complement one another. It proceeds on the assumption that all things are identical to themselves, something that is quite patently not so. That scientists today can speculate so wonderfully and yet so uselessly, no matter how 'rationally', about such phenomena as quasars and black holes, which defy the power of the human mind to conceive in any terms than those of a burlesque abstraction, might be seen as a revenge of the gods, filled with black humour, on those who presume to seek the ultimate meaning of things.

Contradiction is not, however, seen by all philosophers as inimical to logic. For Hegel, of course, it was the motor, the very dynamic, by which thought developed. Far from being a spoke in the wheel of reason, it was the way in which the rational manifested itself.

The interactive process that dialectics involves may be said to be a further way of thinking about the nature of logic. The mediation between opposites, seeking meaning in the gaps that exist between contradictory propositions, gives us a way of going beyond notions of rationality that are trapped within the Aristotelian law of identity. Dialectic is the logic of what is not directly analysable. It contains or gives us a means to access what Hegel called the 'cunning of reason': the way that reason manifests itself over and above the actions and conscious intentions of the actors as it sublates opposing ideas into new configurations.

Like analogy, dialectical thinking assumes a pattern to the world that is not directly knowable. It can therefore explain nothing and so has a limited application if we are seeking scientific explanations. (Misguided attempts to develop a 'scientific socialism' based upon a principle of dialectics have merely underlined this and have tended to disqualify dialectical thought itself, as positivists have not been slow to argue.) However, again like analogical thought, dialectic clearly follows its own logical pattern and adheres to an inherent rationality. All forms of thought are imperfect and are contained within their own metaphysical limits. Analogy lacks the precision of deduction or induction; dialectical thought can easily be distorted into sophism. However, both provide a flexibility of thinking that can enable the resolution of certain problems that deductive and inductive analysis are unable to access. In order to deal with the range of situations that our experience of culture involves, we need to recognise the appropriateness of different types of thinking in different contexts. The world is not ordered rationally as a system that is reducible to deductive and inductive reasoning. It is a property of the structure of the world to evade the category of proof that a narrowly rationalist methodology demands.

The essential point this raises is that it is extremely difficult to analyse any process of thought, and that if we are seeking to understand the functioning of thought within any cultural situation, we must inquire into the modes by which it is realised and conceptualised. Applying our own categories of what is reasonable is fundamentally flawed.

If the principle of identity is central to a Western concept of reason, it has further consequences in terms of how we conceive the world and our relation with thought. In particular, it involves a separation of mind and body that is so ingrained as part of our cultural formation and that is needed in order to maintain clearly defined boundaries between the world of thought and culture and our being as creatures of nature. From this proposition all of our ideas about the structure of the world take shape: cause and effect, free will and determinism, whether the world is structured by material presence or by the perception our minds have of it – all are measured by the assumption of a separation between body and soul or mind. (This may be said to respond consistently to the Christian tradition that equates body with the fall, the soul being what was left as a remnant of our divine nature.)

For within the Western tradition, we view life from the standpoint of the body, and we make a separation between what we are and what our body is. The body is something we inhabit, that we look out from and that restricts us, but is not entirely 'us'. We speak of 'myself and my body', something that is semantically not possible in many languages. The body may be beautiful, it may be exalted in art work, but more commonly it is forbidden. This interplay between our self and our body (which may be conceptualised as thought/soul/mind against matter) defines one of the most significant ways in which Western thought differs from that of other cultures. And this has considerable implications for the way in which cultural frameworks are conceptualised.

How is the world structured and provided with a dynamic? How is solidity maintained in such a way as to make activity within it possible? To consider the issues that such questions raise, we need to focus on the determinisms of dualism.

Dualist thought seems to be central to human thought and the construction of culture. We know that this is a feature distinguishing us biologically as a species: the human brain is divided into two halves having different functions, and there is an imbalance between right and left sides; other animals display no such lateralisation. This imbalance seems to be at the root of the capacity for language and tool-making; it also no doubt explains the propensity for people thinking in terms of duality.

Most creation myths speak of the world as being created due to two gods whose actions separate heaven and earth to make life possible. For instance, to take at random two geographically separate examples: in ancient Egypt, the universe was created when Geb, the god of the earth, and Nut, the goddess of the sky, were separated in order to leave a space between them in which their children could exist. In Japan, the brother and sister deities Izanami and Izanagi were responsible for completing the separation of land and sea. Creation is generally perceived by cultures around the world to be the result of some form of separation or differentiation of elements that results in these elements taking shape as opposing, or complementary, forces, and this process of dualistic separation is repeated in our thought processes.

Dualism seems to be a peculiar human characteristic for thinking about *abstract* concepts. Where we think of concrete elements – a tree, a chair, a table – we can do so in such a way that they have meaning for us in themselves. But once we think about abstract things, they immediately call up their opposite: life/death; male/female; light/dark; self/other; time/infinity; space/matter; right/left; sickness/health; hot/cold. Without their opposite, all of these concepts cease to exist for us, or rather it becomes impossible for us to think about them. What is life without death or male without female? We are here faced with the void that recalls Lichtenberg's renowned bladeless knife without a handle. Abstract thinking seems to require that we mark concepts we are unable to fix in a concrete way in terms of shades of presence and absence that become characterised as opposing principles.

But if dualistic classification is fundamental to human thought processes, there are very different ways of thinking about dualism itself. For most cultures, it is a process of integration, aiming to harmonise opposing concepts: dual concepts simply represent a structural separation within a single substance. A different attitude is apparent among the monotheistic religions that emerged in the Middle East, in which dualism is represented as a clash between incompatible elements. In the Zoroastrian religion, the earliest monotheistic religion, evil is the active principle of matter, created from the conflict between the Wise Lord (Ahura Mazda), who exists eternally in light, and the Destructive Spirit (Ahriman), whose realm is darkness. Creation and the universe will continue until the evil is defeated; humans have a choice of whether to join battle on the side of either good or evil. Life itself is thus a scene of conflict between good and evil.

Making a fundamental distinction between good and evil, Zoroastrianism nevertheless did not inscribe fault within human beings: evil is a fact of creation and humans can do no worse than to help perpetuate it by being complicit with it. As the Judaeo-Christian tradition took shape, however, the fault was displaced from being the result of an elemental battle to become the consequence of human fault: by disobeying God's command we were expelled from the Garden of Eden and forced to live in a world of life and death. We are thus founded in Original Sin, from which we can only be released through belief in the One God. The Christian tradition thus dispenses with the elemental dual nature of creation, which becomes the sole property of a single, male, God. We must worship this one principle, and this was central to Christianity in its fight against pagan idolatry.

When Descartes asserted that 'I think, therefore I am', he was unconsciously drawing on the tradition of Western dualism by giving thought a privileged position in relation to matter. The mind was thus an entity entirely separate from the body, an entity that was incorporeal, indivisible and non-spatial. By doing so he was making of the mind an abstract concept that immediately called up its double: the body. If I only exist because I think, what does this make of matter? Since it is clear that mind must act upon matter, how does this actually happen? The problem is an extension of the Christian idea of the evil quality of matter. God has been replaced by the Mind, but the sensibility accords with the principle established by Christianity. In this sense the Christian tradition made the elemental duality of existence into a moral principle that provides the foundation for the whole Western tradition and in many ways provided the key to Enlightenment ideas.

This final point is important in considering different attitudes to causation. In certain respects, in Western society causation and chance are seen as the determining factors in social explanation. An event is determined either by one or by the other. In general this is another dualism. We look for a cause for a certain phenomenon. For other phenomena we accept the determining role of chance. In medicine, causation is assumed to be the only criterion of sickness. On the other hand, chance is largely the condition of health. So we say that cigarette smoking *causes* cancer. And yet if a smoker lives into his or her nineties and remains in good health, we assume it is chance or fate that that person has survived thus far (s/he has been lucky). Or at least we say that if this person develops cancer while this person doesn't, this is largely a matter of luck or fate. (This may be explained away as a matter of genetics, but it comes to the same thing.) It seems to be largely characteristic of the Western sensibility not to question the idea of chance, which is equated with our condition in the world. In a godless universe, our position here is essentially one that responds to chance. On the other hand, what happens in this life occurs for specific reasons. In a famous anthropological example, it was pointed out that in the West if someone is injured when the roof of a house collapses, it is assumed that the roof collapsed for a reason, but that it was pure chance that it fell on that particular person (see Evans-Pritchard, 1937). In other societies, the concern is much more to do with why that particular person was unfortunate enough to be under the roof when it collapsed. The latter concern is at the root of divinatory practices, which are performed with a view to harmonising oneself and one's society in relation to the world. Divinatory practices in general do not accept a rigid distinction between chance and causality.

In a fascinating study, considering head-hunting practices, especially those of the Kenyah of Borneo, Rodney Needham (1983) argues that causation is a sort of Western myth. Anthropological explanation of head-hunting generally explains such practices in terms of cause and effect: they believe that head-hunting brings prosperity and power. Why they believe this, however, is not clear: there appears to be no causal agent to account for it. This makes it difficult to fit Kenyah beliefs into the framework of a Western discourse focused upon causal relations.

If we return here to consider further issues of duality, we can say that as much as other cultures may perceive duality as central to many aspects of their conception of the world, it is unusual to encounter a dualism between mind and body reliant upon a causal relation between them. The ancient Egyptian conception of the person, for instance, which still has pertinence for understanding African rationality, included no theory of the mind, and regarded the body (the *Khat*) as merely one link in a chain of existence. The person was divided into eight parts, three of which were immortal, and five mortal.[5] What is significant about this model is that human actions were judged within the framework of infinity, not within the limited framework of an individual life. For the Egyptians, what mattered was the extent to which one's conduct ultimately contributed to the immortal *Ka*. This provides a fundamentally different approach towards considerations of what can be considered rational than that which is determined by a Judaeo-Christian tradition of duality as emanating from a single god (whether this be the transcendent god of theology or the philosophers' one of the mind). Interestingly, the ancient Egyptian model of the person seems far closer to some of the findings of modern science that reveal the human body as a force-field concentration, a particular configuration of energy, than are traditional Western notions of mind/body separation.

The denial of the shadow aspect of human rationality – a denial of all that cannot be reduced to the measure of human consciousness and the causal properties by which it is able to explain the world – is not so much a feature of the age of Enlightenment but becomes an essential ingredient of nineteenth-century positivism, which gave to Western rationality its intransigent quality, transforming rationality into an ideology to serve the interests of emergent capitalist society. Insofar as it is encapsulated in shibboleths that remain with us today, such as the idea that society is the outcome of a struggle in which only the 'fittest' survive, or that life is determined by a 'selfish gene' that is concerned only with its own reproduction, Western rationality is not simply a methodology but becomes a metaphysical construction with wide-ranging ideological implications.

Debates today about such issues tend to be polarised around the extremes of universalist assumptions against those of cultural relativism. Yet a universal mentality is not incompatible with different social formulations of it. Thought does not become relativistic simply because it is used differently in different contexts. Relativism is, rather, an ideological formation shaped in reaction to the universalistic claims of a narrow rationalism. Relativism is only legitimate when cultures remain isolated from one another, and then it is irrelevant or even inconceivable. Any contact between cultures (this is as much so between individuals), even the slightest, calls for processes of negotiation that can be difficult to accomplish. It involves adaptation and will often lead to conflict. Relativism is limited by the fact that it shares the same frame of reference as Enlightenment rationalism, and this is a frame of reference that is difficult to exceed. As Max Horkheimer asserts, in today's world even dictators lay claim to reason: if they had the good sense to build so many tanks, other people should be reasonable enough to submit to them (1973: 28).

What should be clear from our discussion is that all forms of logic rely on metaphysical assumptions. Indeed, thought about the world becomes impossible without such assumptions because, as Nietzsche pointed out, our experience of the cosmos is limited by the fact of our human existence: we have to make assumptions about the nature of reality based upon that experience. We cannot judge the cosmos – or anything else for that matter – in its own terms. We can only evaluate it from our own – humanly constituted – point of view.

From this point of view, we can see that different forms of logic are not mutually exclusive: each is necessary to cultural understanding, and we are all constantly using them in different ways in order to solve particular problems in particular situations. Inductive and deductive logic were not suddenly discovered by Renaissance scientists, nor did their findings make analogical thought obsolete or invalid. A shaman who, in the most long-lost 'primitive society' we can imagine, wanted to cook a meal would never have relied upon a series of magic formulae based on analogical principles but would have used his experience as tested inductively and deductively by the society. If deduction and induction have proved more effective at solving certain sorts of problems, it is dangerous to believe they have exclusive access to the truth. Nor should we be blind to the assumptions and limitations that are inherent in using deductive and inductive methodologies. If induction and deduction alone tend to be given scientific status in the Western tradition, we need to inquire into the consequences that have followed from such an ideological imposition.

Reason may be a whole, but it is not the result of any clearly defined process of deduction and induction. Rather, it is an amalgam of different types of logic differently configured in different cultural situations. As such, what we understand as reason within a particular context is inseparable from the ideological, ethical and practical considerations we are applying. To say there is a clearly defined rationality that can be set against 'irrationality', to describe any human thought as being – in and of itself and without taking context into account – illogical, seems to be fundamentally mistaken.

This is to say not that the irrational is not a factor in culture, but that any idea of the irrational can be understood only by the prevailing standards of rationality. Irrationality can never be self-determining, it even lies at the core of what is rational: the world of culture we inhabit is made possible only by a rational ordering of the elemental formlessness that surrounds us. Schelling put this rather nicely:

> Following the eternal act of self-revelation, the world as we now behold it, is all rule, order and form; but the unruly lies ever in the depths as though it might again break through, and order and form nowhere appear to have been original, but it seems as though what had initially been unruly had been brought to order. This is the incomprehensible basis of reality in things, the irreducible remainder which cannot be resolved into reason by the greatest exertion but remains in the depths. Out of this which is unreasonable, reason in the true sense is born. Without the preceding gloom, creation would have no reality; darkness is its necessary heritage. (1989: 34)

Here we see how all claims to rationality are provisional, being formed from out of the shadows that surround us and which we shall never penetrate fully.

In many ways, debates about rationality are vain, because they turn upon too many imponderables: we understand little about the nature of thought, for the chain of relations by which any thought is established is part of a process that is too complex to be disassembled. What is important to take from such debates, however, is that the construction of any cultural formation must, of necessity, be engaged in a rational process that, as Schelling states, draws form from out of elemental formlessness (and would not take shape as a cultural formation unless it followed an internally logical pattern that could have caused it to be accepted by any group of people). That the criteria applied as the foundation to such patterning may defy rational understanding is another matter, but it is impossible to analyse this because such criteria inevitably depend upon metaphysical possibility of one sort or another.

Reason cannot be sundered from its social practice, which takes different customary forms. Max Horkheimer locates this as a difficulty of rationalistic philosophy that originates

> from the fact that the universality of reason cannot be anything else than the accord among the interests of all individuals alike, whereas in reality society has been split up into groups with conflicting interests. Owing to this contradiction, the appeal to the universality of reason assumes the feature of the spurious and the illusory. (1973: 30)

All thinking is rational within its particular frame of reference; what needs to be questioned is not the rationality of belief but the structure within which it is functioning. In this sense, Hegel was right to insist that the rational is what is real. Far from reading this as implying that whatever is perceptible is rational, or that what is rational is necessarily desirable, we need to think about what exactly the framework is within which both the rational and the real are being formulated. This leads us to consider what we understand by reality, and how this conception may be transformed in various ways, especially by means of greater knowledge of the world and the possibilities for freedom this sets up.

Notes

1. The mind/body problem in Western philosophy provides a good example of the former. Almost all of the theories advanced, such as the Cartesian 'ghost in the machine', are rational but illogical, although only in the sense that the result of rational thinking leads to conclusions that are inconsistent with experience; they thus provide hypotheses, which will be further debated, but which only reveal further the intractability of the problem. The mind/body debate in Western philosophy can never be resolved because its founding principle is faulty. Much of the advances in Western science, especially in medicine, are therefore based upon an assumption of a mind/body separation that is almost certainly erroneous. This does not disqualify those advances; indeed it exemplifies Nietzsche's observation about the productivity of error. It should, however, alert us to the need for circumspection about the claims that are routinely made for progress as revealing the superiority of Western rationality. It should also be pointed out that the processes of thought involved in considering the mind/body problem are not at all illogical. If illogical conclusions are drawn from such debates, these emerge from the impossibility of resolving the problems raised. At most this reveals a failure of nerve rather than any lack of logic in the human mind.

2. It is true that we commonly encounter illogical arguments: the editorials of certain daily newspapers provide good examples, as do, as a matter of course, the pronouncements of most politicians. However, these are the result not of a lack of logic, but of being conscious that one is supported by an authority that renders statements beyond the framework of the rational. They are not really illogical because those making such statements do not believe them but rely on the power of rhetoric to carry them along. In this respect religious belief is not logical because it recognises faith as a higher truth than logic. A failure to use logic is generally wilful, for one reason or another; it is not the result of an inability to use the faculty of reason.

3. Nietzsche extended the spider analogy in a critique of empirical positivism:

    The habits of our senses have woven us into lies and deception of sensation: these
    again are the basis of all our judgements and 'knowledge' – there is absolutely no
    escape, no backway or bypath into the 'real world'! We sit within our net, we spiders,
    and whatever we catch in it, we can catch nothing at all except that which allows itself
    to be caught in precisely *our* net. (1982: 73)

4. Nor was it a primitive form of psychology, as Jungian psychoanalysis would have
    it, although it can be said to have combined elements as much from what we now
    consider to be psychology with what is now classed as science. However, it is cer-
    tainly not reducible to this.

5. The immortal aspects being the *Ka* (abstract individuality), the *Ba* (dwelling within
    Ka and having the power to take corporeal or incorporeal form) and the *Khu* (the
    spiritual intelligence, taking the form of 'shining', or 'luminosity'); the mortal
    aspects being the *Sekhem* (the vital force), the *Ren* (the name), the *Khaibat* (the
    shadow), the *Khat* (the physical body) and the *Ab* (the heart).

8

TRANSFORMATORY PROCESSES OF CULTURE:

Knowledge and Freedom

> Therefore, I replied, somewhat at loose ends, we would have to eat again of the tree of knowledge to fall back again into a state of innocence?
> Most certainly, he replied: That is the last chapter of the history of the world.
>
> Heinrich von Kleist

'The history of the world,' Hegel famously wrote in *The Philosophy of History*, 'is none other than the progress of the consciousness of freedom' (1956: 19). Certainly today we live with cultural values that promote freedom as an unqualified aspiration, if not always as a realisation. Few people would even make an attempt to argue against freedom as being inherently to be desired. Even those who in practice act against what we might consider to be the spirit of freedom do so generally in its name. As Marx said, 'Freedom is so much the essence of human beings that even its opponents realise it. . . . No one fights freedom; at most they fight the freedom of others. Every kind of freedom has therefore always existed only at one time as a special privilege, at another as a universal right'

Yet Orlando Patterson, in his magisterial study of its history, reveals a dark side to freedom, showing how its current renown is built on a murky past: its history is inseparable from slavery and repression. Recognising its centrality to Western thought, he argues that it is not the unqualified blessing its advocates assume. Rather, its heritage has a double face, it is both 'the tragic, generative core of Western culture, the germ of its genius and all its grandeur, and the source of its perfidy and its crimes against humanity' (Patterson, 1991: 402). At its worst, he claims, 'no value has been more evil and socially corrosive in its consequences, inducing selfishness, alienation, the celebration of greed, and the dehumanising disregard for the "losers" . . .' (1991: 403). Far from being the essence of human beings, it seems to be a value that has little credence or even significance in many cultures.

Even if we accept this argument, it does not necessarily prove Marx wrong: it may be that freedom is so much the essence of human beings that it becomes an issue in society only when it is threatened or lost. Freedom is taken for granted to such an extent that people think about it or erect it as a value only when their freedom is endangered. People will not accept a state of unfreedom as the condition of existence. Freedom as a value, therefore, can only emerge in societies in which the possibility that it may be taken away becomes a reality. However, what freedom actually means is by no means simple to ascertain.

Hegel, it may be noted, did not posit freedom itself but the *consciousness* of freedom as forming the history of the world. This is significant because it is such awareness that provides history with its main dynamic. It is the demand for freedom that leads to a questioning of the existing order of things, and the demand for freedom can emerge only when freedom itself is denied. It is at such a point that history begins.

This does not mean that freedom itself is necessarily manifest as the dynamic of history. Indeed, from time immemorial wars have been fought for all sorts of reasons but, until the modern era, none was entered into under the colours of freedom. Prior to the American and French Revolutions, freedom was but a latency awaiting realisation. Since then, however, it has increasingly become the central watchword around which social and political conflict is framed and justified. Revolutionaries now pledge themselves to 'liberty or death', but, equally, modern states use 'freedom' as the rationale for imperialist adventures. If Western culture is the home of freedom, to the extent that it can designate itself as comprising the 'Free World' (in distinction to another world that has not achieved this level of illumination), we need, in order to understand the relations between cultures in the modern world, to inquire into the cultural determinisms that constitute such a notion.

Patterson asks why it is that for most of human history freedom has been notable for its absence in the values promoted by different societies. Renown and power for oneself and one's family or clan, imperial glory, valour in warfare, filial piety, the harmony of heaven and earth, altruism, justice, equality, may number among the many qualities recognised in different times and places, but freedom hardly ever (Patterson, 1991: x). It is a significant question that raises key issues about the way in which culture is experienced. In order to exist, consciousness of freedom requires certain cultural conditions to be in place: it is not given to us as a component of existence. As Hegel made plain, freedom is not part of the content of nature, which knows only endless change in a repetitive way, but is realised through the development of the human spirit as an essential element of the experience of culture. Precisely because it is so much the essence of human becoming, it requires particular historical processes in order to allow consciousness of it to emerge in a manifest form. And therefore this consciousness can never be sundered from the social circumstances that give rise to it.

'Man was born free yet everywhere is in chains,' Rousseau famously proclaimed at the beginning of *The Social Contract*. This statement may be one of the more significant in history, for in a sense it opened up the whole modern debate about freedom. It encapsulates a mentality that permeates the contemporary spirit, providing the founding rationale (even if this would have appalled Rousseau himself) for the imperialist impulse of the West, from the civilising mission of nineteenth-century colonialism to the present will to spread democracy and free determination that supposedly animates development programmes and aid packages (as well as armed interventions) in non-Western societies.

It was the rise of capitalism and the growth of individualism that gave the impetus for a surge in the desire for freedom. The revolutionary upheavals of the nineteenth century had their foundation in the stimulus given to a notion of freedom by the American and French Revolutions at the end of the eighteenth century, the ideas of which were conceived in the Age of Enlightenment. Such a will towards freedom can be seen to respond to a yearning for a state of innocence, before the fall, and in Utopia, that would be given shape through the transformation of society. 'Liberty – Equality – Fraternity' were the rallying calls of the French Revolution, and the slogan 'Liberty or Death' has resounded in most revolts in the West during the past two centuries. Modern freedom was given its first most tangible realisations with the American Declaration of Independence and the Declaration of the Rights of Man during the French Revolution. Yet what exactly does 'freedom' mean?

Considered as a concept in itself, freedom is a pure abstraction. As we live in society, so freedom as an absolute value is impossible, because my freedom to act as I wish must very quickly impinge upon the freedom of others. Does freedom include the freedom to oppress, to kill or to harm others? No one, surely, would go so far as to assert this, at least not directly. And yet this issue lies at the heart of any discussion of freedom, since any free action occurring in society – however innocuous – must have an effect upon other people. At what point can it be said that such freedom to act comes to represent an unacceptable restriction of another's freedom? Questions about the nature of freedom therefore turn on how the freedom of one can be ensured without giving it sanction to encroach on the freedom of others, upon how it can realise itself as something of which all people can be part. As such, the question of freedom is less a question of the right to freedom as of how such a right is to be mediated and how it relates to our being in the world along with other people.

As an existential state, freedom is defined against determinism: are we free to act as we wish, or are our actions in some way predetermined? This presents many difficulties and, depending upon one's response, has a powerful impact upon decisions – especially moral decisions – made in society. Christianity, for example, veers uneasily between determinism and the freedom to make moral choices, as do applications of the theory of evolution and much of current concern with genetic theory. The problem of determinism is that it holds out no possibility of moral responsibility. If my actions are programmed within me, then there is nothing I can do to change them. A criminal, therefore, can never reform. In such terms, a belief in determinism is therefore incompatible with free will. Quantum physics and chaos theory in contemporary science give powerful evidence against determinism, by asserting that phenomena are not causally related but connected by chance occurrences. However, if things are not causally related, this also creates moral difficulties for free actions, because in this case criminals can claim that their actions are merely the result of chance: social circumstances are to blame for putting them in a position in which they had no choice but to act as they did. As a condition of existence, therefore, the concept of freedom is difficult to delineate. This presents a particular problem for Christian theology for, if God, who is all-powerful and all-knowing, created everything in his own image and with no power to act for itself, then he must have known that people would rebel against him. He must have determined it. It is he who is therefore responsible for the evil. If, on the other hand, he gave them free will and they used it to rebel, then he is no longer all-powerful and all-knowing.

It was this issue that Schelling addressed in his *Philosophical Inquiries into the Nature of Human Freedom*, in which he argued that freedom is shaped by recognition of the necessity of evil:

> Arbitrary good is as impossible as arbitrary evil. True freedom is in accord with a holy necessity, of a sort which we feel in essential knowledge when heart and spirit, bound only by their own law, freely affirm that which is necessary. If evil consists in strife between two principles, then the good can only consist in their complete accord. (Schelling, 1989: 70)

For Schelling, freedom is a process of recognition; it is not a condition in itself, nor is it something given to us. Determinism and free will are not incompatible, but necessary to one another, indeed each determines the other. Here we see the basis for Hegel's claim that the history of the world is the history of the consciousness of freedom. Starting from the point at which Schelling left it, Hegel developed this notion to show that freedom can be defined as recognition of necessity: we are bound by the limits of what we are and freedom can only take shape through recognition of the fact of our bounded existence. For freedom to exist, there is a need to determine the course of history rather than be determined by it. One must engage with one's own feelings and with those of others to the point at which one perceives no distinction between the two. Essentially it means recognising the needs of the Other as being an element of one's own needs. The implication is that we cannot be free unless we recognise that our freedom is the freedom of all people. We therefore have to engage actively with the world. This is encapsulated by Hegel's famous statement that: 'Only that which is an object of freedom can be called an Idea.'

This conception of freedom is at odds with the notion of freedom that sustains contemporary Western culture, whose foundation lies in Enlightenment ideas of rights that have been shaped primarily by liberalism. A liberal understanding refuses the problematic between freedom and necessity, taking as its foundation an assumption that a person's condition is freely determined, or at least would be if it were not otherwise constrained. The basis of liberal freedom is therefore to provide the conditions that make free determination possible. As such it elides the existential distinction between freedom and determinism, situating freedom as an absolute and naturally given right owing nothing to social circumstances: we are free unless our freedom is taken away from us in one way or another.

Liberalism's view of liberty involves three main elements, which concern personal freedom, the rights of individuals and the autonomy of individuals and societies. Personal freedom is essentially a negative freedom: the absence of constraint, coercion or obstacles to the satisfaction of what one wants to do. This means that each person should be able to choose their own goals from different alternatives. People are free because they are under no coercion by others but have the power to act in accordance with their own wishes. This is given in utilitarianism's absolute freedom to pursue happiness providing that this does not impinge upon the happiness of others. This assumption of the natural rights of individuals leads to a belief that, in order to be protected, such rights should be formally inscribed in the structure of society. Each person should be considered to be an autonomous entity and should be enabled to live free from any external compulsion to submit to others and so be forced to abandon that autonomy. Such principles are to be guaranteed by processes of representative government, freedom of speech and the right to have and dispose of property, and supported by due process of law. The constitution of the United States was the first to set these points down as principles, which later formed the basis for the Universal Declaration of Human Rights, drawn up by the United Nations in 1948 as the four basic freedoms: freedom of speech and expression; freedom to worship God; freedom from want; freedom from fear. Freedom, from a liberal point of view, takes human activity as its realm of concern, refusing any metaphysical constraints to the possibility of self-realisation. As such, it stands as the guarantor of humanity's absolute freedom to exist *in the world*. It refuses to acknowledge any greater authority, whether it be imposed from without (the fact that one's situation in the world is determined by the nature of existence itself, whose workings we do not understand) or from within by the structure of society. This is based upon a conception of the state as an impersonal entity having no other interest than that of satisfying the requirements of its members, since it exists only as the sum total of all those citizens who comprise it. Its authority is therefore impersonal and disinterested. This principle is perhaps summed up by the phrase 'justice is blind', which seeks to establish as a principle the fact that the law treats all citizens equally. The great achievement of liberalism is that it has been able to provide the foundation for a pluralistic society offering considerable opportunities for those people who have the means to take advantage of them. Is this enough, however, to constitute the conditions of genuine freedom?

Hegel's complaint against liberalism was that it puts forward what are effectively a set of abstract principles that fail to give sufficient weight to objective conditions and refuse to acknowledge the weight of necessity. It does not take account of why people make the choices they do: any choice is determined by external forces that effectively control it. For instance (even if this is not an example that Hegel himself would have been likely to choose), we can say that economic freedom and the idea of a free market are principally concerned to maintain existing power relations and serve the interests of those who already have the greatest economic power rather than to guarantee freedom in its generality. Freedom in such circumstances, although it may appear to be guaranteed, in reality is severely circumscribed. This effectively means that the freedom on offer is nothing more than the freedom to submit to existing conditions. Such a notion of freedom fails to take into account – or rather succumbs to – the demands of necessity.

Against such abstract concepts, Hegel[1] put forward a concrete and historically situated view of freedom. He asserted that the whole of human history was part of a process of the development of a consciousness of freedom through which the world would be transformed. Freedom is not contained in the establishment of impersonal rights but is a principle of human becoming itself that is realised through people, as part of their own struggle. Freedom in this sense transcends the wishes of individuals and becomes manifest as part of a general will rather than as an assertion and realisation of the interests of those who comprise it. The latter, which is the essential feature of liberalism, is nothing but a capitulation to the expediency that mediates between existing relations, and claims to freedom on such a basis can only favour those who are already in positions of power. In order to go beyond this, it is necessary to try to understand freedom not as an undifferentiated right, but as an existential impulse within people. It is necessary to give the concept of freedom a historical dimension.

As such, freedom parallels the notion of sovereignty. It takes shape first through the establishment of a divine chief, when the impulse towards freedom is contained in this sole figure. In such societies, there is no freedom to form individual opinions and the chief embodies the concept of freedom for the whole society. (This does not mean that the individual chief is an individual free to do as he or she wishes; indeed in many societies chiefdom was an onerous task that conferred no special privileges: the periodic sacrifice of the king that was a feature of many societies and the fact that the king was often regarded as accursed highlights an essential ambivalence about the status of chiefdom in many societies.) As the structure of such a society congeals into institutional forms in which those in positions of authority assume freedom as a personal right, which in seventeenth-century Europe gave rise to the absolutism of monarchy, so it provides the conditions for a wider realisation of freedom. The Enlightenment was thus situated in an attempt to abolish institutions based on custom and replace them with reason, a central step in the process of the becoming of freedom. The French Revolution was a direct manifestation of this will towards freedom, but the French revolutionaries misunderstood the nature of freedom by conceiving it not as a process but as an abstract principle that could be codified as a symbol. In so doing they failed to respond to the exigencies of concrete reality and the existing society. This meant that they failed to transform the structures of society in the direction required by freedom by means of reason and sought to impose it through the guillotine, thus negating its very principle.

It is here that the essential difference between the liberal and Hegelian views of freedom is revealed. Where the latter sees freedom as a value standing outside human endeavour, but that only reveals itself through such endeavour, the liberal view sees it as manifesting itself as that endeavour. The Hegelian view of freedom is therefore centred in processes of social and cultural activity, while the liberal takes a transcendent view in which such processes are determined by human activity itself. We might exemplify this by saying that where Hegel saw the history of the world as being the progress of the consciousness of freedom as revealed in the actions of people but not being reducible to that activity, liberals see the history of the world as consisting only of such activity and thus consider that the realisation of freedom can be effected only by means of self-mastery and the free pursuit of one's own interests.

In analysing the development of the consciousness of freedom, Hegel neglects one historical circumstance that was undoubtedly determining. Freedom is not simply an aspect of the realisation of a will to freedom taking shape in a struggle against its concentration in rigid forms that could be abused by absolute monarchy. We owe to Orlando Patterson examination of how the consciousness of freedom was due as much – and no doubt more significantly – to the negation of its contrary. The seventeenth and eighteenth centuries were not just the eras of Absolutism, they were also those of the expansion of mercantilism, especially to the point of trade in human beings as chattels and the institution of the most brutal form of slavery the world has ever witnessed. Without understanding the process of slavery, it is clear that the possibility of freedom remains undetermined.

Patterson sees slavery as present in most of human history. It is tied in with social cohesion and inevitable conflict and its roots can be seen to lie in conflict between societies, especially war, an inevitable residue of which is the taking of prisoners. Most societies, as we have seen, are fundamentally ethnocentric, that is, they see themselves as the centre of the world and project themselves outwards from that centre. Other peoples are perceived as enemies and may not be considered to be properly human at all. In its rudimentary state, a society maintains its coherence and integrity only in relation to others. A simple way of doing this is to say, in effect, that 'they are barbarians, unlike us'. The equilibrium of society is here not sufficiently stable to allow the incorporation of otherness within its structure: prisoners of war are therefore unable to become part of such a society except as a surplus share that confers prestige and facilitates the cohesion of the tribe. In this way they become slaves, which is a way of giving them a place within the society without making them part of the society itself. Slaves are therefore not human beings. They are socially dead, having been dishonoured by their defeat in war, which precludes any return to their own society. They cannot regain their former status and no revolt against such slavery is possible. Having been dishonoured, any return to their former condition is out of the question. No consciousness of freedom can develop because any realisation of it is precluded in a definitive way.

What is significant here is that in most societies what matters is not personal freedom as we understand it today, but membership of society. Freedom as a value can only take shape when the structures of society break down, causing an economic element to be introduced into slavery and destabilising the status of *all* people. As this occurs, so slaves cease to be seen as prestige symbols, but gain a value in themselves. Slaves therefore become things. They are no longer socially dead, but become elements of value in an exchange system. This introduces two aspects: slaves are now desired for their own sakes; they are no longer merely a surplus that can be used to represent a display of wealth. This in turn creates a threat of slavery; it is no longer simply a consequence of defeat in war. In effect anyone can become a slave, not simply someone who has been dishonoured. Slavery thus begins to permeate the whole society. People become afraid of being made slaves. And it is this that brings with it the will towards freedom. If one feels that one has been unjustly made a slave, a desire to fight against the injustice begins to become inscribed in a way that had not been possible previously.

Orlando Patterson has charted a clear pattern of how freedom took shape in ancient Greece and in the ideology of Christianity, which is too complicated for us to consider in detail here. However, what is significant to note is that the reason freedom assumed such importance in Western culture is precisely because nowhere else did the essential condition for its realisation emerge, and that essential condition is one that deflates any assumption of Western superiority as representing the march of progress. For Patterson convincingly shows – and it is hardly a comforting conclusion – that the condition of freedom is its opposite. It can be realised only in circumstances in which unfreedom reaches such a level that it becomes intolerable. As such its realisation required the merciless form of slavery based on the principle of exchange that in the seventeenth and eighteenth centuries created the objective conditions for freedom as a value to come to the fore as a *human* value.

In this respect, the assumption made by Western discourse that it has made itself the home of freedom is problematic. Far from being a natural value that all should share, and in default of which most Western writers 'have assumed that something is wrong with the rest of the world and with the majority of human history during which no one ever thought it necessary to express and cherish freedom as an ideal' (Patterson, 1991: x), it can be seen to gain its prestige from the fact that it needed to struggle against the injustice and perversity of the society in which it emerged.[2] Nevertheless, it has established itself as a value that is promoted and reproduced in the way in which we are educated and gain understanding of the world through knowledge.

In accordance with the argument Orlando Patterson makes, as it became the central value of modern society, freedom gave to contemporary culture a shape that allows personal identity to take multiple forms that would have been inconceivable in earlier eras. The consciousness of freedom that exists today makes it difficult for rulers and governments to impose their will by force (although this does not mean that they do not seek out more subtle means of doing so). The fact that people have the freedom to act as they wish within the limits set only by the personal freedom of others and that all persons are equal before the law, that we have an individual right to choose our destiny and make decisions free from direct internal and external constraints, is by no means a negligible achievement and may even be said to be, in its depth and power, superior to any other single complex of values conceived by mankind. It is, Patterson asserts, the source of Western intellectual mastery and the mechanism of its creativity.

At the same time, however, in its liberal form it has tended to place a burden on people that leads to a breakdown of social ties and enhances the alienation we feel from our sources of being. In this process, freedom itself has gained an ideological gloss that has shown a tendency to absorb and codify the urge to which freedom itself responds. Revolt itself becomes institutionalised and indeed is perceived to be part of the developmental process, so that freedom becomes tamed, fixed as a requirement to be fulfilled in a global world that presents us with infinite possibilities for knowledge and adventure. Such a notion of freedom very much represents the triumph of the liberal ideal of freedom as self-realisation against the Hegelian understanding of freedom as the unfolding of universal consciousness.

Francis Fukuyama (1992) has famously – and not to say perversely – asserted that liberal freedom has prevailed as the realisation of the universal consciousness Hegel announced. Perversely, because the past two centuries have been played out against the background of two contrasting ideas of liberty – that of liberalism and that of Hegel. It does seem that Fukuyama's attempt to make Hegel (and even Marx) a forerunner of liberal democracy tries to deny an irreducible problem inherent to capitalist society. For Hegel's critique of liberalism is still relevant: the liberal idea of freedom is inscribed within the current structure of society and must accede to the legitimacy of the current world order and so institutionalises injustice. The traditional liberal view, as exemplified in different ways by Isaiah Berlin and Karl Popper, is that Hegel's idea of freedom leads to totalitarianism. Again, there is some legitimacy in this view to the extent that it leaves open the possibility for an authoritarian figure like Stalin to assume to himself the historical destiny of freedom.

We should, however, question whether there is not something fundamentally mistaken in the presupposition of a progressive unfolding of history that is shared by both liberal and Hegelian conceptions of freedom. Cioran makes no bones about his contempt for any historical determinism of freedom, either as guaranteed by rights or as the consciousness of the human spirit: 'Becoming excludes an absolute fulfillment, a goal: the temporal adventure unfolds without an aim external to itself, and will end when its possibilities of movement are exhausted. The degree of consciousness varies with the ages, such consciousness not being aggrandized by their succession' (1975: 146). This ferociously understated denunciation of the pretensions of progress contains a warning for anyone who proclaims any triumphalist view of historical becoming. There is always a certain ambivalence, or even irony, in seeing the history of the world as the consciousness of freedom, for, as

Cioran has demonstrated, the construction of history itself is a form of enslavement. Is progress really necessary for the development of existence, or is it, as Cioran asserts, a delusion that itself enslaves us?

Freedom as part of mankind's process of self-realisation – whether in liberal or Hegelian terms – is guaranteed, or intended to be guaranteed, in modern society by the socialisation process itself through the institution of a system of education that will prepare the individual for participation in society as a free person: access to the educational process will aid the development of personal autonomy. Free access to education thus is an essential component of any society that strives to realise freedom, and this is summarised in the notion that all people should receive a liberal education, something that adds a further aspect to the notion of natural rights. A liberal education should not simply provide the child with moral virtue, but also be a springboard for creating the conditions of freedom. If freedom is the freedom to choose, then in order to have the ability to make proper choices we need to be able to distinguish between the alternatives available. Education is intended to give us the intellectual means to do this, at least according to the strictures involved in the idea of a liberal education that underlies the social rationale for education and ties together knowledge and reality with ideas of freedom. In order to be a free individual, there is a need for an education that provides the possibility for the individual to be able to cultivate and develop the mind to the full range of human understanding. Education is thereby a tool of freedom, freeing the mind from error and illusion and enabling citizens to make correct decisions on the basis of proper information. At least this is the ideal. How well is it realised in practical terms?

Like freedom, we tend to take education for granted as a universal good, yet like freedom, too, our idea of education is historically determined and has rarely lived up to its proclaimed aim. Prior to the nineteenth century, in fact, education was a privilege reserved for the ruling class, and it was not until the parallel upheavals of the French and Industrial Revolutions that the idea of a liberal education for all became accepted as desirable. Even then, the idea that it was a universal good was very much a minority view: the spread of education was due to a variety of needs within European society; the becoming of individuals may have been a pious aspiration, but as frequently it was seen as a threat to the effective process of disciplining that was undoubtedly the primary concern of education. Certainly the main concern of politicians, employers and other interested parties in education was not then, and has rarely since been, in the learning process itself but that it should effectively train and discipline pupils for the needs of work and the demands of a market economy. This fundamental tension in the education process was well noted by Gramsci in the 1920s: 'The tendency today is to abolish every type of schooling that is "disinterested" (not serving immediate interests) or "formative". . . . Instead, there is a steady growth of specialised vocational schools, in which the pupil's destiny and future activity are determined in advance' (1971: 27). This 'crisis' of education reflecting a fundamental clash between the aims of politicians and those of educationalists has become increasingly acute in recent years, as politicians have increasingly sought to intervene in the educational process, reducing even higher education to the level of vocational training. This raises a question mark over whether it is possible for education any longer even to aspire to fulfil the notion of a liberal education and facilitate the development of a young person's creative and imaginative faculties in the realisation of freedom. Indeed, in Britain the politicisation of education has reached such a point that it may be wondered whether it can still genuinely be called 'education', and would more accurately be termed 'training'. If it retains any integrity given current political dictates, it is due to the fact that the socio-cultural process of education – and the demands of students – resists such political pressure at numerous points and in numerous ways, no matter how many bureaucratic mechanisms politicians introduce to control it.

Of course, the ideological agenda of education has always been apparent to working-class people and other excluded groups, to the extent that resistance to it remains strong among such groups and children may be sent to school not because their parents think it does them any good, but because they are legally compelled to do so. Despite the institution of universal free education, there remain today whole classes of people who are effectively excluded or unable to participate in the education process for one reason or another.

Nevertheless, education itself is an essential, founding condition of culture itself that is manifested not only in schools and other forms of organised education, but in all aspects of our lives. Any culture that did not pass down its accumulated knowledge to new generations in a systematic way would not survive for long. The forms of education available within a particular society will be determined by the cultural needs of that society. These may differ widely, but all will be based in a fundamental need and have the dual task of maintaining the internal cohesion of the society while protecting it from external dangers. A society lacking education is a contradiction in terms: no society that kept its members ignorant of the information necessary for its continued reproduction could flourish, and would be unlikely even to take shape as a society in the first place.

At the same time, however, all societies also restrict knowledge in one way or another, directing it so that it will serve the reproduction of that particular society. The process of education is always as much one of the disciplining of knowledge as it is of gaining it. As Raymond Williams put it, education 'expresses . . . certain basic elements in the culture, what is thought of as "an education" being in fact a particular selection, a particular set of emphases and omissions' (1961: 145). Even when education is tied in with a process of human development, this is not its necessary condition. Equally such development is not undetermined, but is always channelled in certain directions.

Centred in the '3 R's' of reading, writing and arithmetic, today's elementary learning is based upon procedures of initiation into the values of the dominant society, a cosmopolitan, literate one founded in middle-class tenets. This makes the pursuit of knowledge in a disinterested way as an end in itself difficult if not impossible to achieve. The spread of education is almost always down to the practical needs of society: overwhelmingly, education is 'interested'. Pierre Bourdieu has perhaps been instrumental in exposing the ideological factors that militate against education ever being genuinely disinterested. For him, the primary purpose of education in today's society is to enable the child to gain the cultural capital or skills necessary for the reproduction of society and maintain the cultural ascendency of the dominant class. Education, he claims, is structured to initiate the child into class values so that, by means of an unconscious process by which the appropriate rules are internalised and become accepted truths, we learn to accept the place assigned to us within society. Knowledge is thereby disciplined rather than gained. And as much as the apparent discourse is concerned with opening up access to the widest possible number of people, in actual fact the concern is really much more with restricting or excluding people from genuine participation. What Bourdieu calls a habitus provides a site and a radius within which possibilities, while being presented as unlimited, are in fact severely restricted, and the way this is done makes it difficult to break down analytically. This means that a discourse of inclusion playing upon the fact that everyone has rights and equal opportunities conceals the repressive mechanisms actually in place. Education functions to give substance and validation to beliefs and assumptions so that sufficient flexibility is allowed for variation, but only within carefully defined limits. This very flexibility serves the illusion of freedom we are offered, which, far from resulting in the establishment of any form of collective identity, freezes human relations in terms of concepts and value judgements that serve the interests of the dominant class. In addition, the education process sets up a tension within the individual between the values of their immediate community and those of the dominant class, which controls the ordering of educational priorities.

Educational policy lies at the heart of this and explains why it is a political rather than an educational issue. In this respect, literacy – doubtless the middle-class value *par excellence* – is a central theme, instituting the 'Great Divide' that separates civilised from primitive, educated from ignorant, and establishing the developmental schema upon which educational achievement is to be judged, so serving the purpose of collapsing culture into nature by suggesting that something as overwhelmingly cultural as education is in fact a natural process that takes an evolutionary shape so that only 'developed' societies have proper education.

In this way, education is equated with knowledge, but in a particular way. It is assumed that only someone who is educated at school really has proper knowledge, and that literacy is a process of civilisation. The most advanced countries are therefore the most literate and the most educated. This also sets up an evolutionary pattern defining developed societies and separating them from those that are 'underdeveloped'.

Literacy is defined as the ability to read and write, but what exactly is meant by 'read and write'? An Amazonian Indian, to survive in the jungle, needs to be able to read complex signs and indications. He must be able to understand patterns made on trees, the tracks of animals, and so on. This is not something that happens naturally. It is a learned activity involving many years work. Yet we call such people illiterate. Why is it that we do not consider this a form of literacy? If we go to the jungle, do we not become illiterates?

In a revealing anthropological study conducted in the southern United States in the early 1980s, Shirley Heath (1983) looked at educational skills in different communities. She showed how different literacies were at play in different situations and that school education was only part (and not always the most significant part) of how children learn the skills necessary for them to participate in the society to which they belong.

Heath's study was treated by educationalists as evidence of a failure of education, but does it not rather bring attention to the way in which different communities have different needs and aspirations as regards education? There is not necessarily any inadequacy involved in a lack of reading ability if this is not necessary for existence in the society in which one lives. Heath shows that children who did not do well at school were not necessarily uneducated. They were still being taught at home the essential skills to prosper in communities whose needs were not always served by the reading and writing skills taught at school. This alerts us to the fact that even in a land like the United States, culture is sufficiently variegated that different cultural forms require different skills in order to endure in relation to the world that surrounds them.

If it may be said that every society has to be literate in the skills necessary for its reproduction, the meaning of literacy needs to be considered within an expanded arena: it is not exhausted by the idea of being able to read books. Survival in any society entails the gaining of knowledge about its norms and requirements, and the socialisation process is also necessarily an educational process. Illiteracy is therefore not a natural condition that is corrected by education. Rather, it is created by socio-cultural processes within which one form of literacy is defined as being universally applicable. In this respect education and the development process are interlinked and placed under the rubric of a power relation. What is called 'illiteracy' occurs only within a society that is unable to transmit knowledge in terms that are appropriate or even acceptable to those classes of people that become characterised as illiterate, and this bears witness to the fact that the society is unable to address issues of social inequality but can only reproduce them.

If the movement in education is towards human development, today this is directed to preparing young people for a position in society that serves middle-class social hegemony. The primary concern is no longer self-discipline as it prepares them for their occupations, but rather to be consumers, to learn how to partake of what the consumer society has to offer: how to spend increasingly becomes the central value of society. If it allows the development of a consciousness of personal freedom and knowledge, this is a by-product of this process, it is not central to it. Of course, all education is value-laden and imperfect. Yet we should be aware that training within the framework of a middle-class-orientated Western tradition is not the sum total of the possibilities of education. Rather, it is determined in such a way to make us better able to survive in a capitalist world dominated by certain presuppositions.

The French sociologist Régis Debray (1993) argues that the idea of education in the West has gone through quite radical changes in the course of the ages and is now in the process of another shift. In feudal society, education was controlled by the church and meant interpretation of the word of God. During the Renaissance and Reformation, the period of Absolute monarchy in Europe, education was a matter of pageant and colour: the aim was to dazzle with superficial learning. It was only with the Enlightenment and the French Revolution that the idea of education as a pursuit of truth became entrenched. Increasingly the image is displacing the word as the most important element of society. Television desacralises the image as printing desacralised the word. From the Enlightenment until the Second World War education was the defining myth of our lives. It has now been replaced by the myth of communication. The message no longer matters and meaning has become superfluous. Marketing and management have become the educational principles of our age, and any notion of truth has been replaced by seduction. Instead of truth it is information that is the reality. This presents a somewhat over-schematic frame, but it has considerable general validity. If we accept that truth has been replaced by processes of seduction, what is the value of knowledge itself?

Western philosophy in general functions in an unquestioned belief that it is involved in a quest for truth, and that knowledge is the path by which truth may be revealed. It tends to take it for granted that the accumulation of knowledge leads towards an attainable goal of absolute truth. Truth is thus synonymous with the Western philosophical project, and the only doubt generally entertained about it is to question the status of knowledge. The very idea of a sociology of knowledge, implying that knowledge is contingent upon social circumstances and context and has different meanings in different contexts, is a challenge to analytical philosophy, which is convinced that knowledge must be true in all times and places and cannot be contingent in this way. Yet it is clear that truth as conceived by a rationalist philosopher must be very different from what – say – a Christian mystic considers to be truth, while it would be something very different again from what it might seem to a modern businessman. Likewise the uses to which knowledge is put are very different in different contexts.

If the aim of traditional epistemology is to provide a method to eliminate the errors and illusions in socially constructed knowledge and establish its universally valid basis – either in immediate experience or in reason – in order to guarantee our claims to it and refute scepticism, then a sociology of knowledge threatens the view that either reason or experience can provide a bedrock for the foundation of knowledge. For if all ideas and beliefs are social products and knowledge develops in a progressive but not necessarily in an even way in which all theories contain elements of truth, which take

different forms at particular times and ebb and flow in relation to those circumstances, then what can be the criteria for separating true from false? In
this respect, Hegel draws an analogy with a plant:

> The more conventional opinion gets fixated on the antithesis of truth and falsity,
> the more it tends to expect a given philosophical system to be either accepted or
> contradicted. . . . It does not comprehend the diversity of philosophical systems
> as the progressive unfolding of truth, but rather sees in it simple disagreements.
> The bud disappears in the bursting-forth of the blossom. . . ; similarly, when the
> fruit appears, the blossom is shown up in its turn as a false manifestation of the
> plant, and the fruit now emerges as the truth of it instead. These forms are not
> just distinguished from one another, they also supplant one another as mutually
> incompatible. Yet at the same time their fluid nature makes them moments of an
> organic unity in which they not only do not conflict, but in which each is as nec-
> essary as the other; and this mutual necessity alone constitutes the life of the
> whole. (1977: 2)

Within philosophy itself Hegel and, later, Marx were instrumental in chal-
lenging the truth claims of epistemology and instituting the possibility of a
sociology of knowledge, especially by Marx advancing his concepts of ideology and false consciousness. Besides the directly political applications these
concepts had, by highlighting the way that ideology constructs 'truth' in particular directions with particular aims, Marx was able to show that it is
misleading to think that philosophy is necessarily to be equated with truth. It
could equally be used to mislead and even to distort the truth. Above all,
Marx showed that the dominant ideas in a given society are not the ones that
are the most truthful, but those that give the greatest legitimacy to the ruling
order.

From a different perspective, too, Nietzsche challenged rationalist claims to
truth by speculating on whether truth as such was in fact either desirable or
possible. Using empiricist arguments against the very notion of truth, he was
able to bring doubt to the foundation of certain trends of Western philosophy, including empiricism itself. Truth must be contingent due to the fact that
its criteria are predetermined by various factors, but above all in the final
analysis by life itself: we are limited by the very fact that we live as isolated
beings separated from all that surrounds us, something that inevitably places
a limit upon what we can understand about the world. Yet Nietzsche not so
much denied truth itself as made it 'impossible' from the perspective of our
perception as human beings. In a sense, it seems that the logical conclusion of
Nietzsche's argument is that to be able to determine truth we would have to
cease to be alive.

The significance of Nietzsche's doubt is as far-reaching as Marx's analysis
of the way truth claims contain ideological assumptions, and raises the question of why we have such a need for 'truth' in the first place. Why should we
not instead be concerned with untruth? An obsession with truth is a false
path born from fear, and one that can only lead us back to our starting point.
It assumes that knowledge reveals what had previously been hidden from us,
and arises from a need to understand what we are. It therefore accepts given
concepts unquestioningly, and falsely assumes that a given cause has a

necessary effect: to show that something is false implies there must be something true; to reveal a contradiction is to assume a possibility of non-contradiction.

Nietzsche's response is that the quest for truth is meaningless. The value of knowledge is determined not by the fact that it contains truth but by the extent to which it responds to the needs, aspirations and distortions of a particular form of life. There is no truth as such. We should strive not to attain truth but rather to combat error. Instead of judging truth by some objective standard that assumes it can exist of itself, it is necessary to recognise the circumstances in which the claim to truth can be made: '"By their fruits shall ye know them'. I say of each: 'This is a fruit by which I recognise the ground from which it grew.'" In other words things cannot be known by the end results, but through the process by which that end result has been obtained. Nietzsche claims that hitherto we have not discovered truths but only embodied our errors. The need is to embody knowledge and make it instinctive (see Nietzsche, 1974).

Nietzsche's main concern seems to have been to assert that there are no universal answers and that the most important thing is to provide a context in which experience becomes meaningful, is illuminated and so transformed. It is therefore essential to address real people, not abstractions.

Today, Nietzsche's rejection of truth has been given serious attention, and truth is treated with suspicion. For instance, in recent writings on culture, James Clifford has coherently suggested the possibility of a methodology for a new cultural studies that would bear in mind the sort of critique Nietzsche demanded. Clifford proclaims that it is no longer possible to lay claim to the whole truth in studying culture. The most we can do is to establish 'partial truths' by listening to a multiplicity of voices and rejecting any claims to totality. He asserts that the questions that should be asked are those like 'who speaks? when and where? with or to whom? under what institutional and historical restraints?' (in Clifford and Marcus, 1986: 13). Clifford's idea is that this will give voice to those people who have been excluded from the notion of the 'truth' as constructed by Western discourse. However, this is a long way from Nietzsche's rejection of the concept of truth. It simply relocates truth in a wider context, which represents an extreme form of relativism. This seems to represent a displacement of what Nietzsche meant.

Cultural relativism in general fails to account for the problematic Nietzsche opens up concerning truth because it does no more than relocate a notion of truth in contingent circumstances. To say that truth is partial, as Clifford does, or to see it as no more than the sum total of the cultural circumstances that have given rise to it, as is characteristic of relativistic claims to knowledge and truth, seems to be fundamentally to misunderstand Nietzsche's thinking in this area. In fact it remains firmly within the paradigm of truth claims that Nietzsche exposed. The key to Nietzsche's critique of truth claims lies in the injunction to 'embodied knowledge'. What exactly does this mean?

Knowledge, like reason, is never without a shadow which, in its rationalist form, it denies. No doubt this shadow can be primarily characterised as 'power', as widely recognised in the ambivalent phrase 'knowledge is power'. Rather than reject knowledge as ultimately being illusion, Nietzsche's critique seems to deny its claim to truth as an ultimate end, while inserting it into a moral framework. If we are genuinely concerned with understanding, we need to accept the slippage that is present within all knowledge. Knowledge is shaped by what forms it, by the activity that has been necessary to produce it; it is not plucked out of the air as a mastery of what is known. It can only be measured, therefore, by consciousness of what it doesn't know. This conception of knowledge involves no surrender to arbitrariness or subjectivity. Nietzsche reveals no tolerance of inconsistent argument, but calls for rigorous examination of the facts at issue.

To gain understanding of what is involved here we can usefully consider the significance of the figure of the trickster, an ambivalent character who embodies knowledge by means of artifice and allusion rather than by directly confronting a problem.

The trickster is a figure found in most societies and represents the qualities of paradox. He may be lustful, a lout, a boaster, a liar, a fool, a lecher and a glutton but at the same time arouses affection and esteem. He may be a deceiver, a thief, a parricide, but also an inventor, a benefactor, a magician. He may be a creator, a hero who slays monsters, a thief who steals daylight, fire or water for human benefit; he is the one who brings culture and traditions, but is also a prankster with an insatiable appetite for food and sex; he is vain, deceitful and cunning, a restless wanderer and a blunderer who is often the victim of his own follies. This inventory of qualities is not exhaustive.

> A tale of the Ashanti trickster, Ananse, helps to elucidate the qualities of the trickster: Ananse promised to cure the mother of the high God Nyame pledging the forfeit of his life if he failed. When the old woman died, Ananse was sentenced to death. When the executioners were about to carry out the sentence, Ananse's son, who had burrowed under the ground, cried out in a deep voice:
>
> > 'If you kill Ananse, the tribe will come to ruin! If you spare Ananse, the tribe will prosper!' The people therefore asked for Ananse to be spared, since Mother Earth demanded it. Nyame complied and the tribe prospered.

What we see in this tale is that, through deceit, knowledge is gained and the truth is enacted. In a stagnant situation, symbolised by the old woman's sickness, the community suffers and decays. It is released from its state of decline by a crafty stratagem, in which the trickster reveals how prosperity sometimes requires the sacrifice of what one holds dear in order to release the energies of the earth and bring together the people in their shared generosity.

Trickster knowledge stands in relation to freedom as an image that personifies both humanity's folly and its wisdom in its nobility and foolishness, in all of its heroic and cowardly aspects, and incorporating both coherence and incoherence into a pattern of understanding that can never easily be pinned down. The trickster is the one who stands outside society and is able to see what cannot be seen from the inside, the messenger who brings news of the gods and who poses the riddle that, once posed, brings into play the healing power of the imagination. In this respect, the trickster stands for balance between what is above and what is below, combining animal and human qualities and able to effect ritual transformation. A mover between worlds, he is able to empower by means of divination and showing how the impossible can be made possible. As a mediator he reveals truth by indirect means, not to say through dissemblance. These seem to have been the sorts of qualities that Nietzsche was looking for when he called for knowledge to be embodied.

In this sense, the trickster is opposed to any notion of an all-seeing and all-knowing God as well as to any idea of human perfection. He may be characterised as mankind reflecting on its own identity and refusing to be imposed upon by an external force. The trickster is the one who eats the forbidden fruit, steals fire and refuses to accept that the gods are there to be served. The trickster may at times be a joke figure, but the laughter this provokes is emancipatory, especially since, in laughing at the trickster, people are also laughing at themselves. As the embodiment of the actual and the potential, he represents the world both as it is and how it could be. The trickster incarnates the paradox at the heart of existence reflecting a distrust of rational processes of knowledge. Trickster knowledge thereby involves an accumulation of power at a point of dissolution.

As such the trickster stands for change and revelation, the qualities that Nietzsche saw as essential to genuine knowledge. This also calls for a questioning of the assumptions we make about the relation between knowledge and the truth claims made for it in the belief that it can ever be definitive, for it needs to be subject to change if it is to maintain its vitality (one interpretation of the Ashanti tale recounted above is that the dying old woman stands precisely for the sense of disintegration that occurs when what is decaying is kept artificially alive). Such knowledge needs to be anthropologically founded in the realisation that otherwise it has the power to enslave us. Indeed the accumulation of knowledge as servility is revealed everyday to us on TV quiz shows.

This alerts us to how all knowledge is fragmentary and involves more than a simple quest for truth. Real knowledge is established in recognition that the world does not have sufficient stability that we can state anything definite about it. Such is the basis of knowledge systems outside the West, which perceive a necessary link between secrecy and revelation that must be recognised if the spark of knowledge is to be ignited. In this sense, the value of knowledge depends on the extent to which it makes any conclusive image of the universe impossible. Real knowledge is frequently secret knowledge.

Knowledge, as it is understood through the educational process in Western society as the realisation of freedom, is reductionist of the possibilities of both knowledge and freedom and ultimately reduces the framework of reality itself, for it assumes everything to its own frame of reference, leaving nothing to the shadows. The freedom we have to make choices depends in any society on the way that knowledge is culturally constructed. Truth, insofar as it has meaning, is founded in the contingency of everyday situations. Its starting point is in conversation and sharing for there can be no knowledge without community. Freedom itself needs to be concrete and founded in participation in society, and the grounds for such participation will depend upon how the community constructs its sense of what reality is.

Notes

1. It may be objected that distinguishing so much between liberal and Hegelian conceptions is an over-simplification. In order to depict the cultural flows of Western ideas over the past two centuries, however, it seems legitimate.
2. However, perhaps the generally accepted idea that Western culture is the homeland of freedom ought to be questioned. For instance, we might look further into how far the much vaunted individualism in which liberal ideas of freedom are centred really exists. Christopher Caudwell effectively argued that modern capitalist society creates not individuals but *types*. In the process

   > an inherited character is forced into an acquired mould. . . . Twentieth-century civilisation, the creation of a gospel of unadulterated and economic individualism, has finally become anti-individualistic. It opposes the full development of genetic possibilities by forcing the individual to mould a favoured function along the lines of a type whose services possess exchange-value. (Caudwell, 1946: 24–5)

   Genuine individualism, on the contrary, is the characteristic of nomadic civilisations like the Bedouin or the Tuareg, which allow free individual development. Equally, it might also be said that the Hegelian notion of freedom has been more realised in Asian countries than in the West – especially Japan, where an individual development of capacities has been allowed to take shape in accord with social development (although not unproblematically so). Freedom is also a value, on a different basis, in some religions, especially in Buddhism. This calls for further investigation which it is not possible to follow up here.

9

CULTURE AND THE STATUS OF REALITY

If the doors of perception were cleansed everything would appear to man as it is, infinite.

William Blake

The darkness Schelling saw as the necessary heritage of reality has not been denied in the modern age, but its terms of reference have changed. We may accept this darkness, indeed the events of the twentieth century (the reality of the horrors of the Holocaust or Hiroshima among so many other terrible events) make it impossible to do otherwise, but the modern world is still built on solid foundations, or at least we like to think it is. As the dominant culture in which we live assumes a notion of rationality, so it also takes the reality of the universe as empirical fact. This idea represents the foundation stone upon which many of the advances – especially technological – of the past two centuries have been based, even though the grounds for such faith in the solidity of the world have constantly been questioned. Realism – a nineteenth-century movement that was in many ways ephemeral in its immediate effects – may be said to have dominated ways we have thought about culture for the past century and is as central to our cultural assumptions as is rationalism. Realism is so much a part of our world that, like rationalism, we tend to take it for granted. The prevalent use of everyday phrases such as 'get real' or 'live in the real world' testifies to this dominance. Yet what do such injunctions mean? Is it possible *not* to be real, or to live *outside* the real world? The very use of these phrases as value judgements shows the extent to which a notion of the real today acts as a form of cultural hegemony in our lives. Roman Jakobson defined realism clearly as a trend that 'aims to reproduce reality as faithfully as possible and which aspires to achieve maximum verisimilitude'. This makes clear how realism assumes to itself the possibility of being able to describe actuality accurately in such a way that it makes a claim to constitute reality to the exclusion of all other possibilities. It is a definition that raises many questions about the nature of reality and how what in most eras has been regarded as tremendously problematic can be taken for granted in the modern world. Yet it is also a cultural form with clear historical roots.

The certainty that a realist attitude takes for granted is something new in human history. The idea that reality is what is out there, that it can be perceived or even grasped by the senses, is a recent phenomenon even within Western culture. Most cultures posit an irremediable gap between the reality of the world and our perceptual understanding of it. Taoism, for instance, stresses the fact that the *Tao* cannot be grasped by human perception, but represents a state of being that is not graspable by our perceptual apparatus. In Hinduism, the world is an illusion sustained by the activity occurring within it. Religions may vary in the degree to which they embrace the solidity of the everyday world, but none accept its material actuality as true reality. Philosophers, too, have never seen the reality of the world as anything but problematic. Plato may have subsumed being to reality, so instituting a philosophical tradition wedded to exploration of an objectively existing world, but he still believed that there was a fundamental separation between the appearance of the world and the ideal forms that defined reality itself. Until the nineteenth century, the central tradition of Western philosophy took its cue from this, so that traditionally realism referred to the problem of Universals, not to the fact that the objective world has a real existence that can be accessed. Even empiricism during the Enlightenment did not presume to equate sense impressions with reality, but confined itself to asserting that our sense impressions were the only reliable source of knowledge.

In the nineteenth century, however, a sea change occurred in Western thought that transformed the way that people thought about the world and was crucial in defining the modern age. As an idea, realism lies at the crossroads of various different currents of thinking. It emerged from out of the Industrial Revolution and the rise of technology, especially the invention of photography, which brought new possibilities for the 'realistic' representation of the world. The importance of the invention of photography can hardly be underestimated here: unlike other forms of representation, such as those of painting or drawing, photography showed us – or purported to show us – what was really there. It could be seen to be a purely objective form of portrayal, revealing what existed independently of human perception. The saying 'the camera never lies' captures this sense and remains a resonant phrase, no matter how often it is shown to be based on a false understanding of the nature and practice of photography. At least, if people are fully aware that the camera image can be distorted, whether wilfully or not, the belief that what the camera itself shows is what exists 'in reality' remains a prevalent view in modern society.

Opposing itself to idealism and abstraction, realism assumes that reality is transparent and should be subject to no uncertainty: it is what we see all around us. 'Seeing is believing' may be said to be its watchword. Historically, realism was also founded as a reaction against romanticism. Where the essence of romanticism lay in the urge to make the invisible visible (or perhaps more precisely to *realise* the invisible in ways that would not undermine its non-visibility), realism sought to portray only what was immediately perceptible. If it too might be said to have wished to make the invisible visible, it was with the very anti-romantic aim of revealing that its actual visibility constituted the totality of the real, to show that even though there are some things that cannot be perceived by the human eye, they can be grasped by means of tools that have a wider perceptual range than those of the senses: in other words, by the technology created by humans that extends perception into the invisible, something made possible by the invention of photography. It therefore took as its premise only what could be seen as real. There was nothing ineffable, nothing that could not be captured by perceptual means, even if the human senses were insufficient to this and required the aid of technical sources. Realism may thus be seen as a curious inversion of romanticism: where the romantics had explored a realm of infinite possibilities in an overwhelming universe, realism set clear limits to the world, yet asserting that everything within it is knowable. As such it may be said – against conventional wisdom – that, far from exalting the individual's genius, romanticism saw the human individual very much as an insignificant part of an elemental whole; it was the realist attitude that elevated the human to the status of yardstick for the judgement of the nature of reality and which was really responsible for promoting the idea of individual genius. The extent to which realism won out over romanticism – at least in terms of everyday life – is enshrined in language by the fact that we are always enjoined to 'be realistic' and not be 'romantic', these words having become respectively synonyms for being practical or impractical.

But realism was also a response to a variety of other social and cultural factors. Most immediately, the failure of the 1848 Revolutions, which may be seen as sounding the death knell of romanticism, fuelled a powerful reaction that affected all aspects of European society. The urge was towards an everyday art and a way of thinking that would reflect ordinary living rather than the grand ideas that romanticism had embraced. This also reflected the needs of the newly industrialised world, based as it was on a confidence in science as able to explain and control the powers of nature definitively. A reassertion of Enlightenment ideas in a more positive frame, realism saw science as triumphing over nature and leading to the conquest of the world of invisible forces. As such, religion lost much of its force over people's minds, to be replaced by the new divinity of technology, which seemed to have the potential to liberate people and give them power over the invisible. Politically, too, realism can be seen as both the development of and channelling of utopian ideas into more concrete proposals for social betterment, a movement that would, in a sense, underwrite the growth of socialism.

In the sciences, realism was embodied by the doctrine of positivism, another reaction against romanticism. Comte's rallying cry of 'Order and Progress' aimed to initiate a new form of religion, or rather it would replace both religion and metaphysics, which were nothing but remnants of a superstitious age that the modern age had exceeded. No longer did we need to concern ourselves with abstract speculations. Positivism was the religion of humanity. The god of this religion was science, which could explain all we needed to know about existence.

In asserting that all real knowledge derives from sense experience and can be scientifically observed as alone constituting reality, positivism implies the notions of progress and evolution that would come to dominate social trends in the second half of the nineteenth century. Various consequences follow: knowledge of the world is restricted to experience of the phenomenon itself;

there can be no symbolic meaning or interpretation; everything is explainable by empirical investigation; life is a purely physical activity consisting only of what is visible. The visible is given shape within a particular chronological period and can be understood through a convincing and objectively established presentation of the milieu. No idea affects this presentation; only what is instantaneous and apparent to consciousness exists. As it took shape in the novel, realism was thereby concretised as a representation founded in the reality of the indivisible self, making the verisimilitude of character and milieu the establishing criteria for the veracity of works of art. Fundamental to this movement, therefore, was the view that the self could be regarded as a coherent, indivisible and continuous whole. As such, characters in fiction need to be plausible, and the situation needs to be established in such a way that a clear reciprocity exists between the configuration of the marked surface and the object it represents. Realists both in the arts and in the sciences were concerned with scientific portrayal of the world so forcefully that it has tended to govern the unfolding of culture in unexpected ways.

This has not occurred due to the force of the idea itself; indeed realism as a specific doctrine is not convincing. In the arts, its limitations were soon revealed: in painting, impressionism was to reveal that the attempt to capture immediate sense impressions leads beyond the strictures of realist portrayal into abstraction (a trend that reaches its logical conclusion in the work of Mondrian, which essentially restores to realism its original meaning: the exploration of universals). Indeed, in many ways its prestige comes from the fact that most movements that have followed it (such as symbolism, expressionism, surrealism) have defined themselves against realism and have taken shape as a challenge to it. In addition, in the sciences, disparate findings such as Freud's elaboration of the unconscious and ideas of latent meaning, Einstein's theory of relativity, the findings of quantum physics or the studies of perception conducted by gestalt psychology made it scientifically impossible to accept sense impressions at face value as – in themselves – constituting reality, but they still did not provide the necessary methodological challenge to realism that would have resulted in a paradigmatic shift.

Such findings, therefore, as much as they may undercut the fundamental principles of realism, have done little to undermine its underpinning in modern society. If realism as an idea has little ontological foundation, it has established the framework within which contemporary culture has unfolded, if only to the extent, due to the very fact that most developments within culture have been directed *against* realism, that the discursive authority of realism has remained intact and in one way or another debates about realism are still central to current concerns.

The most astute defender of realism is still probably Georg Lukács, who elucidates the essence of the realist attitude in its most sophisticated form. In Lukács, we see the assumption of reality to the realm of the practical writ large. He shows how, in realism, reality is equated with the social formations actually existing in the world. The task of the realist is to recognise such formations in their integrality: 'What matters is that the slice of life shaped and depicted by the artist and experienced by the reader should reveal the relation between appearance and essence without the need for any external commentary' (Lukács, 1977: 33). Thus the need to 'depict the vital, but not immediately obvious forces at work in objective reality' (1977: 47–8). This means that the realist artist or researcher is necessarily outside what they depict: they must engage critically with given reality and reconstitute it in such a way that it can be acted upon.

As Adorno (1977) shows, however, there is a problem here in that to make this assertion, Lukács must conflate the status of the representation with that of reality itself. Art, for instance, becomes nothing but the sum total of what it represents, and Lukács fails to see that this reduces to the level of illusion what is in fact part of reality, having its own status *as a representation* within the structure of reality: in other words, that it must be seen as having an ontological status distinct from what it portrays. For Lukács, in effect, the means by which art or science is expressed is nothing but a sort of divining rod enabling the artist or scientist to recognise and realise the 'truth' of the thing to be represented.

Admittedly, Lukács is far from being a vulgar realist, accepting only the tangibility of what is empirically present. Reality is not the immediate, but is founded in a play between appearance and essence (indeed it is the purpose of the realist to bring attention to such interplay):

> Great realism . . . does not portray an immediately obvious aspect of reality but one which is permanent and objectively more significant, namely man in the whole range of his relations to the real world, above all those which outlast mere fashion. Over and above that, it captures tendencies of development that only exist incipiently and so have not yet had the opportunity to unfold their entire human and social potential. (Lukács, 1977: 48)

This concept of realism is dynamic, but it still parcels the world up and abstracts the real from people's subjective experiences of it: if we have 'a relation to the real world', then it follows that we do not ourselves constitute that world. This may be said to be the fundamental principle of the realist attitude: the will to act on the world rather than to view the world and oneself as interpenetrating realities.

It is this point that Adorno latches on to in showing how 'Art and reality can only converge if art crystallizes out its own formal laws, not by passively accepting objects as they come' (1977: 160). Where Lukács saw the modern attitude, at least the modernist reaction against realism, as a turning away from real problems, and a capitulation to the alienation of everyday life, Adorno considered that the artist needed to transcend the condition of loneliness in the modern world in order to reveal a truth that is common to all people. The central aim should be to make form and content one. Adorno, indeed, sees Lukács' view of realism to involve a much greater sense of alienation than that of the modernist artist, since it implies an elemental alienation of the artist from the sources by which the creative act is generated: such an artist (or scientist) must assume a separation from what is being depicted or analysed that must of necessity make of the final work an abstraction.

The primary difficulty faced by a realist attitude is that it is unable to hold together its claims towards reality other than provisionally: in striving for a comprehensiveness of experience and meaning, the very means by which this is to be achieved is being constantly interpreted and manipulated, both by individuals and by cultures, in strategic ways that must in their very nature involve omissions and classifications of the data that undermine this very aspiration for comprehensiveness. And this means that since realism cannot be conceptualised other than ideologically, it can also not be separated from personal, social and political motivations. Realism is nothing but one group of depictions whose representations have no more claim than any other to reveal what actually exists. As such it is not a form of objective portrayal but a rhetorical device whose assertion that it is able to view the world in an objective way is false. Yet it is still a discourse whose conventions act as dominant and dominating patterns that remain central to the Western sensibility, and that refuses to accept the legitimacy of contrary views. While it may claim to offer an objective portrayal of reality and to have a status as authenticity, striving to communicate not simply what is there but also the social realities within that world, it is fundamentally reductive and restrictive, not to say *prescriptive*. In particular, in order to present what appears to be an unmediated view, it must conceal the stylistic devices and the processes by which it constructs its world view. But the fact remains that it is still a construction that, in seeking to be objective and yet retain a physical and emotional distance from its subject, lays claim to being an immediate form of representation that bypasses – or strives not to acknowledge – the process of representation itself and, consequently, that denies the reality that lies *within* the representation as such.

In these terms, realism undoubtedly owes its ascendancy as a discourse crucially to the invention of an effective photographic process in 1839, something that both reflected a new world view and made it possible. While there was nothing very revolutionary, or even new, about the camera, whose principle and workings had been known for centuries in the form of the camera obscura, the development of photography was to have enormous ramifications. What was important was the fact that it offered a way for the external world to be easily copied in the form of an image. It was not even so much the principle of reproduction that was new in 1839 as the possibility of infinite reproduction, the fact that, once an image was established, it could be copied again and again. The full consequences of this were probably not fully appreciated until a century later when Walter Benjamin, writing in the 1930s, brought attention to them. At first photography was seen as one scientific discovery among many, a development that would, like the microscope or telescope, add another means of examination of the world to the inventory of items the scientist could utilise. Photography was initially seen as part of mechanisation, a technical means to record the exact likeness of things and then of people. It was a recording device to give a permanent image of the actual nature of things, whether it be a person, a landscape or a scene from daily life. As it became more accessible as a technique, so it soon became popular as a means of providing people with personal mementoes of them-selves and their friends. The fact that such images could themselves also be copied was not at first perceived as being significant. It is only now that we can see that it was this that has made possible all of the technical achieve-ments in the realm of media and communications, from film to the internet.

As the photograph gave a perfect image of the world, so it was seen to render an art of imitation obsolete and usher in possibilities for accurate recording of the objective world that proponents of realism were quick to seize upon. As the Belgian painter Antoine Wiertz was to proclaim in 1855:

> The fame of our age was born a few years ago: a machine which, day in and day out, has been the astonishment of our thought and the terror of our eyes. Before a century has passed, this machine will be the brush, palette, colours, grace, experience, patience, dexterity, sureness, hue, varnish, sketch, completion, extract of painting. . . . If you do not believe that the daguerreotype kills art, well, when the daguerreotype, this giant child, has grown up, when all its art and strength have been revealed, then genius will suddenly slap a hand on the back of its neck and call out loud: Here, you belong to me now! (in Benjamin, 1999: 526–7)

Baudelaire was among those who reacted angrily to such a view. Writing two years later, he lamented that

> a new industry has emerged, contributing not a little to confirm stupidity in its belief and wreck what might remain divine. The idolatrous mob demanded an ideal worthy of itself . . . [a] creed of the refined. . . : I believe in Nature, and I believe only in Nature. . . . I believe that art is, and can be nothing other than, the exact reproduction of Nature. . . . A vengeful God has heeded the voice of the crowd. Daguerre becomes its messiah. The faithful say to themselves: 'Since photography gives every guarantee of exactitude we could desire (they really believe this, the idiots!), then photography and art become the same thing.' From that moment our squalid society rushed, Narcissus like, to gaze at its image on a piece of scrap metal . . . .

The views of Wiertz and Baudelaire essentially sum up the two sides of the argument and reveal the extent to which what was at stake was the represen-tation and – more significantly – the status of reality. They also reveal the extent to which this debate is still with us, as the frame of reference and the substance of the argument – even if the subject matter at issue has shifted from the portrayal of nature to the desirability of forms of communication – are fundamentally the same as that which today is centred on the cultural consequences of the computer.

Photographic reproduction undoubtedly did serve to change the way people thought about art and representation of the world in general. There can be little doubt that its immediate impact was to contribute to turning people against romanticism and become more realistic in their depictions. (What was the point of trying to make the invisible visible when photography could lay out for us all that really existed?) The transparency of the image thus reflected the transparency of the world: reality came to be equated with what was immediately perceptible. Even though, in the longer term, it caused artists to turn away from crude realism and seek elements within reality that photographs could not reveal, so opening the way for what we now call 'modern art' (which reveals that a gap exists between what a photograph can show by reproduction and what an artist can reveal through using the materiality of the medium – whether through the actual painting process itself or by eschewing painting altogether, as in conceptual art – to bring together form and content and make the representation itself, or the means by which it is effected, the central motive point), the invention of photography nevertheless still served to provide us with a framework by which we judge what exists and what does not. It is in this that the realist attitude is founded and which remains with us today, no matter how unsatisfactory it may appear to us to be as a way of explaining the world. It is because we believe implicitly in the authority of the image revealed through photography – often against our better judgement – that we are swayed into accepting the uses by which photography intrudes into our personal space, instituting a process of capture and effect that allows us to use it as a surveillance device that can be a valuable aid in establishing the winner of an athletics race, in catching a criminal or in providing evidence of our own existence. In the process, our personal photograph becomes coterminous with what we are, so that a passport without a photograph is invalid. Photography thus comes to be seen to offer a snapshot (a resonant word) of life that displays everything and reveals society in terms of both its consistency and materiality and yet, paradoxically perhaps, opens up its contradictions. The photographic image also goes beyond Kantian transcendentalism, which indicated that knowledge was limited to the human senses, and, by offering us the opportunity to examine what escapes the eyes, reveals the world to us in marvellous detail (although at the same time it divests everything so examined of anything that responds to the other senses, leading to a privileging of visual evidence, which in turn it restricts to a particular perspective).

And in this, by showing how it was by disclosing the possibility of infinite reproduction that photography initiated the modern media and their potential, Benjamin revealed that where previously the image had been precious and unique, unreproducible in any convenient and accurate way, now it became a simple matter to retain an image of virtually anything: reality became not simply what could be perceived, but what could be captured in the form of a precise image. In the process, what Benjamin called the 'aura' of the work of art was brought into question. It became a commodity, available for a mass audience, so that everyone could participate in the process of making and appreciating 'art'.

Photography thus had a paradoxical effect. It opened up a world of representations, allowing everything to be revealed, captured in its moment of actuality and rendered susceptible to infinite transmission, but, by that very process, it encouraged the realist distrust of the power that images have. Realism reinforced the Christian condemnation of the autonomous image. As we have seen, the embodiment of the world in Christianity has been through the word, rather than through the image. Being the unmediated truth of God, the word should be transparent. As such it is not a representation. With the invention of photography, the possibility of making the image transparent (that is, taking it out of the Platonic realm of appearance and giving it the authority of the word) meant that it became able to challenge the ascendency of the truth claims of the word. Because the camera is transcendent of human perception (and can reveal what exists but is outside the range of human visual capacity), what it records legitimates the realist attitude and makes representation one with perception. In this respect the realist attitude unwittingly gave rise to a problematic of representation and the status of the image that has been gnawing away for over a century before coming to the fore in recent debates, especially those surrounding postmodernism. This raises the question of how we perceive the world and what a 'true' representation of it is.

The invention of an effective photographic process had a deceptive effect, inducing people to believe that, because the camera is an instrument whose working is apparently independent of human intervention, it offers an accurate and objective record of an existing reality. This gave us to believe that we could take the world as a solid entity. Did the evidence provided by photography not give clear proof of it? Even if it is admitted that any photograph is the result of human agency, that the camera does not itself take pictures, and that every photograph must to a greater or lesser extent be manipulated by the photographer, there remains a common belief that what the final photograph actually reveals is an objective record of something that exists or existed at the moment the photograph was taken. While there is a recognition that we must be careful to understand and be aware of the ways in which a photograph might be manipulated or distorted, the photograph retains today an authority based on the fact that it *should* reveal actuality. If it does not, it is due to the mendacity, the lack of skill or the bad luck of the photographer. The real difficulty with this, though, is that the camera is an instrument designed by humans to reveal what our senses would expect to find. It may extend and refine our perceptions, but it cannot escape from our assumptions about what the world looks like: if someone invented a machine that revealed a world completely different from what our senses tell us it is like, it is obvious we should reject it. We are therefore condemned always to work with representations that follow our perception of the world, and have no way of knowing how accurate to reality those perceptions are. The profound influence of the enculturation process must also be taken into account. As we have already seen, our perception of the world is tied in with the way in which we are enculturated into it, and indeed it seems that perceiving the one-dimensional patterns on paper that we call photographs to represent the actual world does not at all come naturally but has to be learned – people who see photographs for the first time are bemused by them and have to be shown how they work. This tends to suggest that there is no pure perception separated from representation. Everything we perceive requires to be represented in order to be present to our sense of reality. Yet saying this does not necessarily take us back to Kantian transcendental categories. What it does clearly indicate, however, is that reality is not as realism would have us believe. The world is indeed unknowable in its own terms, for the process by which we are initiated into society inevitably means that we impose our social and perceptual categories on to it. Contra Kant, however, those social and perceptual categories remain determined by whatever material reality really is, even if we cannot know it as such: they are not pulled out of the air by our perceptual apparatus.

This raises questions of central importance to the study of culture and the relationship between different cultural forms. Our understanding of how cultures come to know one another is very different depending on whether we consider perception to be always the same for all people or whether it may be affected by differences in circumstances or values. The realist attitude – supported by the evidence of photography – would like to believe that there is a basic perception that is shared by all humans. Yet even if we do share the same perception of the world – and this remains by no means certain, for, as we have seen, there are reasons to doubt the accuracy of the photographic record – the value we assign to what we perceive may be very different in different cultural contexts. The ways in which perception is communicated – that is, by means of representation – are similarly complex. In today's world, dominated as it is by visual images that often work by manipulating complex codes of representation, it is important to understand how such representation is being established.

Representation creates a problem for realism in that a realist attitude, taking reality as transparent, does not accept the reality of the representation by which that reality is reproduced. As Adorno indicated in his critique of Lukács, it elides the status of representation, making it merely an empty carrier for whatever message it contains. Where the romantics tried to expose the emptiness of representation, opening it out in order to reveal its symbolic mechanism as a means of revelation, for realists representation was one with the perception of the world. If this is an untenable position, since it can clearly be demonstrated that a distinction must be made between the nature of reality, the perception we have of it, and the way in which we communicate that perception by means of representation, realism conceals the problem under cover of an Enlightenment claim to be seeking the truth of representation: if there is a gap between reality, perception and representation, it is one based on an erroneous movement between them rather than being inherent in the relationship between ourselves and the world. For the realist, the human being employs representation in order to communicate a basic reality. We may do so in an imperfect way, but this is not such to provide us with an elemental problem. The aim should be to make representation as transparent as possible in order to allow it to contain the truth factor of the world. This involves an assumption of a direct correspondence between the mode of representation and reality that can be established and revealed. A representation is therefore a mirroring of a timeless, objective reality. This requires that it denies itself as representation. And it provides us with another reason why language has traditionally been seen in the West as being able more accurately to capture the nature of the world than has the visual image, which contains the problematic of representation within it more obviously than does language. Can such a view, however, satisfy us?

Our senses do not immediately grasp the world around us: they probe it and construct it in ways that make sense to us. The way we perceive the objects around us seems straightforward, for perception happens so fast that we are unaware of how complex a process it really is. Yet complex it is, and in considering this complexity we raise numerous issues relating to the problematic of representation. In the first place, our senses receive too much information, far too much for them to access. It is therefore necessary for all sorts of irrelevant information to be screened out of consciousness in order to make the perception effective for us. Perception is therefore an active process of editing: our senses do not respond passively to the data presented to us, but act on them in ways that are complicated and sometimes beguiling and largely beyond our control. In such a process, how do we make a distinction between what are objective and what are subjective data?

Perception does not exist in itself and is not solely generated from within us by our senses. It is also dependent upon the ways in which the world is represented to us by others. What we perceive is often not what is actually there but what we think should be there because we have been induced to believe it is by means of a complex of representations. Our representations, too, are not and can never be innocent and value-free. They are also in turn affected by our perception, so that a double movement is involved that establishes an inextricable link whereby perception and representation are each constitutive of the other.

It is commonly stated these days that there is a 'crisis of representation'. What exactly is meant by this? Until probably the 1960s the question of representation was hardly an issue. Insofar as it was considered at all, it was a fairly abstruse philosophical problem. In particular, both the empirical and realist traditions have taken representation largely for granted as being simply an empty carrier by means of which data are transmitted. This assumes that representation is the measure of reality and does no more than provide a means of mediation between experience and the actually existing world. The main issue was the validity and classification of evidence, not the process by which representation was effected. In recent years, however, the collapse of the certainties about the neutrality of representation has increased to such an extent that representation has itself become a major subject of study in the recognition that, far from being neutral, it is constitutive of meaning and often in a powerful way.

The complexity of issues raised here can be focused by consideration of colour. Colour is at the root of all of our perception and representation of the world. It is necessary for us to be able to have access to colour in order to make any sense of the world. It is impossible to imagine a world in which there was no colour, or where everything was the same colour. In such a world sight would be useless for we would be able to see virtually nothing: in a completely white world the only distinctions we could make in the world would be between the shadings of sunlight and we should exist in a world of time without space in which the world around us would be uniform and lacking in visual contour and shape. We should have to find our way around by touch and our perception of the world would be irrevocably different. We would be as if blind – infinitely more blind than the blind in our own world, in fact, because at least the blind have some access to the world of sight by the representations that the sighted make to them of it – and it is difficult to see how we would be able to exist at all. Without going deeply into either the philosophy or the psychology of colour (both of which are extremely complex), it is easily apparent that perception of colour is a key aspect of the way we respond to the world. But what is colour? There is a simple answer to this question: no one knows. The only things that seem to be agreed upon are negatives: colour is not what we actually see and it is not an objective property of physical objects. It is assumed, but not known, that physical objects do not have the colours they are perceived as having. Equally, there is no way of knowing whether we all objectively perceive the same colours. We agree that the colour of leaves on a tree are green, not pink, but what you see as green, I may see as pink. We agree not in terms of what we perceive, only on a code by which it may be represented: the colour of leaves is green and this distinguishes it from red flowers. The colour code is therefore symbolic. What we each accept is a system of codification that distinguishes the graduations between colours. Colour blindness does not contradict this but reinforces it. People who are colour blind are unable to see particular elements in the colour spectrum. We know they are colour blind not because they see colours differently from normal, but because they see inconsistently. Someone who is blind to green will still see leaves as green because he has learned that they are green. They are colour blind only to unfamiliar objects: seeing a book with a green cover in a library, for instance, they will mistake its colour. What we can say about colour, therefore, is that it is a dispositional property that is perceiver-independent in some way. And that it has some objective quality whose actual nature is obscured from us. The substance of what it is escapes us.

These difficulties can be further exemplified by comparing the nature of colour with the nature of pain, which raises similar problems. Where is pain located? We may experience it in a particular part of the body. So we say 'my arm hurts'. However, the pain is not literally in the arm. This can be shown by the example of phantom limbs, when people who have had an arm amputated still experience pain in that arm, and also by the fact that no pain will be felt if nerve endings in an organ are diverted away from the brain. Does this mean that it is located in the brain, then? This, too, is unsatisfactory, for pain will not be experienced if the sense of touch is in some way interrupted – as for instance when an organ is anaesthetised – even though the brain itself is unaffected. In some way pain is produced through the relationship between the brain and the rest of the body, by a process that remains mysterious. But we are aware of the physical properties of our bodies primarily through the sensation of pain. If we do not feel pain, then we would be unaware of serious injuries. This of course is one of the great dangers of leprosy: people lose their sensations and can severely damage their bodies without being aware of the fact. In a similar way colour is essential in order for us to distinguish between physical objects. If objects did not have colour, then we would be unable to distinguish them by sight: they would appear as they do in the dark, where they can be distinguished only by touch or smell or taste. What also connects pain and colour is that both are virtual properties that are not physically present. Their reality is thus 'representational'. They are virtual properties that are not physically present.

This means that both function as sensory ideas or representations with a content of their own. They act as mediating representations between ourselves and our perception of the world but not in a way that simply provides us with information about the world as such; they also intervene to structure our perceptions. And we are dependent upon the representations they establish for our construction of the world. Just as we should be unable to see if there was no colour, so if we did not feel pain we should not be able to experience our own bodies. In order to survive, if we could, we would have to learn a completely different way of relating to the world.

To think about the problem in these terms also alerts us to the fact that in their role as mediating elements both pain and colour reveal the extent to which we have difficulty in experiencing the world directly. We know an object only through its appearance as it is established by means of its variations of colour. Equally, we know the wound only through the mediation of pain. In acting as representations, both act as signals to enable us to interact with the world that surrounds us. Without the use of such representations our perception would be fundamentally different, if we could perceive at all.

Equally, colour is part of a culturally and socially established symbolic system; it is not merely an isolated representation. Lacking a code and symbolic system, other animals may have the ability to distinguish colours as such. What they are not able to do is to draw meaning from the colours seen. They do not respond to a code. It is only when they do so that culture can be said to begin. To use the analogy with colour blindness mentioned earlier, an animal is unable to recognise a leaf as being green because greenness is a human symbol. It may recognise the distinction between a green leaf and a red flower, and to this extent it represents the colour to itself, but only to itself. It does not make of it a symbol that can in any way be communicated. To do this, it would need to name the colour and so establish a cultural system. An animal that is colour blind to green, seeing it as red, would never be able to correct its perception, lacking the symbolic code that tells it that a leaf is green. For humans, however, everything we see, hear, feel, touch and taste has the potential for symbolic use. And it is through such symbolic use that communication between us becomes possible. It also serves to separate us from the world. One might even say that the distinction between self and other begins at that point. Aware of ourselves as separate entities, we need to create bridges in order to communicate. These bridges are what we call symbols. Perception is created through a collaborative effort between all five of our senses. This very fact brings into question the realist model that presupposes a transparency between perception and reality in which perception merely reveals what is there. Instead, it is very clear that what is actually 'there', insofar as it can be known, is located for us as a construction made from a consolidation of sense data that is given solidity by the process of perception and representation as much as by the fact that it really exists. It is for this reason that Lacan located everyday life as being the realm of the symbolic as opposed to the imaginary or the real. Irrespective of whether one accepts Lacan's schema in all of its implications, there seems little reason to doubt that this symbolic realm is a determining one for our socio-cultural reality. It becomes necessary, therefore, to look more closely at what exactly is meant by a 'symbol'.

Symbols can be recognised by several factors. As a representation, the symbol is characterised by the fact that it conveys meaning in multiple ways. This distinguishes it from a pure representation. A representation that merely represents is a sign in a neutral form, as we saw in looking at the difference between a sign and a symbol. It is through such meaning that culture is constituted. Culture is thus a web of significances made up from symbols. The *meaning* of a symbol is therefore not an object, having no existence in itself. It only exists in relation to other symbols. It is a construction that can only be understood through its use, and it is from this that social and cultural formations take their characteristic patterns. No symbol has meaning out of the context in which it is to be found. Were it possible to make representation a transparent communicative form as realism would like, it would require the elimination of the symbol: everything would have to be reduced to the level of a sign.

This returns us to further consideration of how the realist attitude continues the distrust of the image characteristic of Western thought by, as we have seen, elevating the image to pure perception conveying a transparent message that traditionally was seen as the prerogative of the word. In his general understanding of representation, Plato made a distinction between appearance and reality that gave representation a status as a mere appearance, suggesting a reality through imitation. Plato therefore argued that a painter, for instance, creates an artificial world. He does not create a real tree, but the mere appearance of one. This was the basis of his expulsion of the poet and the painter from his ideal republic, for Plato insisted that we should not succumb to the lure, or seduction, of images, but seek the reality that the image hides. Painting gained its legitimacy from the fact that it *merely* represented. It did not contain truth within it. Realism takes its substance from this view. It is for this reason, too, that scientific research has sought to deny the problematic of representation, treating its own representations as transparent and direct. Hence the view that the act of writing about culture is purely an objective act of recording reality. Reality in this view exists out there. All the researcher has to do is to reach out and grasp it. This attitude may be expressed in these terms: 'I will tell you what I have witnessed, which is true because I have witnessed it.'

Yet Plato seemed not to recognise that the very discourse by which he made his assertion of the falsity of representation was itself a representation. He was himself guilty of the very fault he perceived in painters to the extent that he used representational signs in everyday conversation. For, as representation, words are as dependent upon symbolic meaning as images. A language restricted to representational signs that conveyed a clear and distinct (or unambiguous) meaning would be able to *say* little. It would certainly be unable to engage in the sort of philosophical speculation characteristic of the Platonic dialogue. Indeed, to condemn symbolic representation in this way is to condemn human culture for, as we have seen, it is only by means of such representations that culture becomes possible. This alerts us to the fact that Plato's condemnation – like the Christian condemnation of idolatry or indeed the realist condemnation of metaphysical and romantic speculation – was ideologically motivated, in his case against his Sophist opponents.

Here is the point at which the 'crisis of representation' in contemporary discourse comes to the fore. The postmodernist and post-structuralist concern with representation is a mirroring of the realist attitude: where the realist denied the reality of representation, the postmodernist insists upon it.

There have been many strands to this, but the essential issue in the context we are considering here turns on the authority of textual evidence. As a reaction to what Derrida has felicitously called the 'metaphysics of presence', the discourse that is loosely defined as postmodernism has sought in multifarious ways to address the problematic of representation. Critical consideration of the phenomenon of postmodernism has tended to concentrate on its relation to modernism (is it a break with modernism, its continuation, or has it created modernism as something against which to measure itself?). It may, however, be more profitable to see it not in relation to modernism but as a continuation – a further refinement – of modernist responses to realism. Where modernism interrupted the transparency of realist discourse by pointing to its omissions and failure to encompass a comprehensive sense of reality, postmodernism reverses the realist frame of reference, inserting an opacity of representation asserting that ultimately nothing can ever be true and that we should be content to explore the processes by which representation constructs the world. Dissatisfied with the metanarrative that remains present within modernism as a continuation of the project of Enlightenment, postmodernism fragments or tears apart the textual authority this discourse assumes, collapsing its distinctions into a play of signifiers. In doing so it strives to reinscribe difference into the process of representation, giving a voice to what is other and celebrating difference itself as initiating us into a realm of possibilities that will lead us beyond sterile ideologies founded in a discourse of power and domination. This has led to the tendency for 'reflexivity' in the process of representation: we need to be aware of the context in which we are writing and make explicit the relationship we have with the subject of study.

This impulse is based in a distrust of all truth claims and leads to a view that we should attempt to present no more than, in James Clifford's phrase, 'partial truths', in recognition that the whole truth evades us: 'Strange behavior is portrayed as meaningful within a common network of symbols – a common ground of understandable activity valid for both observer and observed, and by implication for all human groups. Thus ethnography's narrative of specific differences presupposes, and always refers to, an abstract plane of similarity' (Clifford and Marcus, 1986: 101). Far from being a new impulse, however, this deconstruction of the self's specificity is something that is inscribed within Enlightenment itself as a secondary repression. As Adorno stated in a devastating passage: 'The denial of objective truth by recourse to the subject implies the negation of the latter: no measure remains for the measure of all things; lapsing into contingency, he becomes untruth' (1974: 63). Further: 'The ego's unflinching self-criticism gives way to the demand that the ego of the other capitulate' (1974: 64). Adorno's primary target here is psychoanalysis – centred as he sees it in an analytical situation that disintegrates the ego all the better to reconstitute it insidiously in the analyst's terms on the pretext of giving voice to the Other – but it could just as easily be applied to postmodernism. In particular, as Adorno states, the problem here is not representation, but the elevation of man to be the measure of man, something that postmodernism singularly fails to address, or rather that it elides by making representation the measure of humanity.

From this point of view, postmodernism becomes a parody of realism, rejecting its points of reference so that discourse revolves endlessly on itself. This can be seen explicitly in Baudrillard, who, in conceiving simulation as indistinguishable from the real, but yet not real, effectively cancels any criterion of reality at all. But if this is so, can we not reverse the terms of his argument. Since any point of differentiation becomes impossible to determine, could one not just as easily say that there is no longer any such thing as simulation: everything is real?

This perspective draws upon Nietzsche, the Nietzsche who defined truth as a 'mobile army of metaphors', while refusing the problematic he saw in this about the nature of meaning and values. In this respect, the fundamental impulse of postmodernism, that there is nothing outside the text or the simulation, raises its own problematic. For if there is nothing else, how can the text or the simulation exist? Such worlds can be neither self-created nor self-sustaining, or if they could be it would imply a sort of immaculate conception of forms that would collapse under their own weight. In this way we can say that the postmodernist suffers from a parallel delusion to the realist: where Adorno charged Lukács with failing to distinguish between representation and reality, denying to the representation its own status as representation, the postmodernist elevates the representation to the level of reality. Bourdieu has very well expressed the consequences:

> Language as conceived by Saussure, an intellectual instrument and an object of analysis, indeed the dead, written, foreign language referred to by Mikhail Bakhtin, a self-sufficient system, detached from real usage [and] opened the way to all the subsequent research that proceeds as if mastery of the code were sufficient to confer mastery of the appropriate usages, or as if one could infer the usage and meaning of linguistic expressions from analysis of their formal structures. . . . (1990: 32)

In this conflation of the codes by which reality is understood with reality itself, the debates opened up by the 'crisis of representation' do little more than revolve on themselves, returning endlessly to their starting point. The text is given its own integrity and comes to stand in for the nature of those social relations of which it was, at the beginning, only the representation. If this serves to deny the predominance of one view within discourse and promotes multiplicity and dialogue, it does this in such a way as to reduce the nature of the world to an epiphenomenal one of sign structures that become detached from the actual processes of life. Realism as a desire to limit and transcend the possibilities of the real is transformed into a realm of possibilities unconstrained by any reference to reality. What this does is to give intellectual legitimacy to the technological age we are now entering.

By means of technological developments, such as computers, videos, mobile phones, walkmans, the world may be represented to us as immediately present and give us the illusion that we are in touch with the whole of reality. Consequently the way we experience our surroundings is being transformed. In the process, vision and reality are refocused in such a way that the image assumes a new autonomy divorced from a referent in the external world. The image gains the capacity to mediate a shifting reality so that any stable subject and object relation is broken down and a totality of differences is instituted. The objective world comes to be what we represent it to be, an enduring mental construct subject to constant transformation. We are able to control and manage external stimuli, screening out or allowing us to enter the real world as we will. By means of a multiplicity of representation we are present everywhere and yet at the same time and in the same movement absent everywhere.

Despite this, as noted at the beginning of the chapter, we remain under the sway of a reality principle that has changed little. Indeed, the possibility of a 24-hour society that such technological development has made possible fulfils Enlightenment dreams of a triumph of light over darkness and has served to extend the realm over which the reality principle can maintain its sway. Curiously, though, scientists now believe that the condition of the universe is not darkness but light: darkness is only possible because of the expansion of the universe; in a static universe light would be moving in all directions and we would be suffused with unbearable light all around us. The perception that God brought light appears to be false: it is darkness that is the gift that makes life possible, allowing us the time to rest and take our bearings freed from the glare of unrelenting light. In the realisation of Enlightenment claims to illumination that they have brought, therefore, the technological achievements of the contemporary world may be a doubtful blessing.

10

THE TECHNOLOGISATION
OF CULTURE

The development of technology will leave only one problem: the infirmity
of human nature.

Karl Kraus

The modern world offers a realisation of cultural dominance. We can say that
what was started the moment the first person who forged a tool to aid in the
task of dealing with our situation in the world has reached its apogee with
modern developments that promise not simply an enhanced means of production, but mastery over processes of nature and even perhaps over death
itself, if some of the more fanciful claims of proponents of genetic research
are to be believed. The overwhelming light promised by the Enlightenment
finally seems to be perceptible on the horizon.

Culture may begin in technology, if it does not begin in language: the first
tools must, along with the first efforts to speak, have been the foundation of
what made us specifically human. To consider the impact of technology on
culture is therefore to go to its heart, for without technological development,
the development of culture itself is severely circumscribed. Technological
advancement has certainly been one of the motors that has historically transformed society in radical ways, and it is arguable that it has been technology,
rather than the direct strivings of humans, that has caused the revolutionary
changes in society resulting in the modern world, to the extent that technology may be said to be the main determining feature in the evolution of forms
of society. Progress in cultural forms is certainly tied in with technological
development, and we can see a clear line of progression from the very first
tools to the invention of the computer. For this reason we describe successive
periods in terms of their predominant technologies. From the Stone Age, the
Bronze Age to the Industrial Society or the Information Age, we tend now to
define periods not by the actual activity of humans, but by their dominant
form of technology. And this to the extent that in the Information Age, technology has become so advanced that it stands over us in a way that affects our
whole life. Where in the past we used technology unselfconsciously, taking it
as an aid to our own activity, these days we are increasingly aware of technology itself as something we must not simply use, but also *engage with* in
various ways. We need, at this point, therefore, to consider how significant the
new technologies really are that are said to be in the process of transforming
our lives.

It is often claimed that we are witnessing a fresh revolution that will be comparable in terms of its long-term impact to that of the invention of the printing press. The computer, we are told, gives us new possibilities of perception that will transform our lives. In the global economy increased homogenisation is assumed: the computer, it may be argued, democratises us, and has been responsible for the collapse of the totalitarian regimes that dominated much of the world during the twentieth century, and especially after the Second World War. It offers the possibility of immediate communication with virtually any place on earth. And with immediate communication, too, comes instant gratification. We expect our desires to be satisfied at once (or at least those desires that are connected with communication or, more especially, consumption). Available to us in a trice is a vast archive of cultural wealth – we can visit museums on the other side of the world, listen to an array of different music, buy virtually anything, even arrange for sexual gratification, all without leaving our seat and with no more effort than the amount required to press a few buttons on a keyboard. The advantages of such a powerful apparatus are obvious. It frees us from so many trivial tasks, allowing us to concentrate on essentials. Or does it? Not everyone is convinced.

The writer and filmmaker David Mamet recently declared unequivocally: 'I can envision no device more capable of spreading ignorance and illiteracy than the computer. It is, like the atom bomb, a naturally evolved engine of oblivion, a sign, like the Tower of Babel, that civilisation has run its course' (interview in *The Guardian*, 19 February 2000). Is this simply a perverse refusal to accept progress, a nostalgia for a lost past and a denial of present realities? It would be an error to dismiss such a statement so easily, for it raises questions about current technological developments that need to be asked. Will they lead to a liberation of mankind from its menial tasks, opening up a new realm of freedom, or will they create a new slavery, a dependence on mechanical means that will finally serve to destroy us as a species?

It would be vain to deny great possibilities to current technological developments, of which the computer represents the most symptomatic and progressive form. Certainly they give us a much broader opportunity to explore the world around us, to bring us into contact with myriad experiences that could only have been dreamed of by earlier generations. With such possibilities, however, comes a residue. While there is on the one hand an opening of horizons, at the same time, and almost in the same movement, a closure is revealed. The residue is the shadow that, as we have seen, has always dogged Enlightenment claims of revelation; the closure is that unlimited progress is unsustainable.

In the latter respect, it is surely difficult for anyone aware of the history of culture to see technological development continuing on the scale it has over the past two hundred years. It has without doubt outpaced the ability of human beings to keep up with it and it is hard to see how current developments really usher in a new cultural era rather than stand at the end of one. At best, they have brought us to a point at which we need to take stock. At worst they are the logical conclusion of a chain of development that may result in a catastrophe of some sort. How much further can they go without outstripping any human quality at all? Is Mamet right, then, to see the computer as a new version of the Tower of Babel whose much-vaunted potential in fact leads simply to a dead end in which so much information becomes available that nothing any longer will have meaning? The internet, in particular, initiates endless possibilities for empty babbling and includes no restraining constituent able to provide a context that any medium of genuine communication needs to be for long term effectiveness.

While it is certainly true that technology increases our mastery over the world, the fear – expressed in various forms – is that technology itself increasingly comes to dominate us. This is something apparent from the beginnings of technology. As far back as the Stone Age, when the development of tools gave us greater control over nature, but made us dependent upon the very tools we had created, an increasing alienation is installed by each technological advance. Every new invention leaves us in prey to the advance it implies. Nature gods have now been largely replaced in human consciousness by technological ones, which we fear in the same proportion. How we respond to this process depends on the perspective we have on it.

There seems to be no clear consensus about the real implications and consequences of an extensive embrace of technological advance. There is a general optimism, but one that seems unclear about precisely why it is optimistic, and it is combined with a vague and not so often articulated pessimism. Or rather, more accurately, such pessimism, no matter how well articulated, tends to be eliminated by the surge that technological development has created and that itself provides the legitimacy for an esteem that is difficult to question for, however valid doubts about new technologies may be, they can always be swept aside by the comment that 'you can't stop progress'. It is this very phrase that should give us pause for thought. While it is taken for granted and is in many ways a founding principle of our age, a moment's reflection will reveal to us its falsity: unlimited progress is impossible. Far from it not being possible to stop progress, there is little doubt that it will have to be stopped at some point. The issue here is whether progress as we are currently undergoing it is still a natural process or whether it has gained an ideological thrust that maintains it irrespective of its destination. Does our technological optimism simply depend on an unquestioned assumption of the value and possibility of progress or does it have a deeper foundation? Is pessimism merely a part of a natural fear of the unknown, a reluctance to embrace new and unfamiliar ideas?

Marshall McLuhan remains the most celebrated and still perhaps the most typical of those who have written in support of the benefits the new technology may bring. For McLuhan, the really positive aspect of new technology is that it leads to increased access and involvement, allowing all people to participate in society, to shape their own destinies and be freed from the tyranny imposed by an élite culture situated in literacy. Unlike all previous technological advancements, it is not imbued with a fundamental alienation, but includes people and their desires in its movement. And, as the media develop, so they become available to all people to use. McLuhan's argument is perhaps encapsulated in these two quotations:

> [T]he age of anxiety and of electric media is also the age of the unconscious and of apathy. But it is strikingly the age of consciousness of the unconscious, in addition. With our central nervous system strategically numbed, the tasks of conscious awareness and order are transferred to the physical life of man, so that for the first time he has become aware of technology as an extension of his physical body. Apparently this could not have happened before the electric age gave us the means of instant, total field-awareness. With such awareness, the sub-liminal life, private and social, has been hoicked up into full view, with the result that we have 'social consciousness' presented to us as a cause of guilt-feelings. Existentialism offers a philosophy of structures, rather than categories, and of total social involvement instead of the bourgeois spirit of individual separateness or points of view. In the electric age we wear all mankind as our skin. (McLuhan, 1964: 57)
>
> We know from our own past the kind of energy that is released, as by fission, when literacy explodes the tribal or family unit. What do we know about the social and psychic energies that develop by electric fusion or implosion when literate individuals are suddenly gripped by an electromagnetic field. . . .? [T]he products of electric fusion are immensely complex, while the products of fission are simple. Literacy creates very much simpler kinds of people than those that develop in the complex web of ordinary tribal and oral societies. For the frag-mented man creates the homogenized Western world, while oral societies are made up of people differentiated, not by their specialist skills or visible marks, but by their unique emotional mixes. The oral man's inner world is a tangle of complex emotions and feelings that the Western practical man has long ago eroded or suppressed within himself in the interest of efficiency and practicality.
>
> The immediate prospect for literate, fragmented Western man encountering the electric implosion within his own culture is his steady and rapid transforma-tion into a complex and depth-structured person emotionally aware of his total interdependence with the rest of human society. . . . Fragmented, literate, and visual individualism is not possible in an electrically patterned and imploded society. (McLuhan, 1964: 60)

It is worth giving these two lengthy quotations because they express the essence of much of the optimistic reading of where new technologies are leading us. For McLuhan, the invention of printing severely reduced our possibility of participation in society, and the new technologies are a libera-tion from the tyranny of literacy. Instead of an oral culture in which all people participated, the invention of the printing press created the conditions for the hegemony of the visual. Tactile and sensory impressions were dis-counted and humanity had been led astray into individualism. This led to linearity, regularity and uniformity. The possibilities raised by the new tech-nologies challenge this hegemony. The media reorganise life, expanding our senses and nerves in a global embrace: 'The computer, in short, promises by technology a Pentecostal condition of universal understanding and unity' whose next step 'would seem to be, not to translate, but to by-pass languages in favor of a general cosmic consciousness . . .' (1964: 90). The media are thus seen as extensions of our own senses: they are not abstracted from us in the way 'artificial' means of communications like books and films are. The shift is seen between books or films (which McLuhan characterises as 'hot'), which invite detached contemplation, and the telephone or television (cool), which invite involvement and participation. The distinction between high and low culture is abolished, time and space and other constraints are overcome, and the possibility is opened up of a world of leisure and opportunity. This is tied in with the idea that we are leaving an industrial society to enter a techno-logical one based upon the dissemination of information that technology is so adept at making possible.

There is something of value in McLuhan's critique of literacy, but does it really entitle him to draw the conclusions he does about the new technologies? In what way can it be said that these undermine our reliance on literacy? Everything here depends on an assumption that the new technologies repre-sent a new sensibility, but is this really so? Is it not rather the case that electronic media are a culmination rather than a break with the Enlightenment sensibility based in literacy? Equally, while McLuhan may be right to make a distinction between 'hot' and 'cool' media, it is difficult to see how anything other than the opposite conclusions to those he puts forward can be drawn from this. It is surely precisely the non-participatory quality of 'hot' media like photography or cinema that gives them their value: it means that we recognise them for what they are and do not confuse them with an actuality that is other than that of the medium itself. For all that we may con-fuse the representation that the photograph makes of the world with reality itself, we still recognise the representation as representation and do not mis-take it for actuality. The new technologies, however, from television to the computer by way of the telephone and the motor car, obscure this essential separation so that actuality becomes instituted within the medium itself. In the process, life comes to take shape as an extension of oneself into techno-logical forms, rather than as a reciprocal process of recognition occurring among humans mediated by symbolic forms. Far from returning us to the immediacy of oral culture, however, such interaction with technology can give nothing but an illusion of intimacy. There is no reality contained within this process. Rather than making literacy obsolete, it offers no recourse to any other discourse than that established with literacy, indeed to use a computer requires an additional literacy. At this point there seems to be a curious blindness in McLuhan's analysis: he seems to imagine that use of a com-puter can be learned naturally in a way analogous to walking or speaking, rather than being a learned activity reliant upon exactly the same procedures as traditional literacy. The use of a computer even presupposes that we are already literate, so how can it be said to return us to a pre-literate condition of availability? Rather, is not the computer the logical conclusion of the sen-sibility put into play by literacy, taken either to its highest point or to its *reductio ad absurdum*, depending on your point of view. What it certainly does not do, as McLuhan believes it does, is to offer any return back to the inti-macy of oral culture, except in a burlesque sense: there is a certain sadness in the identification that people establish with characters on television whereby what has no reality other than as it is created by the media gains an actuality that is believed in. This is translated into the relationship people have with machines, and especially with their computer or mobile phones, giving them personal names as though they had personalities of their own, something they would never do, I think, with a camera, or even with a television. Does this imply respect for things, a new kind of animism? Not at all. They give machines names as they name their pets, and the essential message is one of control, it is saying 'you belong to me'.

Even though he was writing almost forty years ago, McLuhan remains symptomatic of ways of thinking about new technology both because the superficiality of his thought is itself a reflection of the lazy analysis that technology induces and because he encapsulates a particular way of thinking that is embedded in the American psyche, which is precisely that which dominates computer mentality and has made Silicon Valley the heart of world technological innovation. Combining unbridled optimism and incisive understanding, on the one hand, with a complete disregard for objective conditions (and consequences) that often beggars belief, on the other, this sort of thinking provides a perfect illustration of the way technology induces complacency and blindness. In this respect, McLuhan provides us with a text that perfectly captures the paradoxes inherent in the information age, paradoxes that are so overwhelming and so richly over-determined that they neutralise each other and make it difficult for us to establish a firm footing when dealing with the phenomenon of technological development within culture.

Let us look, therefore, at some of the other assumptions contained within this mentality of technological determinism. It is said that information rather than money is increasingly becoming the real exchange currency. Is there anything new in this? Money has only ever been a symbol of exchange: it has always been information of one sort or another that has been the real content of any process of exchange. It is not that information has not become more important today, but that the processes of information transmission have changed. It is more significant therefore to inquire about the sort of information that technology will promote and how it will differ from information in the past. It is not information that matters. It is not even access to it; it is rather access to the means of *processing* certain types of information in certain types of way. While there seems little doubt that computers and especially the internet will be central to this, it may not be in ways that we now envisage. In fact, for most people, it is difficult to see how, once the initial euphoria has passed, the internet can be anything other than a treasure trove of useless information. Logistically it is now and will always be unable to fulfil one of its main claims, the claim upon which McLuhan based his whole argument, that of unfettered availability to all. With a world population currently at 6 billion people and set to double in the next fifty years, it is surely apparent that no system will ever be able to cope with anything more than a small proportion of such a number of people engaging with it. Even if it could, the consequence would surely be that it would soon contain so much information that it would collapse under its own weight. It can only function in a meaningful way while its information sourcing and utilisation remain restricted to a comparatively small number of people. As it grows it is difficult to see how it can contain all the activity it will encourage. This will inevitably mean that some sort of curbs will have to be introduced to prevent or restrict unlimited access. In this process, it is likely to be made increasingly difficult to use effectively and so will provide the means for a new élite to codify it for their own benefit. The idea that it is a tool for the empowerment of ordinary people is surely a chimera.

Fears about computers tend to be confined to fanciful ideas about artificial intelligence and their potential to take on human qualities. Those who support the use of computers may be right to ridicule such fears, which may reflect little more than a fear of the unknown that has always accompanied technical advances. Yet if such anxiety is unfounded, it still masks a more profound danger.

Advocates of computerisation assume the disinterested quality of technology: it merely serves human interests. This is to deny the active role of the technology, the fact that it contains certain features that direct the way it can be used. No technology is neutral in its impact. It always reflects the society in which it is born and serves its perpetuation. In this respect, Octavio Paz, reviewing *Understanding Media* at the time it was published in 1964, was already stinging as he emphasised the central issue, which is even more immediate to us now and which we too often refuse to address:

> The systems of the past . . . were at once a criticism of reality and an image of another reality. They were a vision of the world. Technology is not an image of the world but a way of operating on reality. The nihilism of technology lies not only in the fact that it is the most perfect expression of the will to power . . . but also in the fact that it lacks meaning. *Why?* and *To what purpose?* are questions that technology does not ask itself. What is more, it is not technology, but we ourselves, who should be asking these questions. (1974: 160).

In noting the failure to ask these questions, Paz rightly identifies the way the new technology is considered, and which differentiates it from all earlier forms.

The problem, of course, is not computers, but our attitude towards them. Or more precisely, it is the way in which our attitude to computers both emerges from and influences the social expectations we have in our day-to-day lives. They have become, as Paz noted, not an image of the world, but the realisation of wish-fulfilment in a purely passive way: they give us the illusion that they are providing us with a means of control over our lives. Yet in giving us access to such a wealth of information, they are also creating a need that we are expected to have and to satisfy. We are given no choice about whether we want this source of information, which, as Paz rightly notes, is nihilistic in its function, giving no point of reference for what its significance might be, thus voiding its impact. What matters rather is the consumption of the information itself irrespective of its content. We are encouraged to consume, and our social processing increasingly demands that we seek out ever more sensations and experiences without questioning their value or the need we have for them. The experience in and of itself, separated from all that surrounds it, determines our rationale for existing. We are expected to take pleasure in the experience itself rather than placing it in the context of a life experience that responds to its reality in terms of where it has come from and where it will lead. A disjunction is imposed in which every experience is discrete, offered to us as an entity that is to be appreciated for what it is and nothing else. This rapacity for the accumulation of experience and the things that encapsulate it, the openness to possibilities that are dazzling only in their lack of contextualisation, leads to a profusion that is ultimately profoundly disappointing. Symptomatic here is no doubt the growing acceptance of drug-taking, perhaps the one custom in modern society that retains a religious dimension, serving the function of a transgressive action that serves the dominant order. The anguished heart-searching that occurs over the increasing use of drugs barely conceals a cynical complicity in the unspoken recognition of how effective both legal and illegal drug-use is for the maintenance of social cohesion in the contemporary world. It is well known that the innovations in the development of computers in Silicon Valley emerged from the drugs cultures of southern California, and the realisation of the new technologies promises to deliver just the sort of totalitarian illumination that is inscribed in the casual use of drugs that today stands as a kind of ersatz religious experience.

This ideology of information that does not inform has been well explored by Baudrillard, whose analysis remains important, as much as one might deplore the cynical and opportunist posturing that goes with it. Baudrillard's work owes much to McLuhan and provides a critical commentary on it that brings into question much of its optimistic gloss. Ignoring the critique of literacy that underlies McLuhan's argument, Baudrillard takes as given his general interpretation of media technology, but critically reinterprets his conclusions as to where this will lead. Instead of offering an opening to communication, Baudrillard perceives a closure of communication and a self-sustaining system of signs connected together by other signs. Nothing can be allowed to interfere with this flow of signs, not even production, which ceases to respond to needs, but rather creates needs that signify status and singularity. Instead of being individuals interacting in society – either acting in terms of self-interest, as in classic liberalism, or in terms of a manifestation of Spirit, in the Hegelian sense – each of us becomes a cog in a system that is self-sustaining and able to contain any dissidence; in fact dissidence is necessary for the effective functioning of the system and inscribed within it. It demands that we make decisions in terms of set values, as an image of what we think we want to be rather than in terms of economic need or genuine desire. We are carefully manipulated to form only those types of image that serve the sign system, which itself is sufficiently flexible to accept a wide variation of different images that transgress its criteria; indeed it encourages such transgression in order to expand its field of operation, knowing that its structures are sufficiently strong to contain them and turn them to its own advantage. There is therefore no point in resisting the processes of the modern media; it is better to go along with them and accept them for what they are.

Baudrillard both is more intelligent than McLuhan and has a carefully honed sense of irony entirely absent in the latter, but in the final analysis he is just as superficial and his work shares with McLuhan's the fact that it is as much a symptom of the society on which it commentates as a critique of it. The difficulty is that Baudrillard is unable to see anything outside the system of media dominance he regards as defining the reality of today's society. It may be true that this system determines the flow of modern society. However, it does not control it and has nothing like the all-encompassing power that Baudrillard perceives in it.

The supposed dominance of the computer is revealed by its use in remote areas, and those who see it as a means for liberation often cite the sophisticated use made by the Zapatistas of the internet as a weapon in their struggle against the Mexican government and the power of international capital. While there is something undeniably impressive in the way that they have been able to use technology, two crucial factors should be borne in mind. First, that they have access to this technology is only due to sympathisers from the United States. Second, and more importantly, while they may be able to support their struggle more effectively by means of the internet, the fact remains that the struggle became so urgent because their livelihood has been brought into question by an international situation made possible by precisely these new technologies. Furthermore, the internet is little more than a sideshow in their real struggle and no doubt impinges very little on their everyday lives. It may even be argued that it does little more than allow them to tell us directly how much we are exploiting them, making us direct spectators of their plight; it hardly seems to have helped in any way to alleviate their situation. All technological advance – and this is the case in all of human history – favours the ruling powers in one way or another (it may be to the advantage of one section at the expense of others and so allow important changes in the structure of society, but this will always support those already in positions of power). The situation of the people of Chiapas – or of any other group existing outside the narrow confines of the global economy – is certainly not determined by simulated media images, but responds to a reality that is all too present.

Yet the process Baudrillard describes undoubtedly exists and it does impose itself as the dominant discourse of the age. Soon, it is suggested, if you do not have access to a computer, you will not exist. It is for this reason that computer literacy has been so much touted in the Western world, accompanied by dire warnings for those who might be left out of this process. Like any form of literacy, however, the ability to use a computer will undoubtedly lead to the loss of others and will change the status of information that is available to literacy. In particular, the reliance on the mediation of the machine involves the risk of a lack of experiential awareness and has a tendency to initiate a consciousness that only accepts as real what has been given by the machine. Anything not verified by the media will be void. This will include all of those people who remain outside its structures and will doubtless mean the vast majority of people in the world will be wiped from our consciousness as conclusively as if they had been eliminated by an atom bomb. It is no doubt partly in this respect that Mamet sees the computer as having an analogous effect to the bomb. It will establish new relations of inclusion and exclusion, emphasising certain things at the expense of others. In particular, it is almost certain to magnify the alienation and commodification of modern society, not to mention the wealth differentials existing within it, reducing human intimacy to a parody of itself.

Of course, Baudrillard claims that the media revolution means the end of alienation: it offers us the means to participate fully in society, even if the terms of reference on offer are ultimately unsatisfying. Equally, those making more extravagant claims for the value of computer communication still cling to a McLuhanite faith in its ability to restore to us a sense of real intimacy that will transcend the alienation of contemporary life. In a world in which it is so difficult to make personal contact and find people who share one's own interests, the internet offers us the possibility of by-passing problems of how to make personal contact. While it can hardly be denied that computers are able to act as aids to communication in many ways, it still remains that such contact will be mediated by the machine. It will always lack any knowledge of intimacy, because the world the computer contains is a world of distance. It may be able to duplicate the feelings of sight and sound, it might even simulate smell or taste, but it will never be able to give more than an unsatisfactory representation of our most primary sense: touch. Touch is the sense of intimacy and, ultimately, of genuine desire. This is not something that can be replicated for easy consumption. To establish genuine intimacy requires effort and sensitivity to the dynamics of anguish and loss that ultimately are the determinants of all human communication. Far from transcending alienation, it is difficult to see how the computer can ever do any more than emphasise our fundamental alienation from the actuality of the world, reducing us to the role of spectators. We are placed in a position in which we can never participate in anything directly, but are always on the outside looking in.

As Kevin Robins explains: 'Technologies function to mediate, to defer, even to substitute for, interaction with the world. We use them to avoid contact with the world and its reality. Through contact we risk feeling the world as alien; through the sense of touch we risk exposure to its chaotic or catastrophic nature' (1996: 19). With this statement, Robins locates the difficulty involved here: that alienation is inscribed within the function of new technologies. While we shall no doubt from time to time hear stories of people meeting one another through the internet and living happily ever after, it is difficult to see how this could ever happen due to the mediation of the machine rather than despite it. This is because the knowledge we establish of the other person through the computer is fundamentally distorted, cutting out all knowledge of them they do not want us to know and giving no information that would allow any of our senses other than sight and perhaps hearing (the two least reliable and most easily deceived senses) to make any decisions about who they are.

Insofar as the media age in general can provide closeness, it is only against the background of a preliminary distancing. We may not always notice this distance, but it remains there. The effect of this is to seem to close down the distance that in fact exists between ourselves and phenomena existing external to us and to create the illusion of intimacy. This initiates a refusal to lose, so that we now speak of 'win, win situations', and refuse to accept the necessity for loss. We see this in all walks of life, so that athletes train not so much against one another as against the physical limits of their own bodies, businesses compete not primarily against one another but against self-established targets, and so on. We all participate in this process, identifying with sports and film stars, projecting ourselves on to them to the extent that we become winners by proxy, expecting victory and refusing defeat. And yet, there can be no winners without losers and traditionally the humiliation that was brought by defeat was itself salutary. Offering the illusion of victory to everyone is to effect a universal lie that accords with the dynamic of consumerism, namely a capitalist ideology of deferred promise. This process of capture by the environment – an artificial environment created by humans – receives its perfect culmination in the ideology sustaining technological determinism: the computer provides an opening into a world in which there will be no losers because it will give us all equal opportunities for participation. The real danger that computers pose is here revealed, not of machines gaining consciousness and so taking on human characteristics, but of humans conceiving themselves as machines – of infinite possibilities and also infinitely malleable – and unable to think outside such a paradigm. In the process we come full circle in the religious stakes: no longer do we worship the gods of nature or those that transcend nature, but rather we worship the god that makes our functioning in the modern world possible, which is the god of electricity, without whose energy we would be lost. Where once loss was fed back into society as a sign of generosity and a passage to intimacy, the technological world gives without generosity, denying any possibility of a return.

In this respect, Baudrillard is right to say that 'power belongs to him who gives and to whom no return can be made. To give, and to do it in such a way that no return can be made, is to break exchange to one's own profit and institute a monopoly: the social process is out of balance' (1988: 208). This seems to go to the heart of the problematic of today's world. The fact that everything is offered to us as a gift we can grasp, while we are simultaneously denied its realisation, means that any genuine reciprocity of relations is withheld.

This equates with the fact that everything has become a commodity in modern society. It is worthwhile here recalling Marx's definition:

A commodity appears, at first sight, a very trivial thing, and easily understood. Its analysis shows that it is, in reality, a very queer thing, abounding in metaphysical subtleties and theological niceties. So far as it is a value in use, there is nothing mysterious about it, whether we consider it from the point of view that by its properties it is capable of satisfying human wants, or from the point that those properties are the product of human labour. It is as clear as noon-day that man, by his industry, changes the forms of the materials furnished by nature, in such a way as to make them useful to him. The form of wood, for instance, is altered, by making a table out of it. Yet, for all that, the table continues to be that common, everyday thing, wood. But, as soon as it steps forth as a commodity, it is changed into something transcendent. It not only stands with its feet on the ground, but, in relation to all other commodities, it stands on its head, and evolves out of its wooden brain grotesque ideas, far more wonderful than 'table-turning' ever was. (1974b: Vol. 1, 76)

What is significant about this definition is that it brings attention to the religious aspect of the commodity: it serves the purpose of the sacred, and what is essential to understand about the function of commodities is not their manifest content, but precisely the 'metaphysical subtleties and theological niceties' with which they are imbued. And the most grotesque of the ideas this leads to involves the abdication of human responsibility pinpointed by Karl Kraus (1976) when he noted how the development of technology can solve all problems except that of human infirmity, with the implication that since it is precisely human infirmity that created this technology, it merely replicates it.

Ultimately technological advance is the ratification and authentication of Enlightenment. It serves all its claims to progressive development by means of enterprise and inquiry into the nature of things, and stands as the culmination of human culture, reflecting its superiority over nature and making it definitively productive. It reflects a faith in the efficacy of information as a remedy for all of the deficiencies within society. It is claimed that by providing unlimited information via the internet, people are able to make viable choices about their lives and their participation in society. Here is a statement typical of its type: 'Our children would be exposed to myriad opinions, countless voices, alternative news angles and news stories. Immersed in a world of diversity and dissent our kids could develop their own values, their own political and moral positions.' We only have to think about this statement for a moment to wonder what sort of world such a diversity would institute. Everything we know about human society suggests that this sort of undirected freedom contradicts the very nature of freedom and could only lead to a paralysis of values. Every political or moral position emerges from social interaction and by means of collective mediation, and, as we discussed in looking at the nature of knowledge, necessarily involves the withholding as much as the revelation of information. It is difficult to see how anything other than eccentric and polarised viewpoints could emerge in a world in which everyone was obtaining his or her primary information from a myriad of sources provided by the computer. All values are socially founded, feeding back into the individual. Giving a child unlimited access to unmediated and uncontrolled information must lead to a numbness in which, knowing everything, we know nothing. In just the same way as the individual human mind ceases to function effectively if we are unable to forget what is inessential, so collectively we have no possibility of making proper choices if we lack a common value system. In today's conditions, we are today in danger of establishing the conditions for a collective inability to forget, something that will undermine memory itself and make life a simple process of transition from one sensation to another, all equally banal or equally significant but all essentially constituted by torpidity. Extending the brain (freed of its ties to the senses) into domains it cannot reach of itself – or rather that it refuses to reach since its effectiveness relies on its surplus and unused capacity – the ideology of computerisation effectively withholds genuine choice from the lives of all people. We finally become stupefied spectators, projecting ourselves passively into everything, but unable genuinely to participate in anything. For the fact is that common values will be instilled, but this will emerge not from social interaction that allows for the possibility of refusal, but by blanket assumptions set up by the media.

By requiring so much information to be consumed, present-day society has placed a wager on the fact that this will happen, establishing a dynamic that depends upon presenting an excess of possibilities that can only be realised within a very limited frame of reference. Humans have an enormous capacity to enslave themselves. Is the computer an abdication of thinking instituting the sort of debraining machine that Alfred Jarry envisaged at the end of the nineteenth century. Can this be resisted?

In this respect we need to consider once more Walter Benjamin's belief that the development of technology demystifies the aura of the original work of art, instituting a democratising process that enables us all, through mechanical reproduction, to enjoy aesthetic products. Each successive technological development in the realm of communications has opened up the possibilities of literacy and has given all people access – at least in principle – to the great works of art and literature. At the same time, though, the authenticity of the art work is undermined and historically decentred: 'Even the most perfect reproduction of a work of art is lacking in one element: its presence in time and space, its unique existence at the place where it happens to be' (Benjamin, 1970: 222). This leads to the denigration of tradition and a demystification of the ritual and cult aspects not only of art (although here it may be most immediately appreciable), but of all aspects of life.

This is a generalised process affecting every level of society and becoming more clearly distinguished with each successive social change until it may today be asserted that a radical and qualitative transformation is being effected whereby industrialisation ceases to be the motive force, but is replaced by technology, initiating us into what we now call the post-industrial, information or communications age.

If industrial societies were characterised by factory-based production, it was those who controlled the means of production who had ultimate power, exercised by means of a hierarchically organised bureaucratic apparatus, marked by the spread of a market economy and the need for self-discipline, and relying upon a social stability that allowed for an improvement of employees' rights as, in order to maintain stability, workers had to be appeased. In the information age it is not control of the means of production that matters, but control of the means of communication, leading to an increase in the importance of the service sector at the expense of manufacturing, with knowledge, consumption and leisure becoming the key factors. The owners of capital must become experts at managing their interests and need to cede power to a professional managerial class for whom everything can be bought and sold, and for whom value is calculated only in relation to its exchange benefit. This transforms the nature of bureaucracy. Instead of being concerned to maintain discipline within the part in order to protect the overall structure of the organisation, leading to an anonymity that tended towards an insensitivity towards those who belonged to the organisation (the 'faceless bureaucracy' that so much characterised the modernist sensibility), management tactics now rely upon control of the parts through setting targets and incentive schemes. This tends to assume that the whole organisation will hold together in the centre and that processes of control within the organisation are paramount. People become stakeholders and customers, and their interests are supposedly taken into account. In reality, however, this leads to an even greater dehumanisation than experienced under bureaucracy, because it institutes control mechanisms that regulate our possibilities of choice at every point, for the so-called 'stakeholder' ideology provides a transparent means of playing interests off against one another while satisfying none of them, so allowing managers to make decisions on behalf of everyone. A supine work ethic is instituted due to the speed of communication that computerisation has made possible. Fear and suspicion become institutionalised and we are forced to participate actively in our own oppression. In his 1852 story *Bartleby*, Herman Melville delineated the possibility of refusal that a bureaucratised, industrial society still left open. The new technologies effectively close this loophole: today Bartleby would be subject to management targets that it would be impossible for him 'rather not' to meet. To refuse to participate, to seek to chart out one's own possibilities of existence, is no longer an option.

The relentless nature of this control process was well explored by Adorno (1991) in his notion of the Culture Industry. Writing some decades ago when management control was still in its nascent form, Adorno was concerned primarily with its most visible manifestations in the way that popular culture was being used as discipline by means of the media, but his critique has gained urgency in the years since he was writing and we can say that the process he describes has now entered every part of society.

As much as Benjamin saw in mechanical reproduction the possibility of a democratisation of the image in favour of communicative possibilities, Adorno warned that this very process had authoritarian consequences. For real power comes to lie not with the audience, nor with the creators, nor even with the financial backers, but with those able to manage the process by which the product comes into the communicative system. In cinema, for instance, real power lies with the distributors, who determine how the film will be presented to the public. For the most part the success or failure of a film will depend upon the strength of distribution, not upon its inherent qualities. No matter how good a film is, it will fail if it does not get a good distribution deal. Of course, the inherent quality of a particular film will be a factor in how it is distributed. It is not, however, the determining one. A distribution deal depends almost exclusively upon the film's commercial viability, and what determines this is whether or not the distribution company feel they can market it successfully. To decide this, they do not consider the film as a whole; they consider primarily its angle: what are its areas that may be exploited in order that it can be sold? It is in this respect that Adorno points out that what is today called 'popular' culture is decided not by popular will, but by a process of mediation that is always controlled by structures of media management.

This means that in the modern era, the mass media have gained a sort of 'mythical structure' that binds society and in which we are all expected to share. They are an unquestioned presence in our lives and ultimately make our choices for us. While we talk today about the Information Society, the quality of the information we receive is increasingly devalued by being presented in a manageable form that elides any difficult questions about its status. Consent is thus 'manufactured', in Chomsky's felicitous phrase.

In this way control of culture has become the core of every aspect of modern society. There is an increasing trivialisation of real issues, so that everything is progressively absorbed into a nexus of commercialising processes. As Adorno says, 'Imagination is replaced by a mechanically relentless control mechanism' (1991: 55). We end up with a vicious circle in which the Culture Industry no longer addresses real needs but rather creates in accordance with needs it has itself established as being able to be most effectively marketed. Hollywood film production marks this clearly, for the world market is so big that it can create a demand that will ensure the financial success of the film in one part of the world, no matter how good or bad the final product is. What is created is increasingly of little importance.

This carries through into all walks of life. Increasingly, we hear how politics itself has become dominated by presentation and spin rather than by content; in the workplace it is how one presents one's work so that it fits in with the systems of reportage and inspection in place rather than the work itself that determines how successful one will be; in news broadcasting, it is the manipulation of actuality rather than actuality itself that matters. Management structures assume everything to themselves, controlling culture with deceptive ease. Themselves unaccountable they can aspire to little but the perfecting of mediocrity. Being able to stand above the fray in a way that earlier bureaucrats could only have dreamed of, today's managers have been made custodians of all aspects of culture to an extent that even Adorno would no doubt have found inconceivable forty years ago.

In this respect, Adorno was right to argue that culture in the contemporary world is effectively being stolen from us, turned into a pure commodity controlled by the Culture Industry, which has permeated society so much that it does make it difficult for us to recognise our real desires or to realise our wishes. Instead we are prey to management strategies that degrade all cultural forms. The 'repressive tolerance' Marcuse defined has made inroads into every aspect of life, fully involving us in our own oppression. In this process, morality is broken down, along with hope and desire. Everything is controlled. Technology aids management control not by working for particular interests, but by allowing the operation of effective forms of institutional domination. Scientific rationality has become a formalism that underlies and determines a specific type of strategic development that characterises our age.

Nevertheless, the process is not as monolithic as Adorno sometimes makes it appear. His prejudice in favour of an élite art fails to do justice to the extent to which people enter into the control mechanism, which is still far more flexible and open to innovation than he allows. For the fact is that people are not completely overwhelmed: great films continue to be made, wonderful music made, doctors still make inroads into improving health and scientists make vital research, despite all the efforts made by management to make this as difficult as possible. Indeed, the Culture Industry – in this respect I think Adorno was mistaken – has no particular stake in vulgarity: its only rationale is to promote what it can most effectively control and sell. It has no interest in the intrinsic qualities of the product, which may as well be good as bad. In this respect Benjamin was right to see in new technologies a democratisation, providing new opportunities. Adorno's mistake was to see the only way of resisting this as by maintaining a space of authenticity in which to protect what really matters in culture. All art is subject to the process he describes, and indeed must be if it is to survive in modern culture. This applies as much to the music of Schoenberg and the books of Beckett as to jazz music or films: there is no realm of purity that popularisation cannot touch.

In the modern environment perception has shifted towards a ceaselessly changing imagery. Everything is replaceable and a subject is formed who is flexible and productive, infinitely malleable and receptive to signs that are forever exchangeable and transportable to whatever place one wishes. Movement and adaptability rule, but to what purpose?

New technologies do initiate new ways of approaching as well as experiencing and understanding the world, and their promises are not entirely false. The difficulty is to think outside the structures in which such promises are currently delivered to us. The danger is that the media will hold us so much in their thrall that this will become impossible and we shall simply begin to live through second-hand images that are nothing but a substitute for real experience, allowing the medium of the machine to do our experiencing for us. In the nineteenth century it was common for aristocrats to allow their servants to do their experiencing for them. Baudrillard mentions a nice anecdote about Beau Brummel that sums this up: visiting a beautiful region of a myriad of lakes, he asks his servant 'Which lake do I prefer?'. Today, the threat to the human spirit is that we have the means for a generalised complacency in which we can allow our machines to do our thinking for us and to experience and establish culture on our behalf. This means that we become disembodied and fragmented subjects unable to experience reality but only to mimic it. Our danger, perhaps, is not of becoming Narcissus, but of allowing our machines to become the Narcissus, of which we become the ever-distant Echo.

The promises of technology are therefore real but ultimately hollow, serving the needs of expediency in today's consumer society rather than real human needs. If technology is to fulfil the hopes placed in it, it must break away from the narrow confines ideology determines for it. Technology is a human development, and should be recognised in terms of its use-value. We need to ask ourselves the vital questions Octavio Paz posed: 'Why?' and 'To what purpose?'

11

REINTEGRATIONS

> Sooner or later, the forces of life erode every cultural form which they have
> produced.
>
> Georg Simmel

In 1880, Friedrich Nietzsche wrote these words:

> We can think many, many more things than we can do or experience – that is to
> say, our thinking is superficial and content with the surface; indeed, it does not
> notice that it is the surface. If our intellect had *evolved* strictly in step with our
> strength and the extent to which we exercise our strength, the dominant princi-
> ple of our thinking would be that we can understand only that which we can *do* –
> *if* understanding is possible at all. A man is thirsty and cannot get water, but the
> pictures his thought produces bring water ceaselessly before his eyes, as though
> nothing were easier to procure – the superficial and easily satisfied character of
> the intellect cannot grasp the actual need and distress, and yet it feels superior;
> it is proud of being able to do more, to run faster, to be at its goal almost in a
> twinkling – and thus it is that the realm of thought appears to be, in comparison
> with the realm of action, willing and experience, a *realm of freedom*: while in
> reality it is, as aforesaid, only a realm of surfaces and self-satisfaction. (1982:
> 77–8)

This extraordinarily prophetic passage could almost stand as a definition
of life not at the end of the nineteenth century but at the beginning of the
twenty-first. The confounding of a world of surfaces and self-satisfaction
with a realm of freedom defines the dominant perception of the world that
pertains and would like to impose itself as an unexamined truth.

Today's culture uses advances in technology to blur the boundaries between
reality itself and the spectacle of reality that is presented by media more
concerned to repeat the same themes in acceptable terms than to report what
is actually going on in the world we inhabit. In this process, human culture is
becoming reified into a form the media desire, directed by controllers and
managers, whose constant need is with evolving, centralising and controlling
all that exists.

This provides the culmination of the progress of international capital in its
will to control all of the facets of our life and whose advance has seemed so
inexorable and inevitable. Control of culture is its latest stage, but it has been
an element within it since the Renaissance, when culture first became a product that served the prestige of a particular class.

From its beginning in the Renaissance, the notion of a single world, separated into its parts, but determined by a common purpose and functioning as
a whole, has inexorably been imposed by means of technological developments

that have successively facilitated an ever more efficient communications network and imposed standardisation across cultures in terms of time and space.

Here the legacy of European colonialism hangs heavy on our lives today. The era of great empires may have passed, but the issues raised by the colonial legacy remain as central as ever, perhaps even more so. From the sixteenth to the twentieth century Europe effectively colonised the whole world, with cultural consequences for all people. We now live in a world under the sway of information and exchange and it sometimes seems that life in Tokyo or Bangkok is fundamentally the same as it is in London. Our lives have become similar just as they have become fragmented. The sense is that cultural forms belong to everyone and it is legitimate to take very different elements from different sources and cultures and to treat them as though they all belonged to the same order of things. In this it is not only Western economic and political forms that have been transported, culture, too, has been increasingly cosmopolitanised.

Yet in the process a lie has been perpetuated and successively reframed, a lie fundamental to capitalism: that human products are more important than human beings (one might put this more baldly as that culture as such is more important than human beings). This forces us to exist in a world that constantly needs to re-create itself, founding a devouring machine whose inherent dynamism requires that it destroys what it creates in order to create anew continuously, establishing human life in a feeling of flux and uncertainty that provokes both anxiety and excitement. However this process is ultimately totalitarian and self-defeating, especially insofar as it denies otherness and tries to disestablish its dynamic.

The crisis of otherness identified by Marc Augé (1999) is therefore perhaps the most pressing issue that faces us today. Embracing the Other in its difference, appropriating and so destroying its singular qualities, leads to a failure of imagination in which difference is seen everywhere and we become blind to its historical becoming. This means that we are condemned to destroy the very otherness that has made history possible. In so doing, as Ziauddin Sardar (1998) has observed, we are effectively 'colonising the future' and forcing it to dance to our tune, a tune that plays on a single note.

At present there is perhaps a single real discordance in the flow of these processes, which is represented by religious fundamentalism. Fundamentalism is significant insofar as it articulates a generalised disquiet about the movement of global ideas. Whether it is manifested in Afghanistan or in the United States, it does not simply reflect a narrow-minded religious fervour, but stands as reflection of the shaping of globalisation. Its very intolerance is the mirror image of the more successful fundamentalism of the advocates of modernisation and globalisation, and it may even legitimately be argued that the real fundamentalism is not that of the Islamic, Christian or Hindu militants standing against the principles of modernisation, but lies precisely within the modernisation process. In many respects, postmodernism itself is an intellectualised form of fundamentalism, as intolerant and as fixed in its ideas as any of the ayatollahs so stigmatised in the Western media. Indeed, we may say that the great value of fundamentalism is to dare to be Other, to refuse the dogmatism of progress and identity politics.

And here we see also the weakness of the homogenising process of globalisation. In its indifference to content, it leaves open a field of alternatives for the human imagination to exploit, if it only has the will. For the emergence of fundamentalism shows that globalisation cannot override the dialectic of otherness. Fundamentalism is not simply a reflection of globalising processes, it is also its condition. We know that the Taliban, for instance, came to exist only due to the intrigues of the CIA. This alone should give pause for thought about how the otherness thrown out of the front door finds a way of entering by the back.

As much as culture theorists might collude with the dominant global managing structures in positing a world in which culture is to be seen as no more than a representation lacking a referent, taking shape in a virtual form and creating an environment determined by replication, the fact is that the imagination gains its stimulus only from its relation to what is real. If the realm of representation is the only frame of reference, it can do no more than turn on itself and will soon find itself chasing its own tail. Freed of the limits we perceive in the real, the human imagination gets lost. If images simply reflect other images and have no material consequences, it seems more likely to lead to a crisis of perception rather than its transformation into a new framework.

All cultures are characterised by universal features and these features are manifested in cultural forms that may vary considerably, but all have the same basis in the fact of being human. What we share is far greater than what divides us, even if what divides us may be of more consequence, being what leads to conflict and war. We cannot know the Other, but the process of striving to do so creates all meaning within society and is the very condition of our existence. To abandon this striving and accept unlimited difference leads to a condition of desensitisation in which conflict may be lessened but so in all likelihood will reasons for living.

Ziauddin Sardar perhaps defines the real dilemma we face, centred in what he calls the pathological necessity of the West to define reality and truth as its truth and reality, allowing nothing to exist outside that framework. 'Rethinking tradition . . . requires appreciation of authenticity and cultural autonomy. Cultural authenticity means that traditional physical, intellectual and spiritual environments and values should be respected. . . . What is necessary is the unabashed embrace of self-confidence, the pride that dares to walk its talk' (Sardar, 1998: 281). This is addressed to non-Western people, but applies just as much to people in the West itself. The flow of modernity has torn our own traditions from us. A new imaginative force is required that will allow a refashioning of technology divested of its cultural assumptions and also allow a space for the Other to grow in its own terms and simultaneously to contribute to our own growth. It is in this that a genuine experience of culture finds its realisation, allowing us to cross the myriad of boundaries that separate us from one another.

BIBLIOGRAPHY

Adorno, Theodor W. (1974) *Minima Moralia Reflections from Damaged Life*, translated by E.F.N. Jephcott. London: Verso.

Adorno, Theodor W. (1977) 'Reconciliation Under Duress', in *Aesthetics and Politics*. London: Verso.

Adorno, Theodor W. (1984) *Aesthetic Theory*, translated by C. Lenhardt. London: Routledge.

Adorno, Theodor W. (1991) *The Culture Industry*, edited by J.M. Bernstein. London: Routledge.

Ahmad, Aijaz (1992) *In Theory: Classes, Nations, Literatures*. London: Verso.

Alleau, René (1976) *La Science des symboles*. Paris: Payot.

Anderson, Benedict (1983) *Imagined Communities: Reflections on the Origin and Spread of Nationalism*. London: Verso.

Arendt, Hannah (1958) *The Human Condition*. Chicago: University of Chicago Press.

Arendt, Hannah (1961) *Between Past and Future*. London: Faber & Faber.

Arguedas, José María (1985) *Yawar Fiesta*, translated by Frances Horning Barraclough. London: Quartet.

Augé, Marc (1999) *A Sense for the Other: An Anthropology for Contemporary Worlds*. Stanford, Calif.: Stanford University Press.

Bataille, Georges (1986) *Eroticism*, translated by Mary Dalwood. San Francisco: City Lights.

Baudrillard, Jean (1988) *Selected Writings*, edited and introduced by Mark Poster. Cambridge: Polity.

Benjamin, Walter (1970) *Illuminations*, translated by Harry Zohn London: Jonathan Cape.

Benjamin, Walter (1996) *Selected Works*, Vol. 1, edited by Marcus Bullock and Michael W. Jennings. Cambridge, Mass.: Harvard University Press.

Benjamin, Walter (1999) *Selected Works*, Vol. 2, edited by Marcus Bullock and Michael W. Jennings. Cambridge, Mass.: Harvard University Press.

Berman, Marshall (1988) *All That Is Solid Melts Into Air: The Experience of Modernity*. London: Verso.

Bidney, David (1996) *Theoretical Anthropology*. New Brunswick, NJ: Transaction Publishers.

Blechman, Max (1999) *Revolutionary Romanticism*. San Francisco: City Lights.

Bloch, Ernst (1988) The *Utopian Function of Art and Literature*. Cambridge, Mass: MIT Press.

Borofsky, R. et al. (1997) 'Forum on Theory in Anthropology: Cook, Lono, Obeyesekere and Sahlins', *Current Anthropology* no. 38.

Bourdieu, Pierre (1981) *Language and Symbolic Power*, edited and introduced by John B. Thompson; translated by Gino Raymond and Matthew Adamson. Oxford: Blackwell.

Bourdieu, Pierre (1984) *Distinction: A Social Critique of the Judgement of Taste*, translated by Richard Nice. London: Routledge.

Bourdieu, Pierre (1990) *The Logic of Practice*, translated by Richard Nice. Cambridge: Polity.

Bourdieu, Pierre and Passeron, Jean-Claude (1977) *Reproduction in Education: Society and Culture*, translated by Richard Nice. London: Sage.

Buck-Morss, Susan (1977) *The Origin of Negative Dialectics: Theodor W. Adorno, Walter Benjamin and the Frankfurt Institute*. Hassocks: Harvester Press.

Bulhan, Hussein Abdulai (1985) 'Master and Slave Paradigms', in *Frantz Fanon and the Psychology of Oppression*. New York: Plenham Press.

Caillois, Roger (1938) *Le mythe et l'homme*. Paris: Gallimard.

Caillois, Roger (1939) *L'homme et le sacré*. Paris: Gallimard.

Camus, Albert (1962) *The Rebel*. Harmondsworth: Penguin.

Carpenter, Edmund (1976) *Oh What A Blow That Phantom Gave Me!* London: Paladin.

Cassirer, Ernst (1972) *An Essay on Man.* New Haven, Conn.: Yale University Press.

Cassirer, Ernst (1955) *The Philosophy of Symbolic Forms* (2 vols), translated by Ralph Mannheim. New Haven: Yale University Press.

Castoriadis, Cornelius (1987) *The Imaginary Institution of Society*, translated by Kathleen Blamey. Cambridge: Polity.

Caudwell, Christopher (1946) *Illusion and Reality: A Study of the Sources of Poetry.* London: Lawrence & Wishart.

Césaire, Aimé (1972) *Discourse on Colonialism.* New York: Monthly Review Press.

Cioran, E.M. (1975) *A Short History of Decay*, translated by Richard Howard. New York: Seaver Books.

Cioran, E.M. (1987) *The Temptation to Exist*, translated by Richard Howard. London: Quartet.

Cioran, E.M. (1992) *On the Heights of Despair*, translated by Ilinca Zarifopol-Johnston. Chicago: University of Chicago Press.

Clifford, James (1988) *The Predicament of Culture.* Cambridge. Mass.: Harvard University Press.

Clifford, James and Marcus, George (1986) *Writing Culture.* Berkeley: University of California Press.

Cohn, Norman (1975) *Europe's Inner Demons.* London: Chatto.

Debray, Régis (1993) *L'État séducteur.* Paris: Gallimard.

Deren, Maya (1970) *Divine Horsemen: The Voodoo Gods of Haiti.* New York: Delta.

Diamond, Stanley (1974) *In Search of the Primitive. New York:* Dutton.

Dorfman, Artel and Mattelart, Armand (1975) *How to Read Donald Duck: Imperialist Ideology in the Disney Comic*, translated by David Kunzle. New York: International General.

Durham, Jimmie (no date) 'In conversation with Dick Snauwaert', in *Contemporary Artists: Jimmy Durham.* Oxford: Phaidon.

Durham, Jimmie (1993) *A Certain Lack of Coherence.* London: Kala Press.

Elias, Norbert (1994) *The Civilizing Process: The History of Manners and State Formation and Civilization*, translated by Edmund Jephcott. Oxford: Blackwell.

Eriksen, Erik (1965) *Childhood and Society.* St Albans: Triad/Paladin.

Eriksen, Erik (1968) *Identity: Youth and Crisis.* London: Faber.

Evans-Pritchard, E.E. (1937) *Witchcraft, Oracles and Magic among the Azande.* Oxford: Clarendon Press.

Ferry, Luc (1995) *The New Ecological Order.* Chicago: University of Chicago Press.

Feyerabend, Paul (1975) *Against Method: Outline of an Anarchistic Theory of Knowledge.* London: Verso.

Feyerabend, Paul (1987) *Farewell to Reason.* London: Verso.

Finnegan, Ruth and Horton, Robin (eds) (1973) *Modes of Thought: Essays on Thinking in Western and Non-Western Societies.* London: Faber & Faber.

Foucault, Michel (1967) *Madness and Civilisation: A History of Insanity in the Age of Reason.* London: Tavistock.

Freire, Paolo (1972) *The Pedagogy of the Oppressed*, translated by Myra Bergman Ramos. Harmondsworth: Penguin.

Freud, Sigmund (1959) 'The Question of Lay Analysis', in *The Complete Psychological Works of Sigmund Freud*, Vol. XX, translated by James Strachey. London: Hogarth Press.

Freud, Sigmund (1984) 'On the Pleasure Principle', in *On Metapsychology: The Theory of Psychoanalysis*, translated by James Strachey, Harmondsworth: Penguin.

Fukuyama, Francis (1992) *The End of History and the Last Man.* Harmondsworth: Penguin.

Gailey, Christine Ward (ed.) (1994) *Civilisation in Crisis: Anthropological Perspectives* (Dialectical Anthropology Vol. 1). Gainesville: University Press of Florida.

Gay, Peter (1969) *The Enlightenment: An Interpretation, the Science of Freedom.* New York: Alfred Knopf/Penguin.

Glissant, Edouard (1989) *Caribbean Discourse.* Charlottesville University Press of Virginia.

Gouldner, Alvin (1976) *The Dialectic of Ideology and Technology.* London: Macmillan.

Graham, A C. (1985) *Reason and Spontaneity.* London: Curzon Press.

Gramsci, Antonio (1971) *Selections From the Prison Notebooks*. edited and translated by Quintin Hoare and Geoffrey Nowell-Smith. London: Lawrence & Wishart.

Gurvitch, Georges (1971) *The Social Foundations of Knowledge*. Oxford: Blackwell.

Harris, Wilson (1999) *The Unfinished Genesis of the Imagination: Selected Essays*, edited by Andrew Bundy. London: Routledge.

Heath, S.B. (1983) *Ways With Words: Language, Life and Work in Communities and Classrooms*. Cambridge: Cambridge University Press.

Hegel, G.W.F. (1942) *The Philosophy of Right*, translated by T.M. Knox. Oxford: Clarendon Press.

Hegel, G.W.F. (1956) *The Philosophy of History*, translated by J. Sibree. New York: Dover Publications.

Hegel, G.W.F. (1964) *Political Writings*, translated by T.M. Knox. Oxford: Clarendon Press.

Hegel, G.W.F. (1977) *The Phenomenology of the Spirit*, translated by A.V. Miller. Oxford: Oxford University Press.

Heller, Agnes (1984) *Everyday Life*, translated by G.L. Campbell. London: Routledge & Kegan Paul.

Hobsbawm, Eric and Ranger, T. (eds) (1983) *The Invention of Tradition*. Cambridge: Cambridge University Press.

Hollis, Martin and Lukes, Steven (eds) (1982) *Rationality and Relativism*. Oxford: Blackwell.

Horkheimer, Max (1973) 'The End of Reason', in A. Arato and E. Gebhardt (eds) *The Essential Frankfurt School Reader*. Oxford: Basil Blackwell.

Horkheimer, Max and Adorno, Theodor W. (1979) *Dialectic of Enlightenment*, translated by John Cumming. London: Verso.

Howell, Signe (1991) 'Art and Meaning', in Susan Hiller (ed.), *The Myth of Primitivism*. London: Routledge.

Huizinga, Johan (1955) *Homo Ludens*. Boston: Beacon Books.

Ingold, Tim (ed.) (1996) *Key Debates in Anthropology*. London: Routledge.

Jackson, Michael (1998) *Minima Ethnographica: Intersubjectivity and the Anthropological Project*. Chicago: University of Chicago Press.

Jay, Martin (1988) 'Scopic Regimes of Modernity', in Hal Foster (ed.), *Vision and Visuality*. Seattle: Dia/Bay Press.

Jenks, Chris (1993) *Culture*. London: Routledge.

Kahn, Joel (1995) *Culture, Multiculture, Postculture*. London: Sage Publications.

Kleist, Heinrich von (1972) 'On the Marionette Theatre', translated by Thomas G. Neumiller, in *The Drama Review*, vol. 16, no. 3.

Kraus, Karl (1984) *Half-Truths and One-and-a-half Truths*, edited and translated by Harry Zohn, Montreal: Engendra Press.

Kraus, Karl (1976) *In These Great Times*, edited and translated by Harry Zohn, Manchester: Carcaret.

Kuhn, Thomas (1970) *The Structure of Scientific Revolutions*. Chicago: University of Chicago Press.

Lacan, Jacques (1977) 'The Mirror Stage as Formative of the Function of the I as Revealed in Psychoanalytic Experience', in *Écrits*, translated by Alan Sheridan. London: Tavistock.

Lefebvre, Henri (1995) *Introduction to Modernity*, translated by John Moore. London: Verso.

Lévi-Strauss, Claude (1963a) *Structural Anthropology*. New York: Basic Books.

Lévi-Strauss, Claude (1963b) *Totemism*. Boston, Mass.: Beacon Books.

Lévi-Strauss, Claude (1966) *The Savage Mind*. London: Weidenfeld & Nicolson.

Lincoln, Bruce (1989) *Discourse and the Construction of Society*. Oxford: Oxford University Press.

Lincoln, Bruce (1991) *Death, War, and Sacrifice*. Chicago: University of Chicago Press.

Lukács, Georg (1977) 'Realism in the Balance', in *Aesthetics and Politics*. London: Verso.

Mabille, Pierre (1977) *Égrégores ou la vie des civilisations*. Paris: Sagittaire.

Marcuse, Herbert (1978) *The Aesthetic Dimension*. Boston: Beacon Books.

Markale, Jean (1983) *Mélusine ou l'androgyne*. Paris: Retz.

Marx, Karl (1974a) *Economic and Philosophical Manuscripts* in *Early Writings*. Harmondsworth: Penguin.

Marx, Karl (1974b) *Capital: A Critical Analysis of Capitalist Production* (3 vols) translated by Samuel Moore and Edward Aveling. London: Lawrence & Wishart.

McLuhan, Marshall (1964) *Understanding Media*. Cambridge, Mass.: MIT Press.

Merchant, Carolyn (1980) *The Death of Nature: Women, Ecology and the Scientific Revolution*. New York: Harper & Row.

Needham, Rodney (1983) 'Skulls and Causality', in *Against the Tranquility of Axioms*. Berkeley: University of California Press.

Nietzsche, Friedrich (1968) *Basic Writings of Nietzsche*, translated by Walter Kaufman. New York: The Modern Library.

Nietzsche, Friedrich (1982) *Daybreak: Thoughts on the Prejudices of Morality*, translated by R.J. Hollingdale. Cambridge: Cambridge University Press.

Nietzsche, Friedrich (1974) *The Gay Science*, translated by Walter Kaufman. New York: Random House

Nooter, Mary H. (ed.) (1993) *Secrecy: African Art That Conceals and Reveals*. New York: The Museum of African Art.

Obeyesekere, Ganath (1997) *The Apotheosis of Captain Cook: European Mythmaking in the Pacific*. Princeton, NJ: Princeton University Press.

Ong, Walter (1982) *Orality and Literacy: The Technologising of the World*. London: Methuen.

Opie, Iona and Opie, Peter (1959) *The Lore and Language of Schoolchildren*. Oxford: Oxford University Press.

Overing, Joanna (1989) 'The Aesthetics of Production: The Sense of Community among the Cubeo and the Piaroa', *Dialectical Anthropology*, vol. 14, no. 3.

Overing, Joanna (ed.) (1985) *Reason and Morality*. London: Tavistock.

Patchen, Kenneth (1941) *The Journal of Albion Moonlight*. New York: New Directions.

Patterson, Orlando (1991) *Freedom, Volume 1: Freedom in the Making*. New York: Basic Books.

Paz, Octavio (1973) *The Bow and the Lyre*, translated by Ruth Simms. New York: McGraw-Hill.

Paz, Octavio (1974) *Alternating Current*. London: Wildwood House.

Price, Sally (1989) *Primitive Art in Civilised Places*. Chicago: University of Chicago Press.

Rank, Otto (1989) *The Double*, translated by Harry Tucker. London: Karnac Books.

Rank, Otto (1993) *The Trauma of Birth*, Mineola, NY: Dover Publications.

The Rig-Veda: An Anthology (1981) selected, translated and annotated by Wendy Doniger O'Flaherty. Harmondsworth: Penguin.

Rivière, Peter (1969) *Marriage Among the Trio: A Principle of Social Organisation*. Oxford: Clarendon Press.

Robins, Kevin (1996) *Into the Image: Culture and Politics in the Field of Vision*. London: Routledge.

Sahlins, Marshall (1995) *How 'Natives' Think About Captain Cook For Instance*. Chicago: University of Chicago Press.

Said, Edward (1978) *Orientalism*. Harmondsworth: Penguin.

Sardar, Ziauddin (1998) *Postmodernism and the Other*. London: Pluto Press.

Saussure, Ferdinand de (1959) *Course in General Linguistics*. New York: McGraw-Hill.

Schelling, F.J.W. (1989) *Philosophical Inquiries into the Nature of Human Freedom*. LaSalle, Ill.: Open Court.

Simmel, Georg (1950) 'The Stranger', in K.H. Wolf (ed.) *The Sociology of Georg Simmel*. New York: The Free Press.

Simmel, Georg (1997) *Simmel on Culture*, edited by David Frisby and Mike Featherstone. London: Sage Publications.

Steiner, George (1975) *After Babel: Aspects of Language and Translation*. Oxford: Oxford University Press.

Steiner, George (1976) *Extraterritorial: Papers in Literature and the Language Revolution*. New York: Atheneum.

Tambiah, Stanley (1985) *Culture, Thought, and Social Action: An Anthropological Perspective*. Cambridge, Mass.: Harvard University Press.

Taussig, Michael (1993) *Mimesis and Alterity: A Particular History of the Senses*. London: Routledge.

Thomas, Keith (1973) *Religion and the Decline of Magic: Studies in Popular Belief in Sixteenth and Seventeenth Century England.* Harmondsworth: Penguin.

Todorov, Tzvetan (1984) *The Conquest of America*, translated by Richard Howard. New York: Harper & Row.

Todorov, Tzvetan (1993) *On Human Diversity*, translated by Catherine Porter. Cambridge. Mass.: Harvard University Press.

Touraine, Alain (1996) *Critique of Modernity*, translated by David Macey. Oxford: Polity.

Tuan, Yi-Fu (1974) *Topophilia: A Study of Environmental Perception, Attitudes and Values.* Engelwood-Cliffs, NJ: Prentice-Hall.

Tuan, Yi-Fu (1977) *Space and Place: the Perspective of exPerience.* Minneapolis: University of Minnesota Press.

Tuan, Yi-Fu (1979) *Landscapes of Fear.* Oxford: Blackwell.

Virilio, Paul (1994) *The Vision Machine.* London: British Film Institute.

Vygotsky, Lev (1962) *Thought and Language*, edited and translated by Eugenia Hanfmann and Gertrude Vakar. Cambridge, Mass: MIT.

Whorf, Benjamin Lee (1956) *Language, Thought and Reality.* London: Chapman & Hall.

Williams, Raymond (1961) *The Long Revolution 1780–1950.* London: Chatto & Windus.

Wilson, Bryan (ed.) (1970) *Rationality.* Oxford: Blackwell.

Winnicott, D.W. (1957) *The Child and the Outside World.* London: Tavistock.

Winnicott, D.W. (1965) *The Family and Individual Development.* London: The Shenval Press.

Wolf, Eric (1982) *Europe and the People Without History.* Berkeley: University of California Press.

Wolff, Janet (1981) *The Social Production of Art.* Basingstoke: Macmillan.

Yates, Frances A. (1966) *The Art of Memory.* London: Routledge & Kegan Paul.

Index